## ArtScroll Series®

Rabbi Nosson Scherman / Rabbi Meir Zlotowitz

*General Editors*

THE KOHN FAMILY EDITION

# THE ESSENTIAL

*Published by*

Mesorah Publications, ltd

*in conjunction with*

JEWISH LEARNING LIBRARY
A Project of Ohr Somayach

# MALBIM

## FLASHES OF INSIGHT ON BEREISHIS/GENESIS

Edited by Rabbi Mendel Weinbach
Adapted by Rabbi Reuven Subar

FIRST EDITION
First Impression … September 2009

Published and Distributed by
**MESORAH PUBLICATIONS, LTD.**
4401 Second Avenue / Brooklyn, N.Y 11232


Distributed in Europe by
**LEHMANNS**
Unit E, Viking Business Park
Rolling Mill Road
Jarow, Tyne & Wear, NE32 3DP
England

Distributed in Israel by
**SIFRIATI / A. GITLER — BOOKS**
6 Hayarkon Street
Bnei Brak 51127

Distributed in Australia and New Zealand
by **GOLDS WORLDS OF JUDAICA**
3-13 William Street
Balaclava, Melbourne 3183
Victoria, Australia

Distributed in South Africa by
**KOLLEL BOOKSHOP**
Ivy Common
105 William Road
Norwood 2192, Johannesburg, South Africa

---

**ARTSCROLL SERIES®**
**THE ESSENTIAL MALBIM**
© Copyright 2009, by MESORAH PUBLICATIONS, Ltd.
4401 Second Avenue / Brooklyn, N.Y. 11232 / (718) 921-9000 / www.artscroll.com

---

ISBN 10: 1-4226-0927-8 / ISBN 13: 978-1-4226-0927-9


Typography by CompuScribe at ArtScroll Studios, Ltd.
Printed in Canada
Bound by Sefercraft, Quality Bookbinders, Ltd., Brooklyn N.Y. 11232

In Memory of

## Annie Adel Kohn

בלימה רבקה אדל כהן ע״ה
בת ר׳ דניאל ז״ל

לב טהור ברא לי אלוקים

With her purity of heart
she devotedly guided her family.

Dedicated by her family
**The Kohns of Toronto, Canada**

# Table of Contents

# Editor's Introduction

Serious students of *Chumash* and *Nach* have learned to appreciate the classic commentary of Rav Meir Yehuda Leibish Malbim (5569-5640; 1809-1879), popularly known as Malbim. His unique approach to precise analyses of text and his skill in drawing from it enlightening concepts has made his work one of the most valuable resources for those who wish to enrich their understanding of our sacred sources.

The poetic style which characterizes so much of his language makes translation virtually impossible and almost all of his works have therefore been inaccessible to the English-speaking public. It is therefore a privilege to have participated, together with **RABBI REUVEN SUBAR**, in this bold effort to present the essentials of Malbim's commentary on *Sefer Bereishis* as a series of essays carefully adapted from his commentary.

To fully appreciate Malbim's impact on history it is not sufficient to merely study his many works. He must be viewed in the context of the battle which raged in the 19th century between the champions of Torah tradition and the reformers and *maskilim* who challenged it.

Malbim, as a great Torah scholar and rabbinic leader, was uniquely equipped to lead this battle by demonstrating in his writings the wisdom of the Talmudic Sages and the validity of their approach to Scripture and its lessons. Already at the age of 20 he completed his first work *Artzos HaChayim*, a commentary on the first 24 *simanim* of *Shulchan Oruch Orech Chaim* which he had begun five years earlier. When it was published in 1837 with the approbation of the Chasam Sofer, his reputation as a great Torah scholar was established. His collection of *derashos* in *Artzos HaShalom* published a year later made him famous as a homiletic expert. His career as a commentator on *Tanach* was launched with his commentary on *Megillas Esther* (1845) and *Chazon Yeshayahu* (1849).

When Malbim launched his commentary on *Chumash* he began with *HaTorah ve'Hamitzvah* on the *Toras Kohanim* halachic *medrashim* on *Sefer Vayikra*. His motivation was to show how the Oral and Written Law blended together in perfect harmony, counter to the vicious slanders that were being spread by those who had deserted their tradition. In his introduction to this monumental work, he took aim at the leaders of the reform movement who met in 1844 in the German city of Braunschweig to plan a sweeping revision of Judaism. Sensing that it was "a time to act for God against these shepherds who devour their flocks and call themselves rabbis and preachers of their communities," Malbim dipped his pen in tears and thus announced his counterattack:

"This wicked assembly treated Scripture as mythology and compared its lyrics and phrases to the poetry of Homer and the Greeks. I have therefore undertaken to erect for the Written and Oral Law a protective wall, with doors and bolts, to keep out the vile offenders who would defile them; for whom the Talmud is a target for sport and who accused the Sages as being ignorant of Hebrew grammar and the simple meaning of the passages."

Malbim's challenge to those whom he thus criticized created serious problems for him in some of the communities in which he served as spiritual leader. His rabbinical career began at the age of 28 when he became the rav of Vereshneh. An impressive series of other positions included such important communities as the Romanian capital of Bucharest, Mohilov, and Koenisgsberg. He was even offered the position as successor to Rav Akiva Eiger in Posna which he declined because of a prior commitment. Similar offers declined for this reason came from Vilna where he was invited to be chief *darshan* and New York City where he would have been chief rabbi.

Malbim earned the respect of the Torah giants of his time. The Chofetz Chaim, who cited his halachic opinions in his *Mishneh Berurah*, once exclaimed, "How does one merit a great mind such as that of Malbim!" This was a tribute to the multifaceted genius of a Torah scholar who, in addition to his work on halachah and *Tanach*, could write *sefarim* on sermons, Hebrew grammar, and even sacred poetry.

Tributes to the extraordinary piety of Malbim were heard from such great Chassidic masters as the Divrei Chaim of Sanz and Rav Yehoshua of Belz. This explains why the initial reservations in some circles about the innovations of the Malbim, such as the use of question marks in his commentary, gave way to a universal consensus that Malbim's works were the products of what the Belzer called "a pure and saintly Jew."

In conclusion I wish to thank the *Rosh Hayeshivah* of Ohr Somayach, **RAV NOTA SCHILLER**, for initiating this project and the beloved *talmid* **EPHRAIM YAWITZ** for his skillful contribution to this adaptation of the Malbim commentary. Thanks as well to **ELIEZER SHAPIRO** for his guidance and to the ArtScroll staff for bringing the project to fruition.

It is our prayer that this work will introduce its readers to the rich world of Malbim commentary.

Mendel Weinbach

Jerusalem, Menachem Av 5769

# A Word From the Adapter

What you are holding in your hands is *The Essential Malbim,* a selective adaptation of the Malbim's commentary to the Book of *Bereishis.*

Malbim's commentary is intense. Sometimes Malbim answers questions with just one word, or answers questions without asking them; sometimes he uses poetic expressions or oblique allusions. For these and other reasons we have opted not to translate Malbim's commentary but rather to adapt selections[1] from it.

We have added hundreds of original footnotes and urge the reader to use them. Most are sources, but many are explanations important for understanding the text.

# Acknowledgments

*Baruch Hashem* for blessing me and for letting me see this project through to completion.

**EPHRAIM YAWITZ** is a brilliant scholar who deserves credit for the essays through *Parashas Chayei Sarah.* I hope my editing did nothing to diminish his excellent work.

---

1. We omitted, for example, certain sections that we deemed too intricate for a work of this nature, such as certain fine grammatical distinctions. None of our omissions should be viewed as an opinion as to the relative worthiness of any of Malbim's comments, *chas v'shalom.*

I thank all my beloved mentors, starting with my parents, **MR. AND MRS. JEROME SUBAR**: besides everything else, they have taught me to love the Torah, to love everything Jewish, and how to type. Thanks to my beloved brothers **AHARON SUBAR** and **YONATAN SUBAR**. And I thank my wife, especially for knowing when to say, "How's the Malbim going?" and when not to. My greatest thanks go to my in-laws, **MR. AND MRS. SIDNEY STILLMAN**, for raising such an individual.

May Hashem make this volume a vehicle solely for the increase of *Kavod HaTorah*. Amen.

*Reuven Subar*

*Tu B'Av 5769*

# THE ESSENTIAL
# MALBIM

## FLASHES OF INSIGHT
## ON BEREISHIS/GENESIS

# פרשת בראשית
# PARASHAS BEREISHIS

---

## A Perfect World?

וַיַּרְא אֱלֹקִים אֶת־כָּל־אֲשֶׁר עָשָׂה וְהִנֵּה־טוֹב מְאֹד

*And God saw all that He had made, and behold it was very good ....*
*(Bereishis 1:31)*

In describing the creation of the various parts of the world, the Torah repeatedly reports that God "saw that it was good," but only at the very end of the Creation, after the sixth day, does the Torah relate God's judgment of the world as "very good." One Midrash derives from here that even death is ultimately a good creation.[1]

---

1. *Bereishis Rabbah* 9:5,10.

The idea behind this is that the Torah is taking one position in a classic philosophical dispute, whether this world is the best of all possible worlds, which the Torah affirms that it is.

The opinion that this must be the best of possible worlds is based on theoretical considerations: God, Who wants to give kindness, and Who has no limitations of knowledge or power preventing Him from creating a perfect world, would of course do so.

Those who raised objections to this view did so only because the reality of evil in the world seems to contradict it. For this reason, the Torah spells out that if one looks at "all that God had made" as a unified whole, rather than concentrating on specific parts of the world, it is possible to see the total overall perfection. Rambam in *Moreh Nevuchim*[2] develops this idea further, giving examples of how harm to one individual often brings greater good to the world in general.

> **If one looks at "all that God had made" as a unified whole, it is possible to see the total overall perfection.**

This statement of the Torah about the perfection of the whole Creation could only have been placed after the creation of Man, since only the existence of Man as a model of the Divine, controlling and elevating physicality via spirituality, can provide a rationale for the existence of "lower" forms of matter such as animals, plants, and minerals. A narrow outlook on the world would make us wonder why God would create animal life-forms without understanding or plants without the ability to move or to perceive. All of these things seem incomplete and lacking when looked at in isolation, but in the context of Man's goal of bringing the Divine into the material, each is seen to have its place and play its role.

Even death, the ultimate expression of Man's finiteness, is clearly understood to be "very good" when it is grasped as the return of the soul to its Source after completing its assigned tasks in this world.

---

2. *Moreh Nevuchim* 3:12.

# Hashem's Two Systems

וַיַּרְא אֱלֹקִים אֶת־כָּל־אֲשֶׁר עָשָׂה ...
וַיְהִי־עֶרֶב וַיְהִי־בֹקֶר יוֹם הַשִּׁשִּׁי

*And God saw all that He had made ... and there was*
*evening and there was morning, **the sixth day***
*(Bereishis 1:31)*

וַיְכַל אֱלֹקִים בַּיּוֹם הַשְּׁבִיעִי מְלַאכְתּוֹ אֲשֶׁר עָשָׂה

*And God finished on **the seventh day***
*His work that He had done.*
*(Bereishis 2:2)*

A basic principle of Jewish thought is that God runs the world in two different ways simultaneously:

- The natural order of things based on the physical law that has been in operation since Creation. This system takes no notice of human behavior as such and neither rewards good nor punishes evil.

- Divine Providence (*hashgachah pratis*), which is capable of overriding natural law and dealing with people according to their merits; so that, for example, even though the facts of meteorology would require rain to fall from the clouds, if people do not deserve it, it will not be given.

These two systems differ in that the natural system is always in operation, whereas Providence responds solely to people's actions. Natural law therefore seems to operate in a way that flows from above to below, from God's decree at the time of Creation to the world below, while *hashgachah* flows in the opposite direction, from Man's actions below that awaken the response by Hashem.

This knowledge helps us to understand the change in the use of the Name of God in the two parts of the Creation narrative:

until the creation of Man, only the name *Elokim*, signifying natural processes, is used; after Man is created, the four-letter Name, associated with Divine Providence, is used as well.[3]

Another point that becomes clear based on this concept is the fact that the Torah in *Bereishis* 2:4[4] mentions the earth before the heavens, unlike the first verse of the Torah which mentions the heavens first. This indicates the onset of the Providential system of dealing with the world, flowing from Earth to Heaven.

A parable makes all of this even more clear:

A rich supporter of Torah decided to build a *Beis Midrash* and, at the same time, to build factories whose profit would go to support those who studied in the *Beis Midrash*. The factory would be equipped with numerous machines for producing goods, but he gave another order to his servants, that if the students in the *Beis Midrash* would not study with the proper diligence, the machines would be slowed down or stopped, resulting in the students being denied their needs.

In the same way, God set up the natural world to provide people with all their requirements, but from the time of the creation of Man onward, He also arranged that if people do not fulfill their task of serving God, the natural system will be prevented from giving its fruits.

This control system was put into operation on the first Shabbos. When the Torah says that the world was "finished" on the sixth day, it refers to the physical, natural world which operates according to blind laws. The Providential system, on the other hand, only went into operation on the seventh day.

Therefore, the Torah repeats the word "finished" on the seventh day, referring to the implementation of the "switch" that can turn the flow of sustenance on or off based on people's level

---

3. *Bereishis* 2:4

4. "These are the chronicles of the heavens and the earth ... on the day that Hashem, Elokim, made the earth and heavens." Malbim understands the second half of this verse as referring to the completion of Creation, at which time the Providential system began.

of righteousness. The completion achieved on the sixth day was that of the world itself, but the completion that came on Shabbos was the true culmination of God's intent in creating the world, to have a system that would be controlled by the good or evil actions of people.

> **Shabbos was the true culmination of God's intent in creating the world, to have a system that would be controlled by the good or evil actions of people.**

This is what our Sages referred to when they said that until Shabbos, the world was lacking rest. "Rest" was created on Shabbos, meaning that the mechanism for halting the flow of sustenance from the natural world as a result of the failings of people was first put into operation at that time.

# Active Rest

וַיְבָרֶךְ אֱלֹקִים אֶת־יוֹם הַשְּׁבִיעִי וַיְקַדֵּשׁ אֹתוֹ כִּי בוֹ שָׁבַת
מִכָּל־מְלַאכְתּוֹ אֲשֶׁר־בָּרָא אֱלֹקִים לַעֲשׂוֹת

*And God blessed the seventh day and sanctified it; because on it He abstained from all His work which God had created **to do.***
*(Bereishis 2:3)*

Shabbos was the time at which the control over the natural order of things was instituted; therefore it has an intrinsic holiness. But there is another important aspect to this rest; it is not synonymous with idleness, but rather it is: "blessed," since it ushers in the system of *hashgachah* that is even more fruitful than the natural system.

The Torah tells us this by adding to the end of this verse the word *la'asos*, "to do." With this phrase, the Torah informs us that the Shabbos rest was not a passive rest, but rather an opening of a new source of blessing from the higher system of God's way of dealing with the world, above the natural system.

The Midrash[5] makes this point clear by saying that God rested on Shabbos only from the "work of this world" but not from His "dealings with the righteous and the evil," doling out reward and punishment.

The way this blessing of Shabbos demonstrates itself is that Shabbos is the day on which the Divine Providence "descends" upon the world and takes precedence over the natural functioning manifest throughout the week. A parable illustrates this concept:

A king instructed officers to distribute wages to all the king's servants six days a week. On the seventh day, the officers themselves were expected to report to the king to receive the money to be given out the next week.

Since the officers were absent from their usual posts on that day, the impression could be had that the seventh day was particularly lacking in blessing; but a more careful examination of the facts shows that the seventh day was the *source* of all the blessing of the other six days, since that was the day on which the officers received the funds they would distribute from the king.

**Shabbos was the source of all of this miraculous blessing.** This is the concept expressed in the Midrash[6] and expanded upon in the Zohar,[7] that the blessing of Shabbos was seen in the fact that no manna fell on that day. Again, superficially this seems to be the opposite of blessing. Looking deeper, however, we understand that the phenomenon of the manna, supernatural though it was, did indeed fall physically from the sky; thus, it had to be renewed on Shabbos, and actually Shabbos was the source of all of this miraculous blessing.

---

5. *Bereishis Rabbah* 12:10.

6. Ibid. 11:2.

7. *Zohar II,* 88a.

# In Man's Merit

וְכֹל שִׂיחַ הַשָּׂדֶה טֶרֶם יִהְיֶה בָאָרֶץ וְכָל־עֵשֶׂב הַשָּׂדֶה טֶרֶם יִצְמָח
כִּי לֹא הִמְטִיר ה׳ אֱלֹקִים עַל־הָאָרֶץ וְאָדָם אַיִן לַעֲבֹד אֶת־
הָאֲדָמָה: וְאֵד יַעֲלֶה מִן־הָאָרֶץ וְהִשְׁקָה אֶת־כָּל־פְּנֵי הָאֲדָמָה: וַיִּיצֶר
ה׳ אֱלֹקִים אֶת־הָאָדָם עָפָר מִן־הָאֲדָמָה

*All the shrubs of the field were not yet upon the
earth, and all the grasses of the field had not yet
sprouted, because Hashem, God, had not sent rain
upon the earth, for there was no man to work the
land. Mist ascended from the earth and watered the
whole surface of the ground. Hashem, God, formed
the man from the dust of the ground ....*
*(Bereishis 2:5-7)*

The Torah prefaces the details of the creation of Man with two verses that seem irrelevant, dealing with the state of plant life immediately before Man's entry on the scene. The truth is, though, that these verses serve to focus on the cosmic significance of what was about to happen.

Without Man, the physical universe is pointless. This is illustrated by the example of the plant kingdom that existed before the sixth day, but nonetheless lacked permanence because of its two intimate connections with humanity:

**Without Man, the physical universe is pointless.**

- In a purely physical sense, many forms of plant life require care and cultivation by people in order to continue existing; if left on their own, they would become extinct.

- Even those species that grow wild cannot grow without rain, and the rain that is truly beneficial only comes through Man's prayers and righteous actions. Although much rain is derived from evaporation in a natural manner, the "rain of *berachah*" is derived from the "Higher

Waters" in a Providential manner, as a reward for Man's behavior.

These two relationships between Man and the plant world are what the Torah is describing here:

- First, the Torah mentions the "shrubs of the field," the types of trees and similar plants that cannot survive at all without human intervention, which grow in a cultivated "field." About these plants the Torah states: "There was [yet] no man to work the land" in a physical manner in order that these plants could grow.

- In addition, the Torah mentions that the "grasses," the plants that can grow without human attention, had not yet sprouted, since the Providential rain, "*matar*" in Hebrew, had not yet been brought down in response to prayer. Only "*id*," natural moisture (mist, dew) due to evaporation, was present, but the *berachah* needed for growth was lacking.

These factors demonstrated the need for the creation of Man. Man would provide his physical input and direction into the natural world, and, more importantly, would pray and leverage his moral and spiritual merits to bring the Divine blessings into the Creation.

# The Multistage Creation of Man

וַיִּיצֶר ה׳ אֱלֹקִים אֶת־הָאָדָם עָפָר מִן־הָאֲדָמָה

**Hashem, God, formed [va'yitzer] the man from the
dust of the ground ....
(Bereishis 2:7)**

L ashon HaKodesh has numerous words for making or creating, among them those formed from the roots *"bara,"*
*"asah,"* and *"yatzar."*
Each one of these roots has its own precise meaning and is
appropriate in specific contexts. The Torah utilizes each of these
three words with regard to the creation of both Man and animal.

The root *"bara"* always indicates a totally new creation from
no previously existing raw materials. The Torah uses this word
when describing the creation of the souls of animals (*"vayivra
Elokim es hataninim"*), which were not derived from physical
matter. This word is used again regarding the soul of the first
man (*"vayivra Elokim es ha'adam"*). Since Man's soul was qualitatively different from the souls of the animals, it could not be
produced from them.

The root *"asah"* indicates the completion of something that
already exists. Thus we find it used regarding the creation of
the land animals (*"vayaas Elokim es chayas ha'aretz"*), which
were similar to the preexisting marine animals, although more
advanced and perfected. Similarly, we find *"asah"* used in relation to Man (*"na'aseh adam"*) when describing the binding of his
soul to his body, which constituted the completion of his unique
nature as a freely choosing agent, unlike all other beings in the
world.

Lastly, the root *"yatzar"* describes the overall observable
"form" of something. For this reason it is appropriate in the
context of discussing the behavior and character of both animals

and Man, which includes both character traits and the intellect. Concerning animals the Torah states, "*va'yitzer es kol chayas ha'sadeh*," and about Man it says, "*va'yitzer Hashem Elokim es ha'adam*."

Despite this similarity between the "*yetzirah*," the creation of the form of Man and animals, the differences between Man and animals in this area is far more significant. Although there are some characteristics that people and animals share completely, those associated with the physical instincts and visualized as being located in the liver, there are many aspects to human nature that are fundamentally different from the nature of animals. These differences can be divided into two broad groups:

- Those characteristics that Man and animals share but which still have deep differences in detail.
- Those characteristics that are totally unique to Man.

The first group includes many personality traits that are subsumed under the name "*ruach*" in Hebrew and that are seen to lie in the heart. There are five essential differences between the expression of these traits in animals and in Man:

- The traits of animals, such as the bravery of a lion or the industry of an ant, are in reality not nearly as deeply rooted in their essence as are the parallel traits in a person.

As an analogy, Rambam[8] cites the difference between a room lighted by sunlight and one lit by a candle. Even though both could be said to be lit, the quality of the light is not comparable. Similarly, the character traits of an animal are in its animal soul, but those of a person are tied to his human, intelligent spirit.

- Each type of animal excels in only one specific trait, for example, the lion in bravery, the ant in industriousness, *etc.* Man, on the other hand, encompasses all the traits found in animals.

---

8. *Shemoneh Perakim.*

- Even when displaying its particular trait, each species of animal uses that trait in a very limited sphere. For instance, the ant uses its industriousness only to amass grain, while a person can use this trait to gather food, money, wisdom or other possessions.

- A person, unlike an animal, can harbor opposite traits; for example, arrogance and humility, stinginess and generosity, mercy and cruelty, shyness and boldness, or courage and cowardice. The brave lion, though, is never afraid; nor is the industrious ant ever lazy.

> *The brave lion is never afraid; nor is the industrious ant ever lazy.*

- Human character traits are practically unlimited in their quantitative scope. For example, one who desires wealth will never be satisfied with what he obtains. A person who seeks honor will not stop until he is exalted above everyone in a godlike fashion. The animal, on the other hand, has intrinsic limits to the scope of its traits.

All of these distinctions make it possible for human beings to have free choice in the exercise and control of their many character traits. Man can give his rational mind power over his instincts and desires, unlike the beast who is unable to resist the pressure of its drives.

In addition to all these traits, in some sense shared by Man and animals, people have an aspect that animals do not have at all: intellectual knowledge and understanding. Nonetheless, even this aspect of Man is considered to be associated with the physical body, and differs between individuals based on the personal nature of their bodies and brains.

The Torah hints at this by stating that the "*yetzirah*" of Man, his abstract form that is expressed as his intellect, was created "from the dust of the ground," the physical aspect of Man. Even according to the philosophical opinion that thoughts originate in higher spheres and are only "received" by the human mind, that mind still needs to possess a raw intellect that is capable of receiving that flow from above.

The Torah alludes to the various differences between human character traits and those of animals mentioned above:

- The *yetzirah* of Man is described as being from dust, fine particles, and that of animals as being from a clump of dirt, "*adamah.*" This indicates that Man has a compilation of varied and even contradictory character traits, as opposed to the one outstanding trait of each type of animal. Our Sages go farther with this idea, saying that the dust used in Man's creation came from all over the Earth.[9]

- The dust used for the creation of Man was positioned on top of the ground, suspended midway between Earth and Heaven, indicating that the character of Man can be utilized for rising up toward spiritual aims, or for falling into negative behaviors. Man can demonstrate mercy, justice, humility, self-control; or he can become cruel, arrogant, and uncontrolled. He can use his mind for the pursuit of spiritual wisdom, or for deviousness and trickery. Ultimately, the human soul can rise up to enter Heaven … or it can fall and descend toward the opposite.

- Man's creation is described in a phrase that first mentions the *object* of the creative act, Man, and only then mentions the *raw material* for that act, *dust*. This is because the main input for the creation of Man was his spiritual aspect, which derived from God; the ground was a secondary ingredient. Regarding the creation of animals, however, God said, "Let the earth bring forth living creatures," indicating that the earth was the main ingredient in their production, and that they remain forever tied to the earth in their nature.

---

9. *Sanhedrin* 38a.

- The Torah says that "all the animals of the field" were created, en masse, whereas Man's creation is described as that of a single individual. Within each animal species, the particular individuals are indistinguishable; all lions are brave, all leopards are bold, etc. Even within families of animal species the variations are relatively minor. Among people, however, the individual dissimilarities can be enormous, to the extent that different people may seem to be almost like different species.

This is because the human character contains all the varied traits imaginable; and each person chooses how to employ and emphasize those traits. Thus, we find the contrast between people who have mercy even on a fly and those who are cruel even to their own children, and similar examples regarding other traits. For this reason, the Torah describes Man as having been made as an individual, since no two people are alike.

# A Soul From Above

וַיִּפַּח בְּאַפָּיו נִשְׁמַת חַיִּים וַיְהִי הָאָדָם לְנֶפֶשׁ חַיָּה

*... And He breathed into his nostrils the soul of life [nishmas chayim], and man became a living being.*
*(Bereishis 2:7)*

After the Torah describes the creation of Man's body, it proceeds to the more significant aspect of Man, his soul, and informs us of its greatness and its elevated Source. Man's soul originates not from the material body or even from higher worlds, but from God's own "breath," as it were.

The soul is referred to in *Tanach* by three names: *nefesh*, *ruach*, and *neshamah*. The word *neshamah* derives from the root *nasham*, meaning exhalation. In numerous places, *neshamah* actually connotes human (but never animal) breath.

Since *neshamah*, when used with regard to the soul, means the "breath of God," it therefore refers to the highest level of the soul, its Divine and eternal aspect. When the Torah states that "God breathed into Man's nostrils a living *neshamah*," it refers to this aspect of the soul.

Once we picture the *neshamah* as originating within God Himself, there is no room for philosophical speculation about "where the soul was before it entered the body" or similar questions.

We can grasp this concept by thinking of the rays that emanate from the sun, or a drop of water taken from the sea. In a similar way, the *neshamah* comes from the Infinitude of God's Essence.

This concept is further deepened by the phrase, unique in the *Tanach*, "nishmas chayim," which accentuates the fact that the *neshamah* was "living" and active even before its introduction into the body.

When the Torah states that Man, through his completion with his soul, thereby became "a living being," we find ourselves somewhat puzzled: What is special here over and above what is true about the animals, who were also given life?

The truth, though, is that the Torah, through the juxtaposition of phrases, is addressing a basic question about human nature and the nature of the soul.

The soul has been described as consisting of three separate parts, vegetative, animal, and intellectual, or as being a unified whole having these three aspects. The Torah here teaches us, however, that the life of the human soul flows only from the *neshamah*, its highest Divine aspect.

Our Sages[10] elaborated on this: "David HaMelech used the phrase 'Bless, my soul' five times in relation to the soul and to God," drawing parallels between the human soul and God Himself:

---

10. *Berachos* 10a.

- "Just as God feeds the whole world, so the soul feeds the body. This refers to the 'vegetative' aspect of the soul that administers the most basic functions of metabolism.
- "Just as God fills the whole world, so the soul fills the body. This refers to the 'animal' or motive aspect of the soul that affects all parts of the body.
- "Just as God sees but cannot be seen, so the soul sees but cannot be seen. This is said in connection with the intellectual soul that 'sees' and understands."[11]

All of these functions are performed by the *neshamah* that is essentially one, yet manifests itself in various forms, and whose influence depends on the refinement or lack thereof of the body that is assigned to it; and if the *neshamah* is completely removed from the body, the body and all its processes cease to function.

For this reason, the Torah tells us that Man became a living being when the *neshamah* was infused into him, since only the Divine *neshamah* gives him life. This causes his entire life to be qualitatively different from that of animals, and it gives him his unique freedom of choice and his other distinctive qualities.

The *neshamah* permeates the entire body, but its effect differs on different parts of the body depending on their level of spirituality. The brain, which is the most pure and elevated part of the body, exhibits the highest aspect of the *neshamah*, the intellectual. The heart, which is somewhat less elevated, exhibits the motive aspect of the *neshamah*. Finally, the liver displays the lowest "vegetative" aspect.

*Even though the neshamah itself is totally holy and pure, it can only have an effect to the extent of the purity of the "vessel" that contains it.*

Similarly, in different people, each of whose body is refined to a different degree by nature or by his good or bad actions, the *neshamah* is able to exert its influence in a different quantity.

---

11. Only three of the five parallels are brought here.

Even though the *neshamah* itself is totally holy and pure, it can only have an effect to the extent of the purity of the "vessel" that contains it.

In this way, the influence of the *neshamah* on the body parallels God's influence on the world, which only evidences itself to the extent of the purity and refinement of the part of the world where God is revealing Himself.

# Planted in the Garden

וַיִּטַּע ה׳ אֱלֹקִים גַּן בְּעֵדֶן מִקֶּדֶם וַיָּשֶׂם שָׁם אֶת־הָאָדָם אֲשֶׁר
יָצָר: וַיַּצְמַח ה׳ אֱלֹקִים מִן־הָאֲדָמָה כָּל־עֵץ נֶחְמָד לְמַרְאֶה וְטוֹב
לְמַאֲכָל וְעֵץ הַחַיִּים בְּתוֹךְ הַגָּן וְעֵץ הַדַּעַת טוֹב וָרָע: וְנָהָר יֹצֵא
מֵעֵדֶן לְהַשְׁקוֹת אֶת־הַגָּן

*And Hashem, God, planted a garden in Eden, to*
*the east, and placed there the man whom He had*
*formed. And Hashem, God, caused to sprout from*
*the ground, every tree that was pleasing to the sight*
*and good for food .... A river issues forth from Eden*
*to water the garden ....*
*(Bereishis 2:8-10)*

One of the most obvious facts about human beings is the way in which they seem so poorly adapted to life in this world.

When compared with animals, Man seems sorely lacking in his ability to find food, clothing, and shelter. From birth, animals know instinctively how to find food in their immediate surroundings, while Man has to perform a long series of complex actions (plowing, planting, reaping, threshing, etc.) before he has bread to eat. Similarly, in order to have clothes to wear, people have to spin thread, weave, design, and sew. A house is even more complicated and requires even more work. All of this is in contrast to animals who have natural instincts for obtaining these needs, such as the beaver's innate ability to build a dam, the spider's talent for spinning a web, or the way a lion or tiger knows how to stalk its prey without any training or conscious planning.

Knowing this, we must wonder: How was the first man, without anyone to instruct him in the arts of providing for himself, able to survive at all?

The question actually has several aspects:

First of all, a lone individual — even with all the necessary knowledge — would not be able to produce anything, since all the tools he needs must themselves be manufactured, a matter that requires numerous individuals. To make bread, for example, he first needs to have a plow made of metal mined from the earth, refined and shaped. For each subsequent step, he needs additional tools and resources, each of which has to be made by people with specific skills. This is likewise true to an even greater extent with regard to clothing or housing.

Secondly, the acquisition of these skills itself is a matter that could take centuries for an entire society. It might take generations for people to figure out by trial and error that wheat could be cultivated and that it could be ground into flour and made into bread. How could a single person be expected to have this vitally important knowledge at the moment he was created?

Finally, the mind itself could hardly be expected to function in a practically useful manner in a person who had just come into existence. Even to understand the concept of fire and to utilize it requires a significant amount of life experience, repeatedly seeing wood burn and perceiving the cause-and-effect relationship between the fire and the burning of wood to coals, for example.

Even speech would seem impossible for such a person, since words by their nature are abstractions from extensive experience with the world. We see that children take a long time to master the ability to walk, which requires an implicit understanding of balance, something which can only come from repeated attempts and failures over time. How can we imagine the way that the first man was able to perform all these functions immediately?

The answer to these questions is that God — Whose kindness to His creatures leads Him to provide each one with the innate skills needed for its survival: the bee with the ability to build a hive, the beaver a dam, etc. — gives people, instead of these sorts of instincts, a general practical intellect to be utilized to gain in a superior manner the skills that the animals innately have. However, He also provides them with the basic instincts necessary for immediate survival

The primary example of this is a newborn baby's ability to nurse, unconsciously using the principles of physics and engineering to imbibe the milk needed for his survival without having to figure them out or be taught them explicitly.

*A newborn baby uses the principles of physics and engineering to imbibe the milk needed for his survival without having to figure them out or be taught them explicitly.*

In the same way, the first man was like a newborn child in his need for basic survival skills, and therefore God provided him with enough understanding and intellectual sophistication to be able to live. He was given the ability to speak, to walk, to take a piece of fruit into his mouth before he would have been able to figure out these things himself; otherwise he would have perished in a short time.

However, the first man was not given even the slightest bit more than the bare minimum necessary for survival, in order that he should have the opportunity to acquire the rest in his unique human fashion, by experiment, choice, and the exercise of his mind.

It follows, therefore, that God did not provide the first man with a building instinct similar to that of the beaver, for example, since that would have required giving him a huge amount of complex skills and knowledge. The same is true in the areas of agriculture or clothing manufacture. God did not want to give

Man innate skills in all the areas needed for pursuing these occupations; He wanted Man to gain these skills himself through the use of his mind. Even when Adam and Chavah made themselves clothes after their sin, they were crude coverings made of leaves; the "leather robes" were subsequently provided to them by God.

If so, we remain with the question of how Man would survive with only these very minimal skills. The Torah answers this question by informing us that God planted a garden of fruit trees that needed no cultivation or care, and that produced food that was ready to eat. The garden was located in Eden, an area near the equator where the climate was so pleasant and constant that there was no need for shelter. There they could live without clothing since there was no rain; rather, the garden was irrigated by the river issuing from Eden, just as the Nile provides water for Egypt. This was the ideal and perfectly designed place where God placed the first man and where he could most easily fulfill the goals for which he was created.

# The Four Rivers
## of Human Nature

וְנָהָר יֹצֵא מֵעֵדֶן לְהַשְׁקוֹת אֶת־הַגָּן וּמִשָּׁם יִפָּרֵד וְהָיָה לְאַרְבָּעָה
רָאשִׁים

*And a river issues forth from Eden to water the garden; and from there it is divided and becomes four headwaters [major rivers].*

**(Bereishis 2:10)**

The Torah relates that four rivers issued from Eden to several distant parts of the world. Beyond a physical description of geography, we can see in this a symbolism of the different streams of emphasis found among people and nations.

Civilizations have always been tied to sources of water, so

these rivers represent the principal groups among humanity. The rivers issue from Eden, indicating that these rivers are the paths of life from which people would choose after mankind left Paradise. Even though the preferred goal of Adam and Chavah, the first pair of people, was to remain in Gan Eden and to pursue only knowledge and closeness to God, nonetheless the preparations were already set in place for the eventuality of the failure of that approach to life and the entrance of mankind into the larger and more complex world.

> *The preparations were already set in place for the eventuality of leaving Gan Eden for the larger and more complex world.*

According to our Sages, the primary source-river that entered the garden was P'ras, the Euphrates, which was also one of the four derived rivers leaving Gan Eden. This river symbolizes the spiritual path, and for that reason it is associated with the Land of Israel,[12] a place that produces wisdom and prophecy.

The other three rivers are representative of the three other paths of life, those that our Sages refer to in *Pirkei Avos* as the three traits which "remove a person from the world": jealousy, physical desire (lust), and the pursuit of honor.

These three traits are the source of all of mankind's misfortune and suffering. From jealousy and the desire for riches comes dissatisfaction as well as endless frivolous distractions from life's purpose. Physical desire leads to animalistic behavior and the deterioration of people's humanity. The search for honor and prestige brings war and destruction of all sorts. Only those who follow the "fourth river" to a spiritual path are able to escape from the emptiness of endless pursuit of material ends.

Each of these four approaches to life was associated with a specific area of the world where one of the rivers was located.

The river Pishon encircled the land of Chavilah, where "good gold" and "precious stones" were to be found. These items have

---

12. *Bereishis* 15:18.

no great intrinsic worth, but rather are considered valuable due to their rarity; for this reason the Torah emphasizes that they were found "there," meaning that they were not common in all the world, and therefore they were precious. This river symbolizes the rush after wealth, for money and other such things that are not intrinsically important, but which people desire in order to have more than others. (Or, but which people desire because they envy the prestige and power with which they endow others.) The Torah does not call this river the "first," even though it is listed first, but rather "one" or "number one." This indicates that it was not truly first in importance (since that distinction belongs to the Euphrates, the symbol of spirituality) but merely counted first in the list.

The second river, Gichon,[13] encircled the lush, hot tropics, and thus it represents physical passion.

The third river is the Chidekel (Tigris) to the east of Ashur, a noisy river near a land known for its aggressiveness, therefore symbolizing the desire for honor and power. This river is described as "going" rather than "encircling" as are the first two, since the seeker of control and power is more motivated to go from place to place rather than to remain within his own private domain.

Finally, the Euphrates is the river associated with Eretz Yisrael, as mentioned above, and represents the more spiritual life to be found in that Land. For this reason, the Torah does not say that the "name" of this river is P'ras, but merely states that "it is P'ras," since "name" and fame are synonymous, and this path is chosen only by the few and its value is little known.

Our Sages also hinted at this idea when they said that "the Euphrates flows quietly but its fruits bear witness to its importance,"[14] meaning that the greatness of the righteous testifies to the worth of the spiritual path of life.

---

13. Additionally, its name hearkens to "gachon" (Vayikra 11:42) referring to the belly of a crawling snake (Rashi, ibid.), suggesting a lowly attachment to earthliness.

14. Tosafos Bechoros 55b.

# Here to Stay?

וַיִּקַּח ה׳ אֱלֹקִים אֶת־הָאָדָם וַיַּנִּחֵהוּ בְגַן־עֵדֶן לְעָבְדָהּ וּלְשָׁמְרָהּ

**And Hashem, God, took the man and placed him in the Garden of Eden, to work it and to guard it.**

**_(Bereishis 2:15)_**

The concept of free will was intimately interwoven into the whole story of the creation of Man. It expressed itself both in the explicit test of the Tree of Knowledge of Good and Evil and in the availability of the alternative paths of life outside of Gan Eden symbolized by the four rivers, representing jealousy, lust, desire for honor or the pursuit of wisdom and spirituality.

After putting Man's origin into this context, the Torah makes it clear that he was not left without Divine guidance in this vitally important matter. When the Torah tells us that the first man was "taken" and "placed" in Gan Eden, it means that God convinced him of the importance of being there and instructed him to do what was necessary to be able to remain there, as opposed to following the "rivers" of empty material goals. The word for "placed," "_vayanicheihu,_" means putting something in its proper location, and is related to the word "_nach,_" "rested."

> **"Working the garden" refers to positive commandments; "guarding it" refers to negative ones.**

In addition, he was told to "work it and to guard it," indicating that not only was he placed somewhere where it was natural and comfortable for him to stay, but he was explicitly commanded in both a positive and a negative fashion to remain there, as our Sages[15] tell us that "working it" refers to positive commandments and "guarding it" refers to negative ones. After this, he was given the explicit commandment against eating from the Tree of Knowledge.

---

15. _Zohar I,_ 27a; _Tikunei Zohar_ 62a.

# The First Commandment

וַיְצַו ה' אֱלֹקִים עַל־הָאָדָם לֵאמֹר מִכֹּל עֵץ־הַגָּן אָכֹל תֹּאכֵל: וּמֵעֵץ
הַדַּעַת טוֹב וָרָע לֹא תֹאכַל מִמֶּנּוּ כִּי בְּיוֹם אֲכָלְךָ מִמֶּנּוּ מוֹת תָּמוּת

*And Hashem, God, commanded the man, saying,*
*"Of every tree of the garden you may surely eat;*
*but of the Tree of Knowledge of Good and Evil, you*
*must not eat from it; for on the day you eat of it,*
*you shall surely die."*
*(Bereishis 2:16-17)*

When God forbade the first man to eat from the Tree of Knowledge, He prefaced the prohibition with a statement that the fruit of all other trees was permitted. This is the way of the Torah in general, as we find in the cases of the laws of Shabbos, of Shemittah, and others, mentioning first what is permitted, in order to remind us that these mitzvos do not render our lives impossible or inordinately difficult.

Only one day of the week and one year out of seven put restrictions on our working activity; the rest of the time we are free to engage in our occupations. Similarly, the first man had a huge variety of fruit trees from which to choose, and only one that was off limits.

Our Sages go even farther and point out that the Torah actually does not prohibit any form of pleasure totally. For every forbidden food, for example, there is a permitted food that tastes the same.[16] This illustrates that God is only interested in keeping Man away from that which is seemingly good but which ultimately leads to his detriment, as symbolized by the Tree of Knowledge.

The commandment against eating from the Tree of Knowledge seems to be phrased in a redundant fashion, "Of the Tree of Knowledge of Good and Evil, you must not eat *from it.*" This redundancy was part of the cause of the downfall of the first man,

---

16. *Chullin* 109b.

since he took it to limit the prohibition to actually taking the fruit *directly* from the tree as opposed to eating it if it was picked by someone else, and this led to his defense that "the woman gave me the fruit."

According to this, the essence of his sin was that he relied on his own fallible reasoning to find "loopholes" in a clear statement of a commandment. At the very least, he should have considered the matter to be in doubt, since he certainly realized that he could conceivably be wrong. We find similar examples in other places in *Tanach*, such as the prophet in Beis-El[17] who interpreted his own prophecy based on his own logic, or Shimi ben Gera who interpreted his oath to Shlomo HaMelech.[18]

The first man was told that on the day on which he would eat from the Tree of Knowledge he would die. The Torah tells us, however, that he died many years later.[19]

The answer to this contradiction is that immediately after he ate from the tree, death became unavoidable for him. Eating the fruit of the tree resulted in his tendency toward thoughts of jealousy, desire, and the need for honor, and this put the body and soul at odds in a perpetual struggle. In addition, the soul thereby became intimately bound to the body with no possibility of ever separating itself to return to its spiritual source, and therefore the idea of eternal life in this world became something that would be painful and detrimental to the soul. For the body, too, these new tendencies of jealousy and desire were intrinsically destructive, as we are well aware from experience. Death now could be seen as

> **The soul became intimately bound to the body; therefore the idea of eternal life in this world became something that would be painful and detrimental to the soul.**

---

17. *I Melachim* 13. The prophet was told not to eat, yet he ate, basing his decision upon a rationalization.

18. Ibid. 2:8,9.

19. *Bereishis* 5:5.

a necessary escape from the otherwise never-rending torture of life for both the body and the soul.

On another level of understanding, death can be literally seen to begin from the moment of eating of the fruit, since the body began deteriorating and losing the moisture of youth, a process that would eventually end in total death, but that can be considered a bit of death in itself. The Hebrew phrase used in the warning of punishment for eating the fruit, "*mos tamus*," hints through its repetitiveness at this constant process of "many deaths."

A third aspect in which death was immediate is that the soul lost its direct connection to spirituality and its perception of Divine Providence, remaining only with a physical life centered on the body and its needs, a deathlike state for the *neshamah*, and one which our Sages described when they stated, "Evil people are called dead even in their lifetime."[20]

# The Root of All Mitzvos

וַיְצַו ה' אֱלֹקִים עַל־הָאָדָם לֵאמֹר מִכֹּל עֵץ־הַגָּן אָכֹל תֹּאכֵל: וּמֵעֵץ הַדַּעַת טוֹב וָרָע לֹא תֹאכַל מִמֶּנּוּ כִּי בְּיוֹם אֲכָלְךָ מִמֶּנּוּ מוֹת תָּמוּת

**And Hashem, God, commanded the man, saying,**
**"Of every tree of the garden you may surely eat.**
**But of the Tree of Knowledge of Good and Evil, you**
**must not eat from it; for on the day you eat of it**
**you shall surely die."**
**(Bereishis 2:16)**

Besides the commandment to the first man prohibiting eating from the Tree of Knowledge, our Sages[21] derive from this verse an enunciation of the first six of the Seven Commandments given to all of mankind, the "*Sheva Mitzvos B'nei Noach*," each commandment being derived from a word or

---

20. *Berachos* 18b.
21. *Bereishis Rabbah* 16:6, *Sanhedrin* 57a.

phrase in this verse alluding to a similar word or phrase elsewhere in the Torah on the same subject.

Adam was commanded:

- Do not worship idols.
- Do not curse God.
- Do not steal.
- Do not kill.
- Do not commit adultery.
- Enforce law and justice.[22]

Now certainly prior to his sin Adam had no true need for these commandments; after all, whom would he kill, steal from, or commit adultery with? Rather, these six mitzvos, besides being commandments in and of themselves to Adam and his offspring, are also general categories into which all the other 613 mitzvos of the Torah fit:

The 613 mitzvos of the Torah may be divided into two general categories:

- mitzvos pertaining to one's obligations to God;
- mitzvos pertaining to one's obligations to his fellow man.

The first category, one's obligations to God, may be further subdivided:

First, there are the mitzvos that relate to the emotions: love, reverence, and a feeling of subservience to God. All these mitzvos are subsumed under the mitzvah "*Do not curse God.*" Secondly, there are the commandments that in practice prevent a *chillul Hashem*, a loss of awareness of God in the world. These mitzvos are all considered branches of the prohibition "*Do not worship idols.*"

The mitzvos between man and his fellow man fall into four main categories: refraining from the three types of harm to others in their bodies, property, or marital relationship, plus the

---

22. The seventh of the "*Sheva Mitzvos B'nei Noach*," not to eat a limb taken from a live animal, was subsequently given to Noach (*Sanhedrin* 59b, see *Rashi* to *Bereishis* 9:3,4).

general obligation to organize society to make civilization possible. These correspond to *"Do not kill," "Do not steal," "Do not commit adultery,"* and *"Enforce law and justice."*

Thus, all 613 mitzvos of the Torah — which God later gave the Jews to observe as the means to express their gratitude for the greater benefits they received over and above those given to all mankind — can be seen as extensions of the six basic commandments given to mankind in general. These six categories were further concentrated into one single prohibition for the first man, since by refraining from eating that fruit he would have prevented himself from ever developing the attitudes and the kinds of thoughts that would lead to either being disloyal to God or to harming another person.

> **By refraining from eating that fruit, Adam would have prevented himself from ever developing the attitudes that would lead to either being disloyal to God or to harming another person.**

# Man and Woman

וַיֹּאמֶר ה' אֱלֹקִים לֹא־טוֹב הֱיוֹת הָאָדָם לְבַדּוֹ אֶעֱשֶׂה־לּוֹ
עֵזֶר כְּנֶגְדּוֹ

*And Hashem, God, said, "It is not good that the man be alone; I will make for him a helper corresponding to him [literally: 'opposite' him]."*
*(Bereishis 2:18)*

One of the most striking differences between the description of the creation of Man and that of the animals is the way males and females originated. There are three main aspects to the uniqueness of the creation of the first couple:

- Large numbers of animals, both male and female, were created all at once. In contrast, the first man was made alone and then given a mate. One opinion among our Sages even holds that the first human being had the form of man on one side and of woman on the other. [23]
- Animals were not assigned specific mates, whereas the first man was given a particular woman for him alone.
- Unlike female animals that were created from the ground in the same manner as the males, the woman was formed from the body of the man himself.

All these differences point to the unique reasons for creating human beings both male and female over and above the necessities of procreation.

The first fact that must be recognized is that each individual person is already in a sense a "couple," since he is composed of a soul and a body that together possess the ability to "give birth" to a complete, constantly improving individual. If the soul succeeds in controlling the instincts of the body, it will be able to transform the body and infuse it with a spiritual nature, producing constant growth toward higher levels.

> *Each individual person is already in a sense a "couple," since he is composed of a soul and a body that together possess the ability to "give birth" to a complete, constantly improving individual.*

If, on the other hand, the body pursues its own agenda, following the dictates of the imagination, the emotions, and physical desire, motivations that find their roots in the Tree of Knowledge, then the individual loses his uniqueness, and is a member of a species like any animal. In this scenario, the sole form of procreation is the physical, just as for animals. All this explains why Man was created first as a single individual, since he was expected to pursue this internal form of

23. *Berachos* 61b; *Rashi, Bereishis* 2:21.

growth and creativity in addition to the usual reproduction of new individuals after the fashion of animals.

Another very significant aspect of Man's distinction from animals is that each person has his own particular personality and traits, unlike the animal kingdom, where all members of a species are essentially the same. For this reason, large numbers of individual animals of each species, male and female, were created at once, while the first pair of humans were made individually.

Our Sages[24] interpret the Torah's statement that a woman is a "helper opposite" her husband to mean that she either helps him through her similar traits and goals if he merits such direct help, or else he receives benefit from her by means of her opposition to his negative aspects if that is what he needs. In either case, a couple must be "tailor made" for each other, and this is symbolized by the fact that initially, only one man and one woman were made.

Animals have reproductive instincts that have natural limits in time and extent. Their reproductive urge comes upon them during certain seasons of the year, and when this season passes, they lose their urge until the next season. Humans, on the other hand, seem to have a constantly active carnal desire.

This fits very well with the essential difference between Man and the animals: Man's free will. Animals, because they have no way of curbing their desires, were given instincts limiting those desires to certain specific times of year. Man, on the other hand, is given a choice: He can follow his almost endless desires, or he can control them with his mind and use them in the right context for good purposes. The result if he succeeds is much more impressive than the instinctive abstinence found among animals. This idea, as well, is conveyed by the creation of one man and one woman, indicative of the need for a person to express his desire solely toward his spouse and solely in the context of the mitzvos that determine proper marital conduct.

---

24. *Yevamos* 63a.

A final distinction between Man and animals is that Man has a social nature in addition to the physical; therefore, he has an institution of marriage that provides — aside from procreation — friendship and also numerous practical benefits. For this reason, also, Man needed a specific woman created from his own flesh to be his companion and partner.

All of these are implicit in the words of the Torah, "It is not good that the man be alone," meaning that the purpose of the creation of Man would not be served by creating many disconnected male and female individuals after the pattern of the animals; rather God states His plan to make for Man "a helper opposite him" who will provide him with friendship, opportunities for personal growth, and an elevated focus for his desire, providing him with one of the most important expressions of his human greatness.

# The Gift of Language

וַיִּצֶר ה׳ אֱלֹקִים מִן־הָאֲדָמָה כָּל־חַיַּת הַשָּׂדֶה וְאֵת כָּל־עוֹף הַשָּׁמַיִם
וַיָּבֵא אֶל־הָאָדָם לִרְאוֹת מַה־יִּקְרָא־לוֹ וְכֹל אֲשֶׁר יִקְרָא־לוֹ הָאָדָם
נֶפֶשׁ חַיָּה הוּא שְׁמוֹ

*And Hashem, God, had formed out of the ground*
*every beast of the field and every bird of the sky,*
*and brought them to the man to see what he would*
*call each one; and whatever the man called each liv-*
*ing creature, that remained its name.*
*(Bereishis 2:19)*

The origin of language has always been a subject of speculation, with some thinkers considering it an innate ability and others a skill derived from outside influences. The Torah reveals that the capacity for speech is actually a miraculous gift from God to the first man and his descendants.

This knowledge still leaves us with some open questions about the details of the process: Did God give Man a full-blown language or did He teach him bit by bit? If it was given all at once, was it given as a skill to create a language or as complete knowledge of the words and usage of the language? Finally, if words were given explicitly, were they presented as words alone or with the ability to apply them, and how was this done?

*The capacity to create a language from scratch is not part of the mind's basic abilities.*

Reason tells us that a single miracle of instilling a full language into Man's mind is much closer to the natural order than repetitive miracles of bit-by-bit instruction from God, and we know that this is always God's way of dealing with the world, in as natural a manner as possible.

Furthermore, the capacity to create a language from scratch is not part of the mind's basic abilities, which include only imagination and understanding but not producing something from nothing, so we must conclude that God gave Man language as a finished product. Having words without connection to reality likewise seems practically worthless. We are left only with the question of exactly what the procedure was by which God gave this connection to the first man.

This is what the Torah describes when it states that God "brought the animals before the man to see what he would call them." The words and concepts were already implanted in the mind of the first man; seeing the animals was only God's pedagogical technique to enable him to bridge the gap between the abstract (knowing the words) and the actual (putting the words to use).

# Adam — The
# All-Inclusive Being

וַיִּצֶר ה׳ אֱלֹקִים מִן־הָאֲדָמָה כָּל־חַיַּת הַשָּׂדֶה וְאֵת כָּל־עוֹף הַשָּׁמַיִם
וַיָּבֵא אֶל־הָאָדָם לִרְאוֹת מַה־יִּקְרָא־לוֹ וְכֹל אֲשֶׁר יִקְרָא־לוֹ הָאָדָם
נֶפֶשׁ חַיָּה הוּא שְׁמוֹ

*And Hashem, God, formed from the ground all the*
*creatures of the field and every bird of the sky, and*
*brought them to the man to see what he would call*
*each one; and whatever the man called each living*
*creature, that remained its name.*
*(Bereishis 2:19)*

The wonder of the human soul is the fact that it contains so many varied and even contradictory character traits, and our commentators have noted that the traits of every type of animal are potentially present in a person. If one finds an animal with a certain characteristic, he may be sure that it is possible to find that same characteristic in himself to some degree. It was once common to use the names of animals as synonyms for the traits exhibited by those animals: a lion connoting bravery, a horse arrogance, etc.

Rambam[25] uses this approach to explain the symbolism of the four animals mentioned in Yechezkel's vision of the Divine Chariot, and Shlomo HaMelech expresses the same concept when instructing a lazy person to look at an ant,[26] indicating that since he sees the ant working hard, he must also have the ability to be industrious. We can even say that this is the reason for the creation of the various animals with their particular traits, so that those traits could then be reflected in Man.

---

25. *Moreh Nevuchim* 3:1.
26. *Mishlei* 6:6.

Man's multidimensional nature is why the Torah explicitly mentions the dust when describing his creation, since he is similar to dust. Just as dust is composed of many particles, so too, Man is made up of many threads of personality.

This is expressed by the Midrash:[27] When the angels saw that Man succeeded in giving the animals names and in giving himself the name *Adam*, they realized that his wisdom was greater than theirs. Man's ability to give appropriate names to animals came from his perception of all the special traits of the animals *within himself*, a perspective that no angel could have. This very fact was most clearly expressed in the name Adam, which he related to the word "*adamah*" meaning ground or earth, hinting at his own multifaceted nature, like the many grains of the dust of the earth. The animals were also created from the ground, but only Man with his multifaceted self has a name that originates in the granular nature of the ground.

> *Just as dust is composed of many particles, so too, Man is made up of many threads of personality.*

The Torah conveys these concepts to us on the level of a subtle hint when it says: "God formed from the ground all the creatures of the field ... and *brought them to the man*." This could be understood to mean that all the different *traits and characteristics* of the animals were *brought to the man*, i.e., were incorporated into the human soul. Thus, "whatever *the man* would call each living being, that was its name" – i.e., Man, the all-inclusive Adam, was therefore able to give accurate names to all the aspects of himself that he perceived in other creatures.

The Hebrew language has two alternative forms for relating the verb "*kara*," "called," to its object. When the connective between these two words is "*es*," the connotation is one of giving a name to something nameless. When the verb and object are connected with the letter *lamed*, meaning "called to," it means that an *additional* name is given to something already named.

---

27. *Bereishis Rabbah* 17:4.

This distinction in usage applies to the naming of the animals, since God had already given a general name to all animals, "*nefesh chayah,*" living beings. Man added new and particular names for each species, and these names were what the angels were unable to grasp on their own.

# Thy Name Is Woman

וַיֹּאמֶר הָאָדָם זֹאת הַפַּעַם עֶצֶם מֵעֲצָמַי וּבָשָׂר מִבְּשָׂרִי לְזֹאת
יִקָּרֵא אִשָּׁה כִּי מֵאִישׁ לֻקֳחָה־זֹּאת: עַל־כֵּן יַעֲזָב־אִישׁ אֶת־אָבִיו
וְאֶת־אִמּוֹ וְדָבַק בְּאִשְׁתּוֹ וְהָיוּ לְבָשָׂר אֶחָד

*And the man said, "This time, it is bone from my
bones and flesh of my flesh; to this one shall be
called 'ishah' [woman], for from 'ish' [man] was she
taken." Therefore a man shall leave his father and
mother, and cling to his wife, and they shall
become one flesh.*
*(Bereishis 2:23-24)*

A cursory reading of the Torah's account of the origin of woman would seem to indicate that she had no name until Adam called her "*ishah,*" woman. A knowledge of Hebrew usage, however, tells us that the use of the phrase "*l'zos y'karei,*" literally "*to this one* shall be called," rather than simply "*es zos,*" "*this one,*" assumes the prior existence of some name for her.

If we remember the statement of our Sages that the first man was created with both male and female "sides,"[28] we understand that originally the woman was also called "Adam" until the two of them were separated and therefore the name "*ishah*" was an added name.

---

28. *Berachos* 61b; *Rashi, Bereishis* 2:21; "*Tzela,*" literally "rib," can also mean a side, as in *Shemos* 26:20.

The choice of this name instead of "*adamah,*" the feminized form of Adam, can be understood based on the principle given by Radak[29] that among animals, only names that are relevant to age have feminine forms (for example, a young female lamb is a "*kivsah,*" parallel to "*keves*"). This clarifies the difference between the two names for Man, "*Adam*" and "*ish*": Adam is the proper name for a human being and is applicable immediately upon birth, consistent

*Originally the woman was also called "Adam" until the two of them were separated.*

with numerous derivations of halachos which include even a new-born baby in the category of "*Adam.*" "*Ish,*" on the other hand, connotes only an adult, and in halachic contexts excludes minors.

The words of the first man now are quite clear. He reacted to the new reality of the woman as a complete separate being by saying, "This time," now that she is an individual, "flesh and bone originating from my body" rather than a part of me, and I myself am now complete and fit to be called "*ish,*" she shall have the new name "*ishah,*" reminiscent of her origin from "*ish,*" rather than "Adam," one taken from the dust, "*adamah.*"

The Torah now generalizes this to all human couples, and states: Just as the first man left his association with the ground — which was in a sense his physical "parent" — at the time he was split in two and acquired a wife, so too, people born of human parents leave their attachment to their physical origins, their parents, when they become adults and cling instead to their spouses to build a new family.

---

29. *Vayikra* 1:2.

# A Garment of Flesh

וַיִּהְיוּ שְׁנֵיהֶם עֲרוּמִּים הָאָדָם וְאִשְׁתּוֹ וְלֹא יִתְבּשָׁשׁוּ

*And they were both naked, the man and his wife,*
*and they were not ashamed.*
*(Bereishis 2:25)*

We are so aware of the shame we would feel were we to be seen without clothing that the Torah's description of the first couple as being unclothed yet unashamed seems quite strange to us. In the context of their spiritual state, though, it is more easily understood, and on two levels.

First, since they had not yet acquired the "evil inclination," the desire for selfish and unnecessary pleasures that became part of them only after eating from the Tree of Knowledge, they related to their reproductive organs in a purely functional manner just as they related to any other part of the body. They felt no subconscious need to hide aspects of themselves that could lead them to behavior of which they would not be proud.

Secondly, and on a deeper level, before eating from the Tree of Knowledge, their souls were not as permanently and intimately connected with the body as ours are after that sin. The soul had the capability of leaving the body temporarily to commune more closely with God. As a result of this, the body for them played the role that clothing plays for us, a covering of the real self that can be donned or removed at will. The body could remain unclothed since it itself was only a garment and it needed no other garment to hide it.

> **The soul had the capability of leaving the body temporarily to commune more closely with God.**

# The Clever Snake

וְהַנָּחָשׁ הָיָה עָרוּם מִכֹּל חַיַּת הַשָּׂדֶה אֲשֶׁר עָשָׂה ה' אֱלֹקִים וַיֹּאמֶר אֶל־הָאִשָּׁה אַף כִּי־אָמַר אֱלֹקִים לֹא תֹאכְלוּ מִכֹּל עֵץ הַגָּן: וַתֹּאמֶר הָאִשָּׁה אֶל־הַנָּחָשׁ מִפְּרִי עֵץ־הַגָּן נֹאכֵל: וּמִפְּרִי הָעֵץ אֲשֶׁר בְּתוֹךְ־הַגָּן אָמַר אֱלֹקִים לֹא תֹאכְלוּ מִמֶּנּוּ וְלֹא תִגְּעוּ בּוֹ פֶּן תְּמֻתוּן: וַיֹּאמֶר הַנָּחָשׁ אֶל־הָאִשָּׁה לֹא־מוֹת תְּמֻתוּן: כִּי יֹדֵעַ אֱלֹקִים כִּי בְּיוֹם אֲכָלְכֶם מִמֶּנּוּ וְנִפְקְחוּ עֵינֵיכֶם וִהְיִיתֶם כֵּאלֹקִים יֹדְעֵי טוֹב וָרָע

*And the snake was the most clever of all the creatures of the field that Hashem, God, had made. He said to the woman: "Couldn't God have said not to eat from any of the trees of the garden?"*

*The woman said to the snake: "We can eat from the fruit of the trees of the garden; but from the fruit of the tree that is in the middle of the garden, God has said: 'You shall not eat of it, and you shall not touch it, lest you die.'"*

*The snake said to the woman, "You will surely not die; for God knows that on the day you eat of it, your eyes will be opened and you will be like God...."*

*(Bereishis 3:1-5)*

To understand the encounter between the first woman and the snake, it is necessary to realize that at that time all animal life was on a far higher level than after the sin of the Tree of Knowledge; the snake was only the most prominent example of this. The Torah states when describing the punishment given to the snake that it was cursed "more than all the animals,"[30] implying that the other animals were also reduced in their stature. Before the sin, the world was in a state of universal

---

30. *Bereishis* 3:14.

peace, extending even to potentially carnivorous animals which ate grass, just as the prophets[31] state that they will do at the time of *Mashiach*.

The characteristic trait of the snake is stated to be its "cleverness," "*armah*," the ability to plan and plot practical schemes, whether for good or evil. This is distinct from true intelligence which is associated only with Man, and which is closely affiliated with Man's free will. The Torah emphasizes this higher degree of cleverness of all animals, and especially of the snake, when it states that the snake was cleverer than all the animals that "God had made"; that is, when they were in their original state in which God put them, before being reduced by the sin of Man. This especial cleverness of the snake explains why it was found within the household of the first couple, since Adam saw that it could have great practical use and had decided to domesticate it.

Of course, the snake's cleverness turned out to be its own undoing and that of mankind as well. It was precisely that similarity between animal cleverness and human wisdom and choice that caused the confusion of the first woman and ultimately, her and Adam's sin.

The snake professed wonder at God's commandment not to eat from the Tree of Knowledge by saying, "Couldn't God have said not to eat from *any* of the trees of the garden?" using the verb "*amar*," "said," instead of "*tzivah*," "commanded." The snake expressed his lack of comprehension of the need for a *commandment* and a *warning* that the tree would cause death, because God has the power to make any act impossible by nature and instinct. At least, this is how things appeared from the "clever" but animalistic perspective of the snake.

The woman chose to respond to him, but in the process made a subtle mistake of her own. She attempted to describe to the snake the human trait of free will, and said, "We can eat of the fruit of the trees of the garden," even in defiance of a Divine commandment, if we so choose. The Tree of Knowledge, how-

31. *Yeshayahu* 65:25.

ever, she said, is different, since God warned us of its danger and potential to cause death. She emphasized this with the *addition* of a prohibition that God had not actually commanded, "you shall not touch it."

Within her understanding of the commandment not to eat the fruit as a warning against its physically harmful effects, it followed naturally that touching it must also be dangerous. This opened the door for the snake to prove to her that touching the tree had no harmful effect, and ultimately this led to the sin of her eating the fruit itself.[32] We see from here the deleterious results of over-rationalizing the reasons behind Divine commandments and forgetting that they are decrees from God, irrespective of whatever beneficial effects they may possess.

The snake continued with a statement seemingly impugning selfish motivations to God Himself, and to which our Sages have given a very cryptic interpretation. "God knows," said the snake, "that on the day on which you eat of it, your eyes will be opened and you will be like God." The Sages[33] read into this the claim that "God ate from this tree and created the world," an obviously outrageous assertion.

In the context of the snake as a being that possessed a cleverness

> *"God ate from this tree and created the world!" is an obviously outrageous assertion.*

closely imitating but essentially different from human intelligence, these claims have an internal consistency. The snake, with its great technical mental skills, was able to envision the immediate benefits of the pursuit of physical and worldly pleasures toward which the fruit of the Tree of Knowledge would lead them; however, his lack of free will and higher, true intelligence blinded him to the fact that these benefits were outweighed immensely by the

---

32. The snake pushed her against the tree and said, "Just as touching it does not cause death, so too eating it will not cause death" *Bereishis Rabbah* 19:3.

33. *Bereishis Rabbah* 19:4.

negative spiritual consequences of such a path. When our Sages read into the words of the snake the claim that "God ate from this tree and created the world," they meant to represent the snake as saying, "This sort of 'good,' temporary physical pleasure, is the real point of the world, and any spiritual goals are an oppressive distraction from the real purpose."

# The Mind Taken Prisoner

וַתֵּרֶא הָאִשָּׁה כִּי טוֹב הָעֵץ לְמַאֲכָל וְכִי תַאֲוָה־הוּא לָעֵינַיִם וְנֶחְמָד הָעֵץ לְהַשְׂכִּיל וַתִּקַּח מִפִּרְיוֹ וַתֹּאכַל

*And the woman perceived that the tree was good for eating and that it was desirous to the eyes, and that the tree was desirable as a means to wisdom; and she took of its fruit and ate ....*
*(Bereishis 3:6)*

In the Torah's description of the first woman's thoughts before eating from the Tree of Knowledge, we are treated to a rare look inside the mind of a person being swayed by the Evil Inclination. Her decision, the prototype for all wrong decisions in the future, was made in three stages:

First, she saw the practical benefit that would issue from the sin, however small that was. The fruit of this tree would give a person more motivation to pursue the necessities of life with energy, as the Torah states, "the tree was good for eating"; that is, it increased the awareness of actual physical needs. This fact was enough to draw her attention to the tree and make it possible for her to incur the mistakes of the next two stages.

Second, now that she was looking at the tree, she saw that it was "desirous to the eyes," using the word "*ta'avah*" which indicates desire for more than what is readily available and necessary. The fruit would cause one to be open to seeking pleasures that were of less benefit and difficult to attain, and led away from the real point of life.

Finally, she perceived that the tree was *"nechmad l'haskil,"* it was desirable for its ability to empower and enhance the mind. This quality seems quite positive at first, until we notice something about the context in which it appears. This "intellectual" aspect of the tree is only mentioned *after* the fact that it increased desire for pleasures, meaning that the intellect was brought in as an afterthought and as a tool for achieving the goal of physical enjoyment.

If a person uses his mind as his primary decision-making faculty, it will serve him well in determining which desires to follow and which to ignore in order to achieve his practical aims. If, however, the mind becomes the slave of the desires, it will only serve as a huge amplifier for them, enabling the pursuit of complex and unusual pleasures that would

> *The mind as slave of the desires serves only as a huge amplifier for them.*

have been unimaginable without the application of great mental powers.

In the Book of *Mishlei,*[34] Shlomo HaMelech sums up this idea in a single verse, contrasting these two approaches to the use of the mind: "According to his mind a person is praised, but if his heart goes astray it will be put to shame." The heart here symbolizes the raw desires, unfiltered through the criticism of the mind. If one puts the mind in charge, he deserves praise for his intellectual powers, but if the "heart," the source of undifferentiated desires, is in control, then "it," the mind itself, is "put to shame."

The sin of the first woman had such tremendous consequences because she reversed the roles of these two aspects of her personality and allowed the mind to become a mere tool of endless wants and distractions.

---

34. *Mishlei* 12:8.

# Knowledge and Shame

וַתִּפָּקַחְנָה עֵינֵי שְׁנֵיהֶם וַיֵּדְעוּ כִּי עֵירֻמִּם הֵם וַיִּתְפְּרוּ עֲלֵה תְאֵנָה
וַיַּעֲשׂוּ לָהֶם חֲגֹרֹת

*Then the eyes of both of them were opened, and
they realized that they were naked; and they sewed
together a fig leaf and made themselves aprons.
(Bereishis 3:7)*

On the surface, it seems that the result of eating from the
Tree of Knowledge was an improvement in the visual
acuity of the first couple, that "their eyes were opened."
But, of course, we realize that they must have had perfect physical
vision before the sin, and that their lack of embarrassment at their
nakedness was not due to an inability to realize it.

Rambam in the *Moreh Nevuchim*[35] deals with this difficulty
by pointing to the use of the word "*vatipakachnah*" (from the
root "*p'kach*", opening) rather than "*vatipatachnah*" (from the
similar and more common root "*p'tach*"). Rambam explains that
"*p'kach*" refers to a removal of a cover rather than the opening of something that was completely closed, and in the present
context means that they came to understand something that was
previously hidden from them, the shame of being naked.

Before the sin, the procreative organs were perceived by
them as being the same as any other part of the body, useful for
their practical purpose without drawing them toward improper
actions. Afterward, with a newfound tendency to seek pleasure
for its own sake, they became aware of the potential this desire
had to pull them away from the elevated goals they aspired to in
life, and this made them embarrassed enough to feel the need
for clothing.

There is a further level of understanding here. The word used

---

35. *Moreh Nevuchim* 3:2.

here for "naked" is "*erumim*," a very minor variant of the word "*arumim*" used earlier (before the sin) for the same concept. The difference between these two forms is that "*arumim*" refers only to the actual lack of covering, while "*erumim*" connotes a shameful nakedness. Thus we see that, besides their perception, something objective had actually changed with the sin.

This fits very well with the concept that eating the fruit of the tree prompted the soul to be more permanently and intimately connected with the body, unable now to detach itself temporarily to pursue spiritual renewal. Now that the body itself was no longer a removable covering for the soul, it needed its own covering, and now physical nakedness was a source of shame.

> **Now the body itself was no longer a removable covering for the soul.**

# A Fall Into "Reality"

וַיִּשְׁמְעוּ אֶת־קוֹל ה' אֱלֹקִים מִתְהַלֵּךְ בַּגָּן לְרוּחַ הַיּוֹם וַיִּתְחַבֵּא הָאָדָם וְאִשְׁתּוֹ מִפְּנֵי ה' אֱלֹקִים בְּתוֹךְ עֵץ הַגָּן: וַיִּקְרָא ה' אֱלֹקִים אֶל־הָאָדָם וַיֹּאמֶר לוֹ אַיֶּכָּה

*And they heard the sound of Hashem, God, walking in the garden toward evening; and the man and his wife hid from Hashem, God, among the trees of the garden. And Hashem, God, called out to the man and said to him, "Where are you?"*
*(Bereishis 3:8,9)*

When the first couple sensed their nakedness, they rushed to don a makeshift covering. Immediately thereafter, the Torah begins to describe their perception of God in distinctly anthropomorphic language: "They heard the sound of God walking in the garden."

Until now, nothing that appeared physical had been said about God; but here, He seems to be portrayed as almost tangible.

To comprehend this sudden shift, we need to be aware of the Torah's Man-centered perspective. The Torah is not telling us objective facts about God, Who in any case is beyond our understanding, but rather is relating Man's perception of God.

After the sin, Man himself became much more physical, his soul far more strongly attached to and dependent on the body. No longer was he capable of perceiving God "directly" without the use of his physically oriented imagination. Beforehand, the first man and woman had enjoyed the "clear glass" of pure vision in a conscious and calm state, a level of prophecy that afterward was reserved solely for Moses. Now they fell to the lower level of prophecy granted to all other prophets. This level was qualitatively different from that of Moses in that the message came through the senses and in a terrifying manner, as befits a message from God Himself. Now they "heard" a physical voice, and it seemed to them that God was "walking" among them.

The form of the verb "walking" is "*mis'haleich*," a form that usually indicates the reflexive, but on occasion, such as here, indicates a pretending or acting. (A parallel is the word "*mis'rosheish*,"[36] meaning "acting as though one is poor," from "*rash*," "poor.") From now on, God would "put on an act" for prophets who were not capable of reaching the state of pure spirituality necessary for the "direct" vision that both Moses and Man possessed prior to the sin.

> **From now on, God would "put on an act" for prophets who were not capable of reaching a state of pure spirituality.**

The reaction engendered by this new kind of awareness of God was also expressed physically, as the man and woman "hid among the trees of the garden." Before the sin, when their minds were pure and in control, they knew that there was no such thing as hiding from God. Now their minds had become infiltrated by

---

36. *Mishlei* 13:7.

the baser powers of imagination and raw sense-perception; thus, they instinctively tried to conceal themselves physically from God's presence, which they also perceived as physical. In proportion to their distance from Him, he seemed more "real" in a material sense.

God responded to them by asking, "Where are you?" meaning, "How have you fallen from your elevated state?"

# For Your Own Good

אֲרוּרָה הָאֲדָמָה בַּעֲבוּרֶךָ
*The ground is cursed for your sake ....*
*(Bereishis 3:17)*

When God decreed the punishment of Adam for the sin of eating from the Tree of Knowledge, He used a phrase that seems out of place. He said, "*Arurah ha'adamah ba'avurecha*," the ground is cursed "for your sake," using the word "*ba'avurecha,*" which usually implies a benefit. Seemingly, the more appropriate word would have been "*bigla-lecha*" which would imply that the curse is "because of you," i.e., in retribution for what you have done.

In the context of an understanding of the effects of eating the fruit of the Tree of Knowledge, this becomes much more comprehensible:

Eating the fruit caused Man to suddenly turn his sights to desires and illusory needs that were distractions from his actual goal. Thus, he now needed

*He now needed an occupation that would prevent him from following his desires endlessly.*

an occupation that would prevent him from following his desires endlessly, in contrast to his original state where all was prepared and available for his consumption. The curse, however difficult, had an aspect of aiding Man's higher purpose. For this reason, the Torah describes it as being "for your sake," rather than "because of you."

# The World Follows Man

וְקוֹץ וְדַרְדַּר תַּצְמִיחַ לָךְ וְאָכַלְתָּ אֶת־עֵשֶׂב הַשָּׂדֶה: בְּזֵעַת אַפֶּיךָ תֹּאכַל לֶחֶם עַד שׁוּבְךָ אֶל־הָאֲדָמָה כִּי מִמֶּנָּה לֻקָּחְתָּ כִּי־עָפָר אַתָּה וְאֶל־עָפָר תָּשׁוּב

*"Thorns and thistles will sprout up for you, and you will eat the herb of the field. By the sweat of your brow shall you eat bread, until you return to the ground from which you were taken ...."*
*(Bereishis 3:18,19)*

When the first man and woman ate from the Tree of Knowledge, the result was a change in the way the world functioned. Man's punishment for the first sin was not merely a form of pain or discomfort, but an actual reflection of the sin itself in Creation.

Just as the eating of the fruit caused the human soul to be permanently attached and embedded in the body, producing a "mixture of good and evil," so the physical world now began to manifest mixtures of usable produce with waste material.

The Torah gives examples of this in the curse given to Man:

"Thorns and thistles will sprout up for you, and you will eat the herb of the field." Instead of a pure crop of edible food, weed plants will also grow and infiltrate your fields. Even the grain that will grow will have extraneous parts attached to it, straw and bran. If you wish to eat fully prepared food, then only "the herb of the field" will be available, i.e., vegetables. In order to obtain edible food from the grain, you will need to "eat bread by the sweat of your brow," going through the process of threshing, winnowing, grinding, and sifting etc. before flour is ready to be made into bread.

Man has to deal with these sorts of mixtures in the world "until he returns to the ground" and at last separates his own soul from the body, undoing the damage done by the sin of the Tree of Knowledge.

> *Man has to deal with these sorts of mixtures in the world "until he returns to the ground" and at last separates his own soul from the body.*

The Torah states that the body will return "to the ground from which it was taken," in order to prepare for the eventual reconstitution of a purified body from the earth and its reuniting with the soul in a form just like before the sin, at the time of *techias hameisim* (Revivification of the Dead).

# More Than Survival

וַיַּעַשׂ ה׳ אֱלֹקִים לְאָדָם וּלְאִשְׁתּוֹ כָּתְנוֹת עוֹר וַיַּלְבִּשֵׁם

*And Hashem, God, made for Adam and his wife garments of skin, and He clothed them.*

*(Bereishis 3:21)*

In accordance with God's plan, the first couple were given whatever they needed for survival, while the production of anything more was left to them. Thus, God saw to it that even after their sin — which placed the feeling of shame at their nakedness into their hearts — they would be able to have sufficient clothing for the climate outside of the garden.

God did this by putting into their minds the skills necessary for making leather garments, as though they had learned these skills for years. From these basic skills, they would be able to build all of the complex processes of technology.

More than this, though, was given to them at this time. By giving them the ability to produce clothing from leather, God also gave them the intimation that their innate spiritual awareness and understanding – that which had been in their hearts before the sin, and which had been diminished by it – would someday be made tangible and concrete in the form of the *Sefer Torah*, written on parchment made from animal skins.

Just as God gave Adam and Chavah the understanding necessary to continue a humanly dignified life despite their now material orientation, He would also give Mankind the wisdom to reach spiritual heights through the material world. That wisdom would be made available through the most material medium, the skin of an animal, its most superficial and toughest part.

> *That wisdom would be made available through the most material medium, the skin of an animal.*

# The Danger of Eternal Life

וַיֹּאמֶר ה׳ אֱלֹקִים הֵן הָאָדָם הָיָה כְּאַחַד מִמֶּנּוּ לָדַעַת טוֹב וָרָע וְעַתָּה פֶּן־יִשְׁלַח יָדוֹ וְלָקַח גַּם מֵעֵץ הַחַיִּים וְאָכַל וָחַי לְעֹלָם

*And Hashem, God, said, "Behold, Man has become as one of Us [k'achad mimenu], knowing good and evil; and now, lest he put forth his hand and take also of the Tree of Life, and eat and live forever."*
*(Bereishis 3:22)*

After recounting how the first man and woman ate from the Tree of Knowledge, the Torah quotes God's "thoughts" about what should be done with them. The conventional translation of this statement, "now Man has become as one of us," is both cryptic and philosophically problematic, implying as it seems that Man indeed became somehow Divine through this sin.

A different reading of the verse solves all the problems. "*K'achad mimenu*" can mean "as one of his own parts." Before the sin, Man was composed of two separable parts, the body and the soul, and the soul was able to depart on occasion from the body to pursue pure spirituality, a level that throughout the rest of history was reserved for such unique individuals as Moshe and Eliyahu. After the sin, the soul was permanently attached to the body for as long as the person lived, and the whole person became materially oriented like the body. Man was now essentially defined by "one of his own parts," i.e., the body, and his spiritual level had decreased enormously.

Now that this was true, it became a real danger to both body and soul to allow him to eat from the Tree of Life. The soul would be forever trapped in the body with no opportunity to achieve its own fulfillment, and even the body itself would only suffer from

*The soul would be forever trapped in the body.*

eternal decay and pain. Death, however negative in itself, would be the only release from this undesirable situation; and Man had to be distanced from the Tree of Life.

# The Individual

וְהָאָדָם יָדַע אֶת־חַוָּה אִשְׁתּוֹ וַתַּהַר וַתֵּלֶד אֶת־קַיִן וַתֹּאמֶר קָנִיתִי
אִישׁ אֶת־ה'

*And the man [Hebrew: ha'adam] knew his wife,*
*Chavah, and she conceived and bore Kayin, saying,*
*"I have acquired a man with Hashem.*
*(Bereishis 4:1)*

וַיֵּדַע אָדָם עוֹד אֶת־אִשְׁתּוֹ וַתֵּלֶד בֵּן ...

*And Adam [Hebrew: Adam] knew his wife again,*
*and she bore a son....*
*(Bereishis 4:25)*

As long as the human race was limited to one man and one woman, the Torah uses the term *"ha'adam,"* "the man," since he contained within himself the essence of the entire species. Once the next generation was born, though, "Adam" became a proper name, denoting one specific individual.

This name choice signaled a *change* in the workings of Divine Providence, a change hinted at, too, in the Torah's use of the Names of God:

> **The first man contained the essence of the entire species.**

In the first account of Creation, which dealt only with the general categories of natural phenomena, the name *"Elokim"* is used exclusively. This is the name associated with *Middas Hadin*, the strict process of nature.

Afterward,[37] in the detailed account of the creation of Man in general, the Torah uses a combination: The name *"Elokim"* is juxtaposed with *"Hashem,"* the four-letter Name that represents

---

37. From *Bereishis* 2:4 and onward.

mercy, since both the particular aspect of mercy and the general Providence over the species are being described.

Finally, once the Torah begins to discuss the generations of mankind and name *specific individuals* — beginning with Kayin — only the four-letter Name is used. This name is associated with the personal Providence with which God deals with people, rewarding or punishing them in ways not bound by strict natural law.

# Two Sons

וַתַּהַר וַתֵּלֶד אֶת־קַיִן וַתֹּאמֶר קָנִיתִי אִישׁ אֶת ה' וַתֹּסֶף לָלֶדֶת ...
אֶת־אָחִיו אֶת־הָבֶל

*... And she conceived and bore Kayin, saying: "I have acquired a man for God." And additionally she bore his brother, Hevel.*
*(Bereishis 4:1-2)*

The names of the first two children born to Chavah provide a hint of what would happen in their lives, and of the pattern of life for generations to come.

A firstborn son, as we find in so many instances, was intended to be "set aside" for service of God, and was therefore considered far more significant than his younger brothers. This idea is expressed here in Chavah's explanation for the name, Kayin, "I have acquired (*kanisi*) a man (a son) for God." Kayin's mother considered him to be her prime acquisition in life due to his more exalted purpose. As a result of this, Kayin was guided to pursue the cultivation of the land, which was looked upon as a more respectable occupation than raising animals, since it provided an individual with far-greater stability by tying him to a specific location.

The second son, Hevel, was treated by his mother as a

**"She called him Hevel, meaning 'a breath, emptiness.'"**

relative afterthought, since he would be destined to pursue more mundane objectives. For this reason, she called him Hevel, "a breath" or "emptiness," since, relatively speaking, he was much less important. Therefore, he was allowed to engage in sheep-herding, a more humble occupation.

# The Natural Impulse To Serve God

וַיְהִי מִקֵּץ יָמִים וַיָּבֵא קַיִן מִפְּרִי הָאֲדָמָה מִנְחָה לַה': וְהֶבֶל הֵבִיא גַם־הוּא מִבְּכֹרוֹת צֹאנוֹ וּמֵחֶלְבֵהֶן וַיִּשַׁע ה' אֶל־הֶבֶל וְאֶל־מִנְחָתוֹ: וְאֶל־קַיִן וְאֶל־מִנְחָתוֹ לֹא שָׁעָה וַיִּחַר לְקַיִן מְאֹד וַיִּפְּלוּ פָּנָיו:
וַיֹּאמֶר ה' אֶל־קָיִן לָמָּה חָרָה לָךְ וְלָמָּה נָפְלוּ פָנֶיךָ:
הֲלוֹא אִם־תֵּיטִיב שְׂאֵת וְאִם לֹא תֵיטִיב לַפֶּתַח חַטָּאת רֹבֵץ

*It was at the end of some time, and Kayin brought something from the fruits of the ground as a present to God. And as for Hevel, he, too, brought — from the firstborn of his sheep and from their fattest. God turned to Hevel and to his offering; but to Kayin and to his offering He did not turn, and Kayin was very angry and dejected.*
*And God said to Kayin, "Why are you angry, and why are you dejected? Indeed, whether you bring a fine gift or whether you bring that which is not good, sin lies at the door ...."*
*(Bereishis 4:3-7)*

J ust as *every* object and organism in the world follows its own nature, so Man innately *seeks* his true purpose: knowing and serving God.

This is illustrated by the Torah's account of the behavior of Kayin and Hevel who, without prompting, brought offerings to God from their respective produce. The very fact of receiving bounty from God's creation caused the welling up of gratitude that found its most direct expression in the symbolic "returning" of part of the gain to the Giver.

The two brothers, however, differed greatly in the depth of understanding of their obligation of gratitude, and this manifested itself in the form of their offerings in four ways:

- Kayin did not succeed in perceiving the fact that God is the only Cause of all good and of all events in general. Rather, he saw God as an added force working with nature; and therefore he only felt the need to thank Him when the finished product was ready, "at the end of some time." He did not see that at *every* step of the way, God was behind whatever was happening. Hevel, on the other hand, brought "the firstborn of his sheep" to indicate that God's hand was there from the very start.

- Kayin brought only "something from his fruits," a lower quality of produce that he had less need of for his own consumption. Hevel, in contrast, brought the fattest of his flock to show the enormity of his indebtedness to God.

- When Kayin brought his offering, he perceived it as "a present for God," as if God Himself would see it as a present from which He would gain. Evidently, Kayin thought that gratitude was not just his internal obligation, but something God actually benefited from or even needed. Hevel, however, understood that God possesses everything and needs nothing from Man, not even feelings or expressions of appreciation.

- Hevel understood that the externality of an offering is only a way of stimulating a person's internal willingness to "offer himself" in submission to God and His will. The Torah tells us this by saying that Hevel brought "he, too," which can be read "himself too"; he brought himself as an offering, the physical offering serving only as a symbol of this act. Kayin did not achieve this level of understanding; he brought the physical offering for its own sake.

*Hevel brought "himself" as an offering.*

For these four reasons, the Torah tells us that God was pleased with Hevel "himself," and as a result was pleased with his offering; whereas, God was not pleased with the superficial sort of offering brought by Kayin, as it did not include a true submission of his soul.

Kayin reacted to God's lack of satisfaction with his gift in two ways, ways that seem to contradict each other, but that do indeed have something significant in common:

- Kayin was "angry," showing that he thought that his offering was intrinsically good and valuable and should have been accepted.
- He was "dejected" (literally, "his face fell"), feeling that the offering was *not* good enough and embarrassed at having brought such a meager offering.

Both of these reactions were inappropriate, since they focused on the quality of the offering, rather than the spiritual change that the offering is meant to demonstrate.

As a result, God tells Kayin that the offering itself is not the point: "Whether you bring a fine gift" (interpreting the word "*s'eis*" to be related to "*mas'as,*" "a gift"), "or whether you bring a gift that is not good," nonetheless, "sin lies at the door"; i.e., at the "door" that you open to bring the offering, there lie your unrepented sins, preventing God from forgiving you, since you have only tried to distract Him with your gift rather than implementing real internal change.

# Natural Law,
# Natural Punishment

וְעַתָּה אָרוּר אָתָּה מִן־הָאֲדָמָה אֲשֶׁר פָּצְתָה אֶת־פִּיהָ לָקַחַת אֶת־
דְּמֵי אָחִיךָ מִיָּדֶךָ: כִּי תַעֲבֹד אֶת־הָאֲדָמָה לֹא־תֹסֵף תֵּת־כֹּחָהּ לָךְ נָע
וָנָד תִּהְיֶה בָאָרֶץ

*"Therefore, you are cursed more than the ground,
which opened wide its mouth to receive your brother's blood from your hand. When you work the
ground, it will no longer yield its strength to you;
you shall be a vagrant and a wanderer on earth."
(Bereishis 4:11,12)*

The mitzvos of the Torah can be divided into two categories:
those that are based on a natural understanding of people
and society, and those that can only be known through
Divine revelation.

God apportions reward and punishment in accordance with a
person's performance in both of these areas, but there is a difference in the means by
which the punishment is
administered. When a per-
son violates a mitzvah that is
beyond our natural under-
standing, the retribution is
also delivered in a manner

*When a person violates a
mitzvah that is beyond natural
understanding, the retribution
is also delivered in a manner
that is beyond nature.*

that is beyond nature, through special Divine Providence. If,
however, he commits a sin that goes against the dictates of
nature — for example, killing another human being — then the
physical world itself punishes him by "violating" its own laws and
refusing to provide him with his needs.

The first example of this is God's curse of Kayin for killing his
brother. When the Torah speaks of the ground "opening wide

its mouth to receive your brother's blood from your hand," it means that the land will clearly take revenge on you for your act of murder as if it were saying with its mouth that it was doing so.

The way this revenge will be brought about is twofold:

First, the ground "will no longer yield its strength to you" when you work it, a punishment involving sparse gain from the land. Secondly, a more active punishment, the land will refuse to let you rest upon it; rather, you shall be condemned to be "a wanderer on earth."

When Man behaves in a way that ordinary human nature finds repugnant, God causes Nature to react and make itself inhospitable for Man.

# Life as Punishment

וַיֹּאמֶר קַיִן אֶל־ה' גָּדוֹל עֲוֹנִי מִנְּשֹׂא: הֵן גֵּרַשְׁתָּ אֹתִי הַיּוֹם מֵעַל פְּנֵי הָאֲדָמָה וּמִפָּנֶיךָ אֶסָּתֵר וְהָיִיתִי נָע וָנָד בָּאָרֶץ וְהָיָה כָל־מֹצְאִי יַהַרְגֵנִי:

וַיֹּאמֶר לוֹ ה' לָכֵן כָּל־הֹרֵג קַיִן שִׁבְעָתַיִם יֻקָּם וַיָּשֶׂם ה' לְקַיִן אוֹת לְבִלְתִּי הַכּוֹת־אֹתוֹ כָּל־מֹצְאוֹ

*Kayin said to Hashem, "Is my sin too great to bear? Behold, you have banished me today from the face of the earth, and from your Face I must hide; I shall have to wander around upon the earth! Whoever meets me will kill me!"*

*Hashem said to him, "Therefore, whoever kills Kayin will be avenged sevenfold." And Hashem placed a sign for Kayin, so that none that meet him might kill him.*

*(Bereishis 4:13-15)*

Although we usually think of death as the worst possible fate, sometimes things can appear in a different light. After Kayin received notice of his punishment for murdering his brother, he fell into a state of despair. Without a concept of *teshuvah*, he felt that his sin was "unbearable." A look at the world gave him the impression that there were only three possible ways that he could survive and flourish, and all of them seemed closed to him:

- He had no hope of remaining in his original place, since God had banished him from it. "You have banished me today from the face of the earth."
- He did not expect special Providential care, since God had decided to leave him in a state of reliance on natural means. "From your Face I must hide."
- He had no possibility of choosing a new place and fortifying and developing it for himself, since he was condemned to wander from one location to another: "I shall have to wander around upon the earth."

In his state of despondence, he expressed to God his wish to die, saying, "I desire that anyone who will meet me will kill me!"

To this God responded that, in his case, life itself would be part of the punishment. "Whoever kills Kayin will be avenged sevenfold," for the sin of murder, compounded with the sin of violating God's desire that Kayin live to suffer and atone for his sin. In addition, the murderer of Kayin would be far more culpable than Kayin himself, since he had had the opportunity to see the retribution that a murderer received, yet performed the act anyway.

*In Kayin's case, life itself would be part of the punishment.*

This itself is the "sign" that God attached to Kayin, the fact that no one would dare to harm him after they saw the direct natural punishment that the earth had given to him.

# Repairing the Damage
## of Murder

וַיֵּדַע קַיִן אֶת־אִשְׁתּוֹ וַתַּהַר וַתֵּלֶד אֶת־חֲנוֹךְ וַיְהִי בֹּנֶה עִיר וַיִּקְרָא
שֵׁם הָעִיר כְּשֵׁם בְּנוֹ חֲנוֹךְ

*And Kayin knew his wife and she conceived and
bore Chanoch; and he was engaged in building a
city, and he named the city after his son, Chanoch.*
***(Bereishis 4:17)***

**M**urder seems the prime example of a sin that can never be undone; and this is certainly true in a simple sense. However, on another level, there is something that could be done, and this is what Kayin, the first murderer, set out to do when he decided to repent.

Kayin understood that, besides destroying the life of one person, he had also disrupted the order of society and opened the possibility for total chaos among people. This was something that he saw a chance of changing, and for this reason he began the project of building a city, symbolic of fostering order and civilization.

The Torah uses the phrase "*va'y'hi boneh ir,*" "he was engaged in building a city," rather than saying simply "he built a city," to emphasize the fact that Kayin, in his nomadic state, was only able to begin the work of founding the city, but was unable to remain in that place to see it to completion. For this reason, he left his son Chanoch there to oversee the project to its end, and even gave the city the name of Chanoch to solidify this connection.

The descendants of Kayin soon multiplied and continued on this path of developing civilization, progressing on to the development of all sorts of tools and technologies. The Torah[38] tells us

---

38. *Bereishis* 4:17-22.

of the seven generations of the seed of Kayin whom God allowed to flourish in order to perform this necessary task. Even though they would not fulfill the main spiritual goal of the creation of Man, a task that would be dele-

gated to the sons of Sheis, Adam's third son, they had this important secondary function. From the guilt of Kayin and his consequent recognition of the

> **From the guilt of the first murderer ultimately came the constructive forces of organized human society.**

gravity of his destructive sin ultimately came the constructive forces of organized human society.

# Farther Along the Rivers

וַתֵּלֶד עָדָה אֶת־יָבָל הוּא הָיָה אֲבִי ישֵׁב אֹהֶל וּמִקְנֶה: וְשֵׁם אָחִיו יוּבָל הוּא הָיָה אֲבִי כָּל־תֹּפֵשׂ כִּנּוֹר וְעוּגָב: וְצִלָּה גַם־הִוא יָלְדָה אֶת־תּוּבַל קַיִן לֹטֵשׁ כָּל־חֹרֵשׁ נְחשֶׁת וּבַרְזֶל וַאֲחוֹת תּוּבַל־קַיִן נַעֲמָה

*And Adah bore Yaval; he was the first of those who dwell in tents and breed cattle. The name of his brother was Yuval; he was the first of all who handle the harp and flute. Tzillah, too — she bore Tuval-Kayin, who sharpened all cutting implements of copper and iron; and the sister of Tuval-Kayin was Na'amah.*
*(Bereishis 4:20-22)*

The descendants of Kayin, who were the originators of material civilization, reached the apex of their progress in the seventh generation, that of Lemech. Lemech's children were responsible for the start of the main branches of human physical achievement, each branch related to one of the emphases in life symbolized by the rivers issuing from Eden, as explained above.[39]

Yaval began the practice of breeding cattle. The Hebrew word for cattle is *"mikneh,"* which also means "property," since animals were the main form of movable property in early times. This was the beginning of the world of business and finance, and corresponds to the first river, the one associated with gold and precious stones.

The next son, Yuval, invented music, which was originally associated mainly with the pursuit of lust and pleasure. Although music eventually came to have more positive and even holy applications, its origin was for this; therefore it is connected with the second river that symbolizes the pursuit of physical desire.

Tuval-Kayin, the son of Tzillah, was an expert in metalworking, whose main application was in perfecting weapons of war, corresponding to the third river that is related to the desire for power.

The fourth river, P'ras, which leads to Eretz Yisrael and symbolizes spiritual pursuits, is not explicitly associated with anyone mentioned in this *pasuk*. However, our Sages tell us that Na'amah, the sister of Tuval-Kayin, was the wife of Noach and a righteous woman in her own right, so she can be seen to fit into this role.

Besides giving us this description of the way the various aspects of human nature emerged in practice, the Torah also is implicitly defusing a common fallacy made in ancient times: the attribution of creative and inventive powers to various idolatrous gods. Since the skills of government, business, music, and technology are truly impressive, mythology credits their origin to the various deities of polytheism. The Torah makes it clear that every one of these fields was invented by ordinary,

> *The Torah implicitly denies a common error of ancient times: attributing creative and inventive powers to various idolatrous gods.*

---

39. See above: "The Four Rivers of Human Nature" on verse 2:10.

albeit talented, humans with no Divine nature, and thereby strengthens Jewish resistance to influence by idolatrous culture.

# The Beginning of History

זֶה סֵפֶר תּוֹלְדֹת אָדָם בְּיוֹם בְּרֹא אֱלֹקִים אָדָם בִּדְמוּת אֱלֹקִים עָשָׂה אֹתוֹ: זָכָר וּנְקֵבָה בְּרָאָם וַיְבָרֶךְ אֹתָם וַיִּקְרָא אֶת־שְׁמָם אָדָם בְּיוֹם הִבָּרְאָם

*This is the account of the descendants of Adam: On the day God created Man, He made ["asah"] him after the fashion of God. He created them, male and female. And He blessed them and called their name "Adam" [Man] on the day they were created.*
*(Bereishis 5:1)*

The first four chapters of *Bereishis* constitute a setting of the stage for the entire Torah. These chapters detail the creation of the natural world and the crucial changes in the human condition resulting from the sins of the Tree of Knowledge and Kayin's murder of Hevel; they culminate in the birth of Adam's third son, Sheis, who, as his name implies in Hebrew, was the "foundation" of the future of mankind. Now the Torah begins the story of the generations of Man and the great events of history.

The climax of the first ten generations was the disastrous decadence of the generation before the Flood, prompting God to "regret the creation of Man on earth."[40] The question arises as to how God could have made Man in such a way that "all his thoughts are evil all day,"[41] and why Man should be held responsible for his failure.

---

40. *Bereishis* 6:6.
41. *Bereishis* 6:5.

For this reason, the Torah begins its description of history with a reminder of what the original state of human nature was: "On the day God created Man, He made him after the fashion of God."

The Torah here uses the word "*asah,*" indicating completion, to denote the making of Man. This seems odd, since human beings are never really complete in the same way as inanimate objects, since humans must always choose to follow the path of good and to constantly grow spiritually. This usage is only seen to be appropriate when we pay attention to the end of the sentence, which informs us that at the beginning, Man was made "after the fashion of God." This indicates that his spiritual essence was predominant; his physical body could not take control of him to bring him to disobey the dictates of his soul.

In the Midrash[42] on this verse, God says to the angels that "Man will be righteous," since Man was already a complete being, on a pure spiritual level, almost comparable to God himself.

The Torah continues to say that Man was "called Adam (Man) on the day on which they were created," alluding to the fact that only a finished creature can be called by its generic name. "A one-day-old ox is called an ox"[43] because an ox does not grow spiritually during its lifetime. From the moment of his creation until the sin of the Tree of Knowledge, Man was also in a state of completion and perfection.

> **Until eating from the Tree of Knowledge, Man was in a state of completion and perfection.**

Therefore, the responsibility for his state ten generations later could only be his own. By eating the forbidden fruit, he opened the door for the possibility of following the body's desires toward empty pursuits and spiritual self-destruction.

---

42. *Bereishis Rabbah* 8:4.

43. *Bava Kamma* 65b.

# Counting the Years

וַיִּהְיוּ כָּל־יְמֵי אָדָם אֲשֶׁר־חַי תְּשַׁע מֵאוֹת שָׁנָה וּשְׁלֹשִׁים שָׁנָה וַיָּמֹת

*And all the days that Adam lived were nine hundred and thirty years; and he died.*
*(Bereishis 5:5)*

In all the generations from Adam until Noach, the Torah gives the number of years each person lived until having his first child, then the number of years in the rest of his life, and finally the total of these two, his full life span. In contrast, for the ten generations from Noach until Avraham, the Torah gives only the first two figures without calculating the total.

This difference can be understood when we recall the tradition of our Sages that all of the people mentioned in the first instance, from Adam until Noach, were *tzaddikim*, righteous people who achieved the potential of spirituality that they were given. Therefore, the Torah makes two separate statements about their ages: One is in the context of bearing children, representing their significance in terms of continuing the human race; the other gives their own total sum of years, showing that they were each significant in their own right for the level of deeds and wisdom that they reached.

> **The people mentioned from Adam until Noach were tzaddikim, righteous people who achieved their potential of spirituality.**

The generations from Noach until Avraham, however, included both people of great stature, as well as those who did not use their potential in the right way. These generations served solely there to provide the links in the chain from Noach to Avraham; and thus, their years were counted only as a separate number before having children and after, without a total for their own achievement.

# The First Eliyahu

וַיִּתְהַלֵּךְ חֲנוֹךְ אֶת־הָאֱלֹקִים אַחֲרֵי הוֹלִידוֹ אֶת־מְתוּשֶׁלַח שְׁלֹשׁ
מֵאוֹת שָׁנָה וַיּוֹלֶד בָּנִים וּבָנוֹת ... וַיִּתְהַלֵּךְ חֲנוֹךְ אֶת־הָאֱלֹקִים
וְאֵינֶנּוּ כִּי־לָקַח אֹתוֹ אֱלֹקִים

*And Chanoch walked with God for three hundred years after fathering Mesushelach, and he fathered sons and daughters. ... And Chanoch walked with God, then he was no more, for God had taken him."*

**(Bereishis 5:22,24)**

The Torah presents us with an enigma in the character of Chanoch, one of the ten righteous men in the chain from Adam to Noach. Only in his case does the Torah use the phrase "he walked with God"; and when describing the end of his life, the Torah states, "and he was no more," rather than "he died," as it does concerning the others.

These anomalies become understandable in light of the tradition of our Sages that Chanoch went up to Heaven alive, just as Eliyahu HaNavi would in later times. This explains why he is described twice as "walking with God," once during his lifetime, and once again at the end of his life.

During his lifetime he "walked with God," meaning that he served God by seeking wisdom and following God's commandments while still engaging in material pursuits (epitomized in the phrase "he had sons and daughters"). At the end of his days this phrase is repeated, indicating that he became a Heavenly being, like Eliyahu, who would now engage only in direct service and closeness to the Creator.

*Seeking wisdom and following God's commandments, while still engaging in material pursuits ....*

# Total Turnaround

וַיִּקְרָא אֶת־שְׁמוֹ נֹחַ לֵאמֹר זֶה יְנַחֲמֵנוּ מִמַּעֲשֵׂנוּ וּמֵעִצְּבוֹן יָדֵינוּ מִן־
הָאֲדָמָה אֲשֶׁר אֵרְרָהּ ה׳

*And he called his name Noach, saying "This one*
*shall comfort us [y'nachameinu] from our actions*
*and the sadness in our hands, from the ground*
*which Hashem had cursed."*
*(Bereishis 5:29)*

We are accustomed to speaking about the mitzvah of "comforting" mourners, but an examination of the Torah's word for this act, "*nichum*," gives us a much deeper understanding of the process.

A person in a state of mourning has had his entire world thrust into disarray and confusion; though mere "comfort" might make his state more bearable, it would hardly merit being considered a special mitzvah, different from ordinary kindness.

A broader look at the Hebrew language, though, informs us that the root "*l'nacheim*" means to change one's mind (or someone else's), whether in the context of backing out of a commitment, regretting an action, or getting a person to move out of the despair of mourning and back into the positive flow of life. The mourner needs more than comfort; he needs a complete change of attitude, which can come from properly expressed words of understanding and hope.

> *The mourner needs more than comfort; he needs a complete change of attitude.*

This general concept of "*nechamah*" as change of attitude is the clue to Lemech's prayer upon the birth of his son, Noach, that "he shall comfort us (*y'nachameinu*) from our actions and the sadness in our hands." Lemech hoped and foresaw that his son Noach would work to inspire mankind — mired as they were into emptiness and depravity ten generations after the Creation — to turn their actions around. Lemech prayed that Noach would reverse the curse of the ground, a curse which resulted from the deterioration of people's behavior.

A change in action would lead to a change in the situation. Thus, Lemech gave Noach his name, related to both "*nechamah*" and "*menuchah*," "rest," to symbolize the role Noach was to undertake: to bring rest from sadness by means of producing radical change in mankind's behavior.

# Only Human

וַיִּרְאוּ בְנֵי־הָאֱלֹהִים אֶת־בְּנוֹת הָאָדָם כִּי טֹבֹת הֵנָּה וַיִּקְחוּ לָהֶם נָשִׁים מִכֹּל אֲשֶׁר בָּחָרוּ ... הַנְּפִלִים הָיוּ בָאָרֶץ בַּיָּמִים הָהֵם וְגַם אַחֲרֵי־כֵן ... הֵמָּה הַגִּבֹּרִים אֲשֶׁר מֵעוֹלָם אַנְשֵׁי הַשֵּׁם

*The "children of the gods" [b'nei elohim] saw that the daughters of man were beautiful, and they took themselves wives from whomever they chose. ... The "fallen ones" [nephilim] were on the earth in those days, and also afterward ....; these were actually just mighty ones, who were ancient people of fame.*
*(Bereishis 6:2,4)*

At the core of the idolatrous religions of ancient times (and at a deep level, of all of the false religions that survive to our day) is the desire to bring the transcendent down to human level. This is in opposition to Judaism's demand that Man constantly strive toward the unreachable Infinite.

All the mythologies of Egypt, China, Greece, and other cultures featured god-men who "fell" from the Heavens; these played the role of supermen in human society and produced children with tremendous strength and abilities. Rulers of empires were said to be the descendants of such people, giving them unchallenged power, and entitling them to be worshiped as gods.

The practical result of this sort of belief was the portrayal of the behavior of the gods as similar to the worst of human behavior, replete with violence and lust, and destroying Man's most powerful motivation to improve, the desire to imitate God. Instead, whole cults were devoted to specific types of depravity, some gods being worshiped through "sacred harlots," others through human sacrifice.

God in His Torah, beyond merely commanding us to refrain from these repugnant practices, gives us the tools to debunk them and easily treat them with contempt and disdain. The Torah reveals to us exactly who these "b'nei elohim," "children of the gods," truly were. They were nothing but charlatans who deceived unsuspecting women, often married, to consort with them on the pretense, perhaps based on their genuine strengths, that they were supernatural beings.

"The b'nei elohim saw the daughters of man"; in other words, they followed their desires that were aroused by what they saw, and they invented the claim of being "b'nei elohim." Their children called themselves "nephilim," those who "fell" from Heaven, and claimed to be descendants of gods. The Torah makes sure that we see these people in their true light, as "just mighty ones," but most importantly, as mere people, flesh and blood, and in no sense Divine.

This sort of skepticism of exaggerated claims of origin or greatness by powerful people has been one of the central aspects of the true Jewish personality as cultivated by the concepts of the Torah. It has enabled the Jewish people to focus on true understanding of God without distraction by "cults of personality," in all their forms.

> **Skepticism of exaggerated claims of origin or greatness has been one of the central aspects of the true Jewish personality.**

# Long Life — A Blessing?

וַיֹּאמֶר ה׳ לֹא־יָדוֹן רוּחִי בָאָדָם לְעֹלָם בְּשַׁגַּם הוּא בָשָׂר וְהָיוּ יָמָיו
מֵאָה וְעֶשְׂרִים שָׁנָה

*And God said, "My spirit shall not struggle within Man forever, he being even flesh ["**b'shagam hu basar**"]; and his days shall be a hundred and twenty years."*
*(Bereishis 6:3)*

I n the generation before the Flood, God saw that people's physical desires were leading their minds so far astray as to let them convince others and even themselves that they were Divine (see "Only Human," above). The potential benefits of long life were being outweighed by the tremendous erosion of spirituality that such an extended association with the body caused to the soul.

God decreed, therefore, that His "spirit," in the form of the human soul, should not be forced to struggle ("*yadon*") with Man, that is, with Man's body, "forever," for such a long time that the soul could not go on fighting.

In such a lengthy battle, the soul itself would become like the body, coarse and materialistic. This is what the Torah means when it quotes God as saying, "*b'shagam hu basar*," that even the soul would become like flesh, experiencing the physical desires of the body as its own, and thereby being unable to carry on a struggle whose existence it no longer perceived.

> **God then decreed that the maximum human life span would decrease gradually until reaching 120 years.**

God then decreed that the maximum human life span would decrease gradually until reaching 120 years, brief enough that death would be well within a person's imagination of his future, and also not enough time to do endless evil deeds.

Despite this change, Man's negative behavior continued, as the Torah relates: God saw that "Man's thoughts were bad all day."[44] Shortening the life span could only help to weaken the physical drives that tempt people to sin, and to give those whose sins were motivated by desire the chance to regret them in moments of seriousness or in old age. But a person whose whole thought system justifies and even glorifies his evil behavior will be unaffected by a mere lessening of the intensity of his desires, because his mind will keep them alive and present "all day."

This is the state in which God found the world immediately before the Flood, leaving no option other than severe punishment.

# Whose Fault?

וַיִּנָּחֶם ה' כִּי־עָשָׂה אֶת־הָאָדָם בָּאָרֶץ וַיִּתְעַצֵּב אֶל־לִבּוֹ

**And Hashem regretted having made Man on earth,
and He was sad about his [Man's] heart.
(Bereishis 6:6)**

The great Flood in the generation of Noach is unparalleled in history as a virtually complete destruction of mankind in preparation for a totally new beginning. An event of this scale raises the question of how God's Creation could have come to such a total state of failure, given that His infinite wisdom went into designing it.

The Torah deals explicitly with this problem when it tells us that "God regretted having made Man on earth." God's "regretting" is a way of saying that at this point, He had no other way to save the Creation other than to destroy mankind almost to the very last person. When the Torah emphasizes that the "regret" was over Man's being made "on earth," this means that Man was

---

44. *Bereishis* 6:5.

overly influenced by the powerful pull of the newly created material world. A world that still had the power to produce people and things of great size, strength, and perfection constituted a greater temptation than would be the diminished world of subsequent eras.

God "regretted" and took action with regard to Man's creation only in the context of the specific sort of tests with which Man had to deal. There is no statement of God considering His entire Creation to be in any sense a "mistake" that had to be somehow redone; only that Man's particular situation was too much for him.

This can be compared to an artisan who fashions a perfect object, only to see a destructive person come along and ruin it to the extent that it had to be made again from scratch. Certainly no one would consider this to be an indication that poor design or craftsmanship went into the object originally. Similarly, it was only people's improper choices that led to the necessity to afford a new beginning on Creation, and in no way does this indicate that God had produced anything less than a perfect world. On the contrary, the tremendous potential of the pre-Flood world made it a test too difficult for Man, even though it could have been used for greater good than a lesser sort of world.

Only Man's free will caused the world to fall into such a state that mandated the Flood and mankind's new beginning. The Torah makes this point when it says that "God was sad about his (Man's) heart," the heart symbolizing the free will of a person to choose good or evil.

# The Punishment
# of the Animals

וַיֹּאמֶר ה' אֶמְחֶה אֶת־הָאָדָם אֲשֶׁר־בָּרָאתִי מֵעַל פְּנֵי הָאֲדָמָה
מֵאָדָם עַד־בְּהֵמָה עַד־רֶמֶשׂ וְעַד־עוֹף הַשָּׁמָיִם.
*And God said, "I will wipe out mankind whom I cre-
ated from the face of the earth — from man to animal, to creeping things and to birds of the sky ...."*
*(Bereishis 6:7)*

T he Torah on a number of occasions seems to associate the
idea of punishment with animals and even inanimate
objects, a concept that demands a clear explanation.
Liability for punishment should always be a function of free will,
a quality that only humans possess. How can animals be said to suffer for their misdeeds?

The key to this puzzle is the general principle that the Torah speaks

> *Liability for punishment should always be a function of free will, a quality that only humans possess. How, then, can animals be said to suffer for their misdeeds?*

from the perspective of a human-centered world, a world where
the free choice of people is the main, and really the only, subject
of interest. From this viewpoint, the world, and in particular the
animals, exist to help man in a physical sense, and also to provide him with tangible examples of all sorts of character traits: the
courage of the lion, the industry of the ant, etc. If man uses these
aids to his self-development, they themselves acquire worth. But
if he ignores the lessons he could learn from them — or, worse,
if he learns the opposite, using traits in inappropriate ways and
becoming more "animalistic" himself — then the animals take
on a negative value, and their destruction becomes a means of
teaching the right path.

An extreme case of this idea was at the time of the Flood, when

God said, "I will wipe out mankind … from man to animal …," stating clearly that the punishment of animals was a part of the punishment of man. Both of these punishments provided future generations with the same fearful object lesson: The Creation exists for a purpose, and when this purpose is not fulfilled, there is no justification for the world's existence.

Our Sages express this in a parable of a king who prepared an elaborate celebration for his son's wedding. When the son subsequently angered him, not only did he have his son executed, but he destroyed everything that was in readiness for the wedding as well. The king thus demonstrated that these things had no intrinsic worth, but were valuable only as long as the celebration was planned.[45]

Similarly, just as man needed a completely new start at the time of Noach, the animal world, which exists for man's growth, also had to be reduced to a minimum, one pair per species, and then given the chance to begin again.

# Noach's Paradox

וַיֹּאמֶר ה׳ אֶמְחֶה אֶת־הָאָדָם אֲשֶׁר־בָּרָאתִי מֵעַל פְּנֵי הָאֲדָמָה
׳ה ... וְנֹחַ מָצָא חֵן בְּעֵינֵי ה

*God said, "I will wipe out mankind whom I created*
*from the face of the earth …." But Noach found*
*favor in the eyes of God.*
*(Bereishis 6:7,8)*

God in His Infinite Wisdom has arranged the world in a way that includes not only a physical order, but also and more importantly, a spiritual order that functions in different ways depending on the moral choices made by people.

---

45. *Bereishis Rabbah* 28:6.

Our Sages[46] tell us that God's "preferred" manner for dealing with the world is one of directed Providence, rewarding good and punishing evil, and driving Creation toward an overall goal of improvement. However, if this way of running the world is for some reason not applicable, and the world would seem to have no merit whatsoever to allow its continued existence, there is a "backup" approach of Heavenly Kindness. This approach was in effect during the time before the first man was created, when there was no possibility of choice, and it can be invoked at any time in history when there are insufficient numbers of righteous people to merit the world's continued existence.

This principle explains the statement of our Sages[47] that *Mashiach* will come in a generation that is either "totally righteous" or "totally undeserving." The arrival of *Mashiach* when people are all righteous needs no explanation, but why should he come in a time when mankind has hit some kind of absolute bottom?

*"Why should Mashiach come in a time when mankind has hit some kind of absolute bottom?"*

The answer is that at that time, God will be "forced," so to speak, to invoke His Infinite Kindness and ignore completely humankind's spiritual level, bringing an undeserved but effective Redemption. The prophet Isaiah refers to this concept when he quotes God Who will say at that time, "I looked and there was none to help ... and then My Arm brought salvation."[48]

Paradoxically, at the time of Noach, this rule of God's Providence led Noach's righteousness to cause, in a sense, the catastrophe of the Flood. If there had been no one meritorious at all at that time, God's Kindness would have kept the world functioning normally; punishment would have been withheld, since

----

46. *Pesikta Rabbasi* 40; *Shemos Rabbah* 30:13; *Bereishis Rabbah* 12:15; see *Rashi, Bereishis* 1:1.

47. *Sanhedrin* 98a.

48. *Yeshayahu* 63:5.

it would have served no positive purpose. God does not destroy except when that destruction brings some greater constructive gain, and in this case, only pure destruction would have been possible.

The presence of Noach, though, changed the entire picture. Under these circumstances, wiping out all of mankind with the exception of Noach and his family would be a constructive act, not only creating the possibility of a new start, but also protecting these few righteous people from corruption by the decadent majority. Now the principle of *din*, God's strict judgment, was applicable, and the destruction of the Flood as a punishment for mankind's sins was more productive than indiscriminate Kindness. This is why the Torah includes the statement that "Noach found favor in the eyes of God" at the end of the section recounting God's decision to punish Man with the Flood, since without Noach's merit, the Flood would not have been possible within the system of Divine Providence.

The Midrash[49] compares this to the owner of a vineyard who decided to prune almost all of his vines because he found one branch with luscious clusters of grapes. Without the good grapes, there would be no purpose in pruning the remainder of the vineyard, but their presence made it a useful and necessary act. Similarly, Noach's presence made the Flood a constructive rather than purely destructive event, and therefore it became God's preferred course of action.

(Translator's note: Our Sages interpret the verse in Yeshayahu[50] describing the Flood as "the waters of Noach" to mean that Noach himself took some responsibility for the punishment of everyone else. Since the Flood took place for his spiritual benefit, he acquired an overwhelming obligation to use it for that benefit; and if he would not do so, the suffering of those who were punished would be his fault.)

---

49. *Bereishis Rabbah* 29:2.

50. *Yeshayahu* 54:9.

# פרשת נח
# PARASHAS NOACH

## Noach and His Generation

אֵלֶּה תּוֹלְדֹת נֹחַ נֹחַ אִישׁ צַדִּיק תָּמִים הָיָה בְּדֹרֹתָיו אֶת־הָאֱלֹקִים
הִתְהַלֶּךְ־נֹחַ: וַיּוֹלֶד נֹחַ שְׁלֹשָׁה בָנִים אֶת־שֵׁם אֶת־חָם וְאֶת־
יָפֶת: וַתִּשָּׁחֵת הָאָרֶץ לִפְנֵי הָאֱלֹקִים וַתִּמָּלֵא הָאָרֶץ חָמָס: וַיַּרְא
אֱלֹקִים אֶת־הָאָרֶץ וְהִנֵּה נִשְׁחָתָה כִּי־הִשְׁחִית כָּל־בָּשָׂר אֶת־דַּרְכּוֹ
עַל־הָאָרֶץ

*These are the progeny of Noach: Noach was a righteous man, pure in his generations; Noach walked with God. Noach fathered three sons: Shem, Cham, and Yafes. And the earth had become corrupt before God, and the earth was full of crime. And God looked at the earth and behold it was corrupted, for all flesh followed a decadent way upon the earth.*
*(Bereishis 6:9-12)*

Every force in Creation is by necessity a force *for* creation, for producing new and different combinations of phenomena that never existed before. From this it follows that the three aspects of human nature — the physical body, the spiritual soul, and the connection or union of these two (which is a reality in its own right) — each has its own way of "reproducing" and being fruitful.

The body, superficially similar to that of an animal, produces physical progeny just as animals do. The transcendent soul brings new ideas and understandings into the world, increasing knowledge and understanding of God. Finally, the connection between body and soul that is the essence of Man's special nature as a "living, speaking being" creates the revelation of the spiritual within the physical, which is most typified by the pursuit of justice and optimal interpersonal relationships.

> **The body produces physical progeny; the soul brings new ideas and understandings into the world. The connection between body and soul creates the revelation of the spiritual within the physical.**

The Torah introduces Noach to us with a description of how he produced "progeny" of each of these three aspects. First, he is called by the two titles of "*tzaddik*" and "*tamim*," "righteous" and "pure." Together these indicate that he lived a life of honesty and decency with others and that he did this not for selfish reasons, but purely from principle. This is the example of Noach's creative power in the realm of human interactions.

The Torah continues to state that Noach pursued knowledge of God and "walked with God," producing the spiritual "progeny" of the soul.

Finally, he had three sons, the children of his body. These children, who would be the progenitors of all of mankind after the Flood, were the product of a man who typified positive creative energy at all levels. Thus, these three sons would be able to continue all of these levels, making possible a continuation of humanity that would be more than merely the preservation of a physical species.

The relevance of Noach's success in these three areas goes beyond merely serving as a basis for appreciating his personal greatness; Noach's real significance is that he was the diametrical opposite of all the trends of his time; his survival amid their destruction was the clearest statement of God's rejection of their way of life. Therefore, the Torah details the way the people of Noach's generation failed in exactly the same three areas in which he excelled:

First, the world was "corrupt before God," meaning that awareness of God was diminished, resulting in a failure to pursue the growth of the soul. Second, the world was "full of crime," the opposite of justice. Finally, "all flesh followed a decadent way upon the earth"; their earthly matters violated even the obvious and natural dictates of decency, more fundamental than any laws based on reason, leading them to murder and other violent behavior.

This total deterioration condemned them to annihilation, while at the same time, it served to highlight Noach's greatness in resisting the trend. Not only did Noach remain good, but he was even creative and productive in his goodness.

# Two Sides of Noach

נֹחַ אִישׁ צַדִּיק תָּמִים הָיָה בְּדֹרֹתָיו.
***Noach was a righteous man, perfect in
his generations.
(Bereishis 6:9)***

Our Sages communicated the depth of their concepts about life in the form of disputes, some of which seem to us at first to be rather inscrutable:

"Rabbi Yehudah said, 'If Noach would have been in the generation of Moshe or Shmuel he would not have been considered especially righteous.' Rabbi Nechemiah said, 'He would have been even more righteous than he actually was.'"[1]

Why would these great minds have played this game of "What if?" and how is it meaningful to argue about something that seems to exist only in the realm of imagination?

> **Why would these great minds have played the game of "What if?"**

These questions force us to the conclusion that Rabbi Yehudah and Rabbi Nechemiah are focusing on different aspects of Noach's actual personality, each illuminating one aspect of it and complementing the other's insight.

The Torah describes Noach with two adjectives: "*tzaddik*" and "*tamim*," "righteous" and "perfect." "Righteousness" here refers to his acts and behavior, while "perfection" means the purity of his intent in performing them.

Rabbi Yehudah regards Noach's acts as his point of departure, and tells us that living in a corrupt generation of that magnitude took an unavoidable toll from the quantity of his spiritual output. If he would have lived in a time when there were other great people from whom to learn, he would have certainly achieved more.

Rabbi Nechemiah looks at Noach in terms of inner quality, and says that the very fact that he was isolated and opposed by his peers, frustrating as it may have been, purified his intention by ensuring that he had no ulterior motivation to be good. If he would have lived in the time of Moshe, he would have been tempted to pursue righteousness for the sake of honor or some other gain, but as it was, he acted solely for the sake of Heaven.

Together, Rabbi Yehudah and Rabbi Nechemiah illustrate in the Torah's description of Noach a picture of someone who struggled with the challenge of a very difficult era, and utilized the struggle itself to engender greatness of deep quality even if its superficial quantity was less than it might have been otherwise.

---

1. *Bereishis Rabbah* 30:9.

This discussion parallels another one[2] in which Rabbi Yehudah and Rabbi Nechemiah make their points in a different way. The Torah describes Noach as walking "with God," while Avraham Avinu is described as "walking before God."[3] Each Sage explains this distinction in accord with the aspect of Noach's life on which he chose to focus.

Rabbi Yehudah, looking at Noach's actual level of achievement, says that "Noach was like the young son of the king who had to walk along with his father, while Avraham was like an older son who could walk ahead." Noach needed constant help from God to succeed, while Avraham had reached a level of independence where he could "walk alone" without constant assistance.

Rabbi Nechemiah looks at the contrast between Noach and Avraham differently, again ignoring the superficial aspect of a simple comparison of levels but rather spotlighting the two different challenges that Noach and Avraham faced in their respective generations. "Rabbi Nechemiah said that Noach was like the friend of a king who was stuck in the mud. The king said to him, 'Instead of remaining in the mud, come walk with me.' Avraham, on the other hand, was like the friend of the king who was providing light for the king from a window. The king told him, 'Rather than giving light from the window, come give light before me.' Similarly, God said to Avraham, 'Instead of giving your light from foreign countries, come give it in Eretz Yisrael.'"

The spiritual conflict in Noach's time was a struggle with physical desires; even though people recognized God's existence, they had difficulty overcoming temptations, and God, seeing Noach's willingness to succeed in this area, pulled him out of the "mud" of materialism to spiritual heights.

In the time of Avraham, things were exactly the opposite: Mankind's behavior in the physical realm was more or less satisfactory. (This was partially the outcome of the reduction of the intensity of the world's physicality after the Flood.) However,

---

2. *Bereishis Rabbah* 30:10.

3. *Bereishis* 17:1.

they had fallen into the intellectual errors of denial of God's Providence and the consequent worship of idols. Avraham alone recognized the truth about God, and was shining this light in private for himself in places where he could not publicize it, and God told him to come to Eretz Yisrael, the appropriate place for him to begin disseminating his ideas to the world.

Again, Rabbi Yehudah and Rabbi Nechemiah complement each other, giving a full view of Noach's entirety. Noach was engaged in a head-on conflict with physical desire; only help from God could make victory possible when fighting to control drives that are, after all, necessary aspects of human nature. Avraham Avinu, in contrast, was working to restore people's ideas to what should have been their natural state; therefore, he could pursue this goal "independently," without specific intervention from God to combat any innate and essential resistance.

The comparison of Noach and Avraham provides a complete picture of what Noach was struggling against and how he succeeded.

# The Ark — Real and Symbolic

עֲשֵׂה לְךָ תֵּבַת עֲצֵי־גֹפֶר קִנִּים תַּעֲשֶׂה אֶת־הַתֵּבָה וְכָפַרְתָּ אֹתָהּ
מִבַּיִת וּמִחוּץ בַּכֹּפֶר

*"Make for yourself an ark of gopher wood, make the*
*ark with compartments, and cover it inside and out*
*with pitch."*
*(Bereishis 6:14)*

When God commanded Noach to build an ark, the goal was more than just physical survival for Noach, his family, and the animals he brought inside. The ark, by its very design, was meant to symbolize the new form that the world would take after the Flood, a form that would make a return to the sorry state of mankind before the Flood impossible.

The world before the Flood had a nature in which it was very difficult for the spiritual to control and subdue the physical, which was intense and overwhelming. Afterward, this physicality would be less dominant, and man would no longer be able to fall into such degradation.

This idea was illustrated by the use of very light wood in the construction of the ark, leaving it to float easily above the water that covered the remains of "the world that was." Furthermore, the ark was made in such a way that it contained numerous sections, symbolizing the fact that mankind would no longer be one united group living together, but would disperse into various groups in different places. This ensured that even if one subset of humanity deteriorated to a stage where they deserved punishment, the result would not be the destruction of the whole world. Lastly, the ark was covered inside and out with pitch. On the physical level, this prevented leaks; yet, it symbolized the fact that God would constantly protect the spiritual survival of the new order of things, and in particular the unique great people who would arise, especially Avraham Avinu and his descendants.

In these three ways, the world after the Flood would be both lessened and strengthened. Lessened, in that the great potential inherent in the powerful physicality of the pre-Flood world would be gone. Neither would there be the simple unity of all mankind, nor the purely independent strivings of special individuals for the pinnacles of greatness without personal assistance from God. Yet, in this case, "less is more," and the "lessened" world would be more sustainable in a spiritual sense, and would ultimately provide the stage for the emergence of the Jewish people and for the Giving of the Torah.

*The great potential inherent in the powerful physicality of the pre-Flood world would be gone; neither would there be the simple unity of all mankind.*

# Two Aspects of Survival

וַיֹּאמֶר ה' לְנֹחַ בֹּא־אַתָּה וְכָל־בֵּיתְךָ אֶל־הַתֵּבָה כִּי־אֹתְךָ רָאִיתִי
צַדִּיק לְפָנַי בַּדּוֹר הַזֶּה

*And **Hashem** said to Noach, "Come, you and your
entire household, into the ark; for it is you that I have
seen to be righteous before Me in this generation."*
*(Bereishis 7:1)*

The commandment to Noach to bring animals into the ark
seems to be repeated in the Torah, with a slight change:

First Noach was told that one pair from each species
would come to him to survive the Flood: *"And Elokim said to
Noach... from every living thing, from all flesh, bring two of
each into the ark to survive with you ... from every type that
crawls upon the earth, two from each will come to you to
survive"* (6:19,20).

A few verses later, however, the Torah records that he was told
to bring *seven* of each species of "clean" animals, and two of
each species of "unclean" ones: *"And Hashem said to Noach ...
'from every clean [domestic] animal, take for yourself seven
of each ... but from the [domestic] animals that are not clean,
two ...'"* (7:1,2).

What is the explanation of this seeming contradiction? There
are clues in the second instruction to Noach that help clarify the
matter:

- In the second instruction, the four-letter Name of God,
  *Hashem*, is used, as opposed to the name *Elokim* that is
  used the first time Noach was told to gather animals.

- In this section, only *"beheimos,"* domestic animals, are
  mentioned, as opposed to the previous section where
  "everything that crawls upon the earth" is included.

- In the second section, Noach is told to take his "entire
  household" into the ark with him.

All of these facts indicate in this instance God is speaking to Noach on a *more personal* level than He had previously:

In the earlier instruction, Noach was told to bring enough specimens of all types of animals to ensure their perpetuation. Here, on the other hand, God is giving Noach permission to save some of his own private domesticated livestock among his other possessions, "his household."

Here, the four-letter Name is used, since it represents the more particular type of Providence in action here, in contrast to the general Providence at work in the preservation of animal species overall.

From this we see that in the previous verses, God is laying out the plan for the earth's survival. Here, Noach *himself* is being rewarded for his own personal righteousness, over and above the protection he and the inhabitants of the ark would receive as a result of their world-rescuing mission.

Noach was told to bring two pairs of unclean animals and seven pairs of clean animals, all this in addition to the single pair of the same species brought to ensure basic survival. He was also permitted to bring any of his own household property so that he could feel "at home" in the ark.

All of this was not only for Noach's personal benefit; it also served a larger purpose in ensuring that the achievements of the ten pre-Flood generations would not be lost. The animals that came in by themselves were all wild animals, even those from the same species as the domestic ones that Noach added to them.

> *Noach brought with him the products of technological invention up to his time, so that the world would not have to begin again from scratch.*

Two wild oxen, two mountain goats, etc., were all that would have been preserved if Noach had not brought some of his own flock with him, and the process of domestication would have to have been repeated after the Flood.

Similarly, Noach brought with him the products of technological processed invention up to his time, and presumably the knowledge of how to produce them as well, so that the world would not have to begin again from scratch in a material sense. God wished to destroy the moral degradation of the pre-Flood world, but He had no desire to destroy all of the physical progress that had been made up until that time; and, in His personal mercy on Noach, He provided for the continuity of civilization after the Flood.

These two aspects of God's relationship to the world at the time of the Flood became real and evident in the opposite order when the Flood actually began. First, seven days before the Flood, "Noach did everything as he was commanded by *Hashem*."[4] The four-letter Name for God is used to show that here the Torah is describing Noach's preparation for the Flood by bringing his own possessions into the ark and setting it up as his home.

Afterward, on the day of the Flood itself, Noach and his family entered the ark "because of the water of the Flood," a reaction to the physical threat to survival; all animals, whether "clean" or "unclean," arrived in single pairs "to the ark," for preservation rather than for Noach's personal use. All of this was "as *Elokim* commanded Noach,"[5] showing God's general concern for the existence of Creation rather than His specific care for Noach and for human civilization.

The preparation seven days earlier was done consciously and deliberately, corresponding to the fact that Noach's intentionally acquired property and the intelligent products of human ingenuity were being preserved. The actual entry into the ark was motivated by the instinctual fear of the "water of the Flood," in consonance with its purpose of saving the world's natural order, which functions by nonconscious physical law. Together, these two sides of God's way of dealing with the world guaranteed its continued existence.

---

4. *Bereishis* 7:4,5.

5. Ibid. 7:7-9.

# Contrary to Nature

וַיְהִי לְשִׁבְעַת הַיָּמִים וּמֵי הַמַּבּוּל הָיוּ עַל־הָאָרֶץ ... בַּיּוֹם הַזֶּה
נִבְקְעוּ כָּל־מַעְיְנוֹת תְּהוֹם רַבָּה וַאֲרֻבֹּת הַשָּׁמַיִם נִפְתָּחוּ

*And it was after seven days that the waters of the Flood was upon the earth. ... On that day, all the fountains of the vast deep burst forth, and the windows of the Heavens were opened ....*
*(Bereishis 7:10,11)*

T he Flood in the time of Noach is the classic example of Divine punishment of man; therefore it was necessary that it take place in such a way that would be practically impossible to attribute to natural circumstances and to dull its impact.

The Torah tells us three features of the Flood that illustrate this emphasis on its supernatural quality:

- First, it was predicted in a prophecy to Noach as the Torah states, "And it was after seven days," from the time God told Noach that the Flood was coming until the water arrived.

- Secondly, "the waters of the Flood was upon the earth," from the first minute, it was a huge flood rather than a small storm that gradually gained in intensity like any natural flood.

- Third, the "fountains of the deep" and "the windows of Heaven" opened simultaneously, releasing boiling water from deep underground pools

*Noach and his family had no choice but to immediately enter the ark to save their lives.*

and all the water vapor in the atmosphere which instantly condensed and began to fall in an obviously miraculous fashion.

Noach and his family had no choice but to immediately enter the ark to save their lives, and they did so with the undoubted realization of an unparalleled supernatural event.

# The Duration of the Flood

וַיִּגְבְּרוּ הַמַּיִם עַל־הָאָרֶץ חֲמִשִּׁים וּמְאַת יוֹם
*And the water overpowered the land for*
*one hundred fifty days.*
*(Bereishis 7:24)*

The Torah gives two different figures for the duration of the Flood: 40 days, and 150 days. If we examine the words of the Torah carefully we can reconcile these two numbers.

The actual rainfall and upflow of underground water lasted only 40 days; after that the water level began to recede. For 150 days, however, it was impossible to perceive this fact since the highest mountains were all covered. The Torah states "*va'yigb'ru ha'mayim al ha'aretz*," "the water overpowered the land," meaning that the water covered the land and made it invisible.

When the Torah stated earlier, "the water overpowered greatly over the land,"[6] it meant that the water level was rising until it was seen to rise above the mountains, but here the same phrase means only that the water was still above the land even though it was receding day by day. (The root "*gavar*" is one of many that can indicate both a change in state and a continuation of the changed state; other examples are "*kam*" meaning "stood" or "was standing," "*amad*" with a similar meaning, "*chayah*" meaning "became alive" or "remained alive," and "*hayah*" meaning "came into existence" or "continued to exist.")

When the Torah states that "God remembered Noach"[7] it

---

6. *Bereishis* 7:19.
7. Ibid 8:1.

means that after 40 days, He stopped the increase of the water level, giving the land time to dry out completely before a full year had elapsed from the beginning of the Flood. A year, say our Sages,[8] is the maximum duration of a Divine punishment.

Only after 150 days when the ark rested on a relatively low mountain in Ararat did Noach realize that the waters had receded to a significant extent. From that time on, it was possible to see how "the water level continued to decline" by looking at where it reached on the side of the ark. When it reached the bottom of the ark, the "top of the mountain was visible."[9]

> **A year, say our Sages, is the maximum duration of a Divine punishment.**

# The Raven and the Dove

וַיְשַׁלַּח אֶת־הָעֹרֵב וַיֵּצֵא יָצוֹא וָשׁוֹב עַד־יְבֹשֶׁת הַמַּיִם מֵעַל הָאָרֶץ:
וַיְשַׁלַּח אֶת־הַיּוֹנָה מֵאִתּוֹ לִרְאוֹת הֲקַלּוּ הַמַּיִם מֵעַל פְּנֵי הָאֲדָמָה

*And he sent out the raven, and it kept going back and forth until the waters dried from upon the earth. And he sent forth the dove from him to see whether the waters had subsided from upon the face of the land.*
*(Bereishis 8:7-8)*

As the Floodwaters receded, Noach sent out two birds on two different missions to determine the state of affairs outside.

First, he sent a raven, considered in ancient times to be a bird with almost supernatural powers of perception. Noach watched

---

8. *Seder Olam* 3.
9. *Bereishis* 8:5.

as it flew "back and forth" without flying far away, and he interpreted its motions and sounds as a weather report.

Our Sages[10] point out Divine Providence in the availability of the raven for this task: Of all the birds in the ark, only the raven reproduced during the Flood, making it possible to send one out without risking the possibility of its loss and the extinction of the species.

Afterward, he sent out a dove (or perhaps a carrier pigeon, known for its swift flight) for an actual exploratory mission, "to see whether the water had subsided from the land." (Sending a dove did not endanger the species, since Noach had taken seven pairs of domesticated doves, in addition to the two wild ones that had come on their own, as explained in "Two Aspects of Survival" to verse 7:1.)

The first time he sent the dove, it returned without having found a place to rest, even though it had flown far away, unlike the raven. After seven days, he sent it out again, and it returned with an olive branch that was still fresh ("*taraf,*" from "*teref*" meaning edible and moist), indicating the presence of a live tree above water level.

> **Noach knew that the world was returning to its normal state.**

Seven days later, the dove, a bird that retains something of its wild nature even after being domesticated, flew away for good, and Noach knew that the world was returning to its normal state.

# A Pleasing Sacrifice

וַיִּבֶן נֹחַ מִזְבֵּחַ לַה' וַיִּקַּח מִכֹּל הַבְּהֵמָה הַטְּהוֹרָה וּמִכֹּל הָעוֹף הַטָּהוֹר וַיַּעַל עֹלֹת בַּמִּזְבֵּחַ: וַיָּרַח ה' אֶת־רֵיחַ הַנִּיחֹחַ וַיֹּאמֶר ה' אֶל־לִבּוֹ לֹא אֹסִף לְקַלֵּל עוֹד אֶת־הָאֲדָמָה בַּעֲבוּר הָאָדָם כִּי יֵצֶר לֵב הָאָדָם רַע מִנְּעֻרָיו וְלֹא־אֹסִף עוֹד לְהַכּוֹת אֶת־כָּל־חַי כַּאֲשֶׁר עָשִׂיתִי

---

10. *Sanhedrin* 108b.

*And Noach built an altar to God; and he took of every pure animal and from every pure bird, and he brought burnt-offerings upon the altar. And God smelled the pleasing aroma, and God said in His heart: "I will not continue to curse the ground again because of man, since the impulse of man's heart is evil from his youth; nor will I continue to smite all life again as I have done."*
*(Bereishis 8:20,21)*

After the Flood was finished, and all the animal species returned to living "in their families" each with its own kind rather than all together in the ark, Noach saw fit to bring an offering to thank God for His kindness in restoring the world to its order. He saw a clue indicating his obligation to do this in the fact that God had commanded him to take many more clean animals than necessary either for the survival of the species or for his own consumption, since meat-eating was not yet permitted.

Our Sages[11] liken this offering to the one brought by the first man celebrating the creation of the world, taking their cue for this comparison from the Torah's use of the definite article, "the altar,"[12] as opposed to "an altar," indicating that Noach brought his offering on the same altar as had Adam, and for a similar purpose.

The Torah expresses God's "pleasure" with Noach's offering with the phrase "God smelled the pleasing aroma," "*rei'ach nicho'ach*," a phrase used throughout the Torah in connection with offering.

The concept of a burnt offering is the submission of the physical and the "release" of the more elevated spiritual essence,

---

11. *Bereishis Rabbah* 34:9.

12. The phrase "the altar" seems perfectly justified, referring to "an altar" mentioned in the beginning of the verse. Perhaps, though, the entire phrase is otherwise superfluous, thus indicating the Midrashic explanation. (Ed.)

symbolized by the volatile aroma that wafts upward, "*rei'ach*" meaning aroma being related to "*ru'ach*," "the spirit." God perceived Noach's pure intentions of thanks for the salvation of the world and of himself and his family from destruction and his hopes for the future as flowing upward beyond the limitations of his physical body, and was pleased with the new potential inherent in mankind.

This is what the Midrash[13] hints at when it states that God "smelled the fragrance of Avraham being (potentially) burnt in the furnace and that of Chananiah, Mishael, and Azariah being thrown into the fire." Contained in Noach's intense desire and hope for the success of mankind after the Flood was all the greatness that would eventually be revealed in his descendants' actions, and this was what caused God such great pleasure.

> **God "smelled the fragrance of Avraham (potentially) being burnt in the furnace."**

Noach's subjugation of his physical nature to his spiritual side and his ability to pass this achievement on to his progeny was the impetus for God's decision not to "curse the ground again because of man." The Hebrew word used here for "because" is "*ba'avur,*" which means "for the sake of" as opposed to "*biglal*" which means "as a result of." The previous curses of the land at the time of Adam and in the Flood itself were intended for Man's own benefit: to weaken his physical strength that had been misused, and to make it easier for him to focus on the spiritual. Man's life span and energy had been reduced, and now God saw that there was no need for further such reduction, since Noach demonstrated that it was possible to succeed spiritually with the level of strength that he had.

From now on, the source of Man's temptation to sin would no longer be the raw physicality of the world, which had been tamed to a great extent. Instead, "the evil impulse of his youth" would be Man's major challenge. This refers to the fact that a person begins

13. *Bereishis Rabbah* 34:9.

life in an animalistic state, devoid of intelligence; by the time his rational faculties appear, these faculties are at a disadvantage.

Now there would be no more point in cursing either "the earth," the physical nature of the world, or "smiting all life," the animals that symbolize the many character traits within a person, since these were already on a level compatible with a successful struggle for good. Now each individual would be charged with working against the negative images and ideas acquired in childhood and overcoming them with the intelligence of his mature soul.

# The Spiritual Rainbow

וְהָיָה בְּעַנְנִי עָנָן עַל־הָאָרֶץ וְנִרְאֲתָה הַקֶּשֶׁת בֶּעָנָן: וְזָכַרְתִּי אֶת־
בְּרִיתִי אֲשֶׁר בֵּינִי וּבֵינֵיכֶם ... וְהָיְתָה הַקֶּשֶׁת בֶּעָנָן וּרְאִיתִיהָ לִזְכֹּר
בְּרִית עוֹלָם

*"And it shall be, when I place a cloud over the earth*
*and the rainbow will be seen in the cloud, I will*
*remember My covenant between Me and you ....*
*And the rainbow will be in the cloud, and I will look*
*upon it to remember the eternal covenant ...."*
*(Bereishis 9:14-16)*

God's choice of the rainbow as the symbol of His covenant with Noach was based on the concept that the rainbow is considered a reflection of God Himself.

*The rainbow is considered a reflection of God Himself.*

The Midrash[14] connects the word "keshet," "rainbow," with the root "hekesh," "a comparison," indicating that the rainbow is compared with an "image" of God. The same thought is found

---

14. *Bereishis Rabbah* 35:3 (see *Berachos* 59a).

in Yechezkel's vision of the Divine Chariot,[15] where the "appearance" of God is likened to a rainbow.

We can understand this comparison in terms of the process by which the rainbow is produced. If there are no clouds, there is nothing to split the white light of the sun into a spectrum; on the other hand, if the clouds are too thick, the light will not be able to penetrate to form the rainbow. Only if a thin cloud layer is present will the rainbow be seen.

The analogy is to God's spiritual "light" that He sheds upon the world: When that "light" contacts angels or other purely spiritual beings, it is not split into any specific forms of Divine interaction, such as kindness or strict judgment, since these beings have no need of such direction from God. On the other hand, when the Divine influence impinges on "thick," materialistic sorts of people, it cannot penetrate at all. Only when it contacts a person who is like a thin cloud in that he has refined his physical nature to the extent that he can perceive God's "light" does that "light" exhibit its entire spectrum, the seven ways of dealing with the world known as *Sefiros*.

The Torah uses two expressions when mentioning the rainbow: It will be "seen in the cloud," and it will "be in the cloud." The physical rainbow will only be seen, since it is basically an optical illusion, with no tangible presence in the cloud itself. From the vision of this rainbow of physical light, we are to infer the existence of the Divine "spectrum" of different attitudes toward the world that will actually be present in the "cloud" of human nature after that nature has been permanently refined by the change the Flood wrought in Creation.

---

15. *Yechezkel* 1:28.

# A Natural Sign

וְהָיָה בְּעַנְנִי עָנָן עַל־הָאָרֶץ וְנִרְאֲתָה הַקֶּשֶׁת בֶּעָנָן: וְזָכַרְתִּי אֶת־
בְּרִיתִי אֲשֶׁר בֵּינִי וּבֵינֵיכֶם וּבֵין כָּל־נֶפֶשׁ חַיָּה בְּכָל־בָּשָׂר וְלֹא־יִהְיֶה
עוֹד הַמַּיִם לְמַבּוּל לְשַׁחֵת כָּל־בָּשָׂר: וְהָיְתָה הַקֶּשֶׁת בֶּעָנָן וּרְאִיתִיהָ
לִזְכֹּר בְּרִית עוֹלָם בֵּין אֱלֹקִים וּבֵין כָּל־נֶפֶשׁ חַיָּה

*And it shall be, when I place a cloud over the earth,"*
*and the rainbow will be seen in the cloud and I will*
*remember My covenant between Me and you and*
*every living being among all flesh, and never again*
*will the waters become a flood to destroy all flesh.*
*The rainbow will be in the cloud, and I will look upon*
*it to remember the eternal covenant with the world,*
*"... between God [Elokim] and every living being*
*(Bereishis 9:14-16)*

Even though the rainbow is a natural phenomenon that appears regularly under certain physical conditions, it was fitting to serve as a sign of God's covenant with Noach and his descendants for the following reason:

For a rainbow to be visible, it is necessary for the clouds to be thin enough to allow the sun's rays to pass, and they must cover only part of the sky, leaving the rest clear. Before the Flood, the world had a more intense nature, producing people and animals and plants of great size and power, and these people possessed more powerful physical desires with which they had to struggle. This same extreme aspect of nature caused every rainfall to be accompanied by a very thick cloud cover that filled the entire sky, and so a rainbow was an impossibility.

> **The rainbow was not an arbitrary symbol.**

Afterward, with the intensity of Nature reduced, a thin partial cloud cover could develop, producing a rainbow.

Thus, the rainbow was not an arbitrary symbol; it was a demonstration of the less intense sort of struggle with physicality that would now take place, a struggle that would no longer present the risk of mankind falling to the level where a total destruction would ever again be required.

The sign of the rainbow could be given in two different ways:

In a time when people were behaving in a generally proper fashion, rain would fall regularly and the clouds would never get so thick and widespread as to prevent the appearance of a rainbow visible to people on earth. This is described by the Torah when it quotes God as saying, "When I place a cloud over the earth, the rainbow will be seen in the cloud."

If, however, mankind would fall to a state where their destruction was almost imminent, and rain would be withheld for a long period, the rain that would descend afterward would be accompanied by clouds totally covering the sky. Here, too, God promises that "the rainbow will be in the cloud" since they will be thin enough to create a rainbow, although visible only from above. This symbol, though, is only for God himself, Who says, "I will look upon it to remember the eternal covenant with the world." In this case, the covenant is described as being with "every living being," i.e., even animals. When mankind alone is not deserving of being saved, the "merit" of the animal world — which at least functions according to God's plan — would prevent the catastrophe.

For this reason, too, the name *Elokim* is used here, denoting God's natural way of dealing with the world, as opposed to His special Providence on human beings.

# The Sons of Noach

וַיִּהְיוּ בְנֵי־נֹחַ הַיֹּצְאִים מִן־הַתֵּבָה שֵׁם וְחָם וָיָפֶת וְחָם הוּא אֲבִי
כְנָעַן: שְׁלֹשָׁה אֵלֶּה בְּנֵי־נֹחַ וּמֵאֵלֶּה נָפְצָה כָל־הָאָרֶץ

*And the sons of Noach who emerged from the ark were Shem, Cham, and Yafes — Cham being the father of Canaan. These three were the sons of Noach, and from these the whole world was spread out.*
*(Bereishis 9:18,19)*

The three sons of Noach were not just individuals; they were prototypes and progenitors of three different types of people with different directions in life.

Shem was the example of a person with intellectual and spiritual goals, the seeker of intrinsic "good." Yafes was the practical-minded builder of successful nations guided by decent man-made laws and rules, that which is "useful." Cham set the negative example of a life of pursuit of physical satisfaction and animal desires, that which is only "pleasant." The world would not be complete without these three types of people, and therefore the Torah states that these were the sons of Noach "who emerged from the ark" to found a new world.

> **Shem was the example of a person with intellectual and spiritual goals, the seeker of intrinsic "good."**

# The Tower of Bavel

וַיְהִי כָל־הָאָרֶץ שָׂפָה אֶחָת וּדְבָרִים אֲחָדִים: וַיְהִי בְּנָסְעָם מִקֶּדֶם
וַיִּמְצְאוּ בִקְעָה בְּאֶרֶץ שִׁנְעָר וַיֵּשְׁבוּ שָׁם ...
... וַיֵּרֶד ה' לִרְאֹת אֶת־הָעִיר וְאֶת־הַמִּגְדָּל אֲשֶׁר בָּנוּ בְּנֵי הָאָדָם:
וַיֹּאמֶר ה' הֵן עַם אֶחָד וְשָׂפָה אַחַת לְכֻלָּם וְזֶה הַחִלָּם לַעֲשׂוֹת
וְעַתָּה לֹא־יִבָּצֵר מֵהֶם כֹּל אֲשֶׁר יָזְמוּ לַעֲשׂוֹת

*And the whole earth was of one language and uni-*
*form lifestyle [devarim achadim]. And it was when*
*they traveled from the east [mikedem], they found*
*a valley in the land of Shinar and they settled*
*there ....*
*... And God went down to look at the city and the*
*tower which the sons of man had built. And God*
*said, "Behold, they are one nation with one lan-*
*guage for all, and this they have started to do. And*
*now, should it not be withheld from them all they*
*proposed to do?*
*(Bereishis 11:1-6)*

In the generations immediately after Noach, people followed a tradition of life that could be traced directly back to Noach and his family. First of all, they had a common language, which, according to our Sages,[16] was Hebrew. Furthermore the Torah tells us that they had in common "*devarim achadim,*" which can mean either that they followed a uniform lifestyle, or that they had "few possessions" and were not overly concerned with material things.

In the time of Peleg, however, their approach to life changed. They traveled "*mikedem,*" which can mean "from the east," but can also denote a change "from the past."

The first aspect of this change was the decision to form a large

---

16. *Tanchuma* 19; *Targum Yonasan.*

kingdom, headed by Nimrod,[17] in the valley of Shinar. Rather than spread out and fill the entire Earth as God had commanded them to do, they began to build permanent homes in this area, using bricks and mortar that were readily available there.

*Even among idol-worshipers, there would always be disputes about which idol was more powerful.*

The next step was to decide to build a tower which, according to their distorted beliefs, would "bring down" blessing from the constellations, which they considered to be the source of all benefits. Not only did the originators of this idea want to do this for themselves, but the plan was to unite all people in this denial of God and worship of human power.

God saw not only the seriousness of their sin in the present, but also the future consequences. The Torah expresses this by saying that "God went down" and looked at the practical repercussions of their behavior. He saw that without decisive action, they had every chance of achieving their goal and corrupting mankind completely: They were "one nation" without different customs to separate them; they spoke "one language" which gave them clear communication; and they had already "started to do this," so they were past the hardest stage of any project, getting it off the ground.

God decided to stop them before they reached the stage that would require large-scale destruction of mankind, and for that purpose He chose to confuse their languages and spread them throughout the world. This would actually be good for mankind, since as a result any thoughts of denial of God would no longer be universally accepted. Even among idol-worshipers there would always be disputes about which idol was more powerful, a fact that would foster a return to the recognition of the One God Who is above all other powers.

---

17. *Pirkei d'Rabbi Eliezer* 24.

# Terach's Journey

וַתְּהִי שָׂרַי עֲקָרָה אֵין לָהּ וָלָד: וַיִּקַּח תֶּרַח אֶת־אַבְרָם בְּנוֹ וְאֶת־
לוֹט בֶּן־הָרָן בֶּן־בְּנוֹ וְאֵת שָׂרַי כַּלָּתוֹ אֵשֶׁת אַבְרָם בְּנוֹ וַיֵּצְאוּ אִתָּם
מֵאוּר כַּשְׂדִּים לָלֶכֶת אַרְצָה כְּנַעַן וַיָּבֹאוּ עַד־חָרָן וַיֵּשְׁבוּ שָׁם

*Sarai was barren, she had no child. And Terach took
his son Avram, and Lot, son of Haran, his grand-
son, and his daughter-in-law Sarai, the wife of his
son Avram, and they departed with them from Ur
Kasdim to go to the land of Canaan; they arrived at
Charan, and they settled there.*
*(Bereishis 11:30-31)*

**B**efore Avraham Avinu left his family at God's command to go to Eretz Yisrael, his father Terach had set out with the same goal. What was Terach's motivation in doing so?

We are told that Terach's son Haran died in Terach's lifetime in "Ur Kasdim."[18] Our Sages[19] elaborated on this, explaining that "Ur" here means the fire of the furnace into which Nimrod threw Haran after his brother Avram was miraculously saved from the same fate. This was one of the reasons prompting Terach to leave the realm of Nimrod, a descendant of Cham, for the land of Canaan, then inhabited by Terach's kin, the sons of Shem.

*This was a first step in distancing Avram from the false beliefs of his immediate ancestors.*

He took with him only Avram, Avram's wife Sarai, and Lot, who also was suspect in Nimrod's eyes as a possible avenger of his father's blood. Terach's other son Nachor, who had not defied Nimrod's idolatry, remained behind.

---

18. *Bereishis* 11:28.
19. *Bereishis Rabbah* 38:13.

This was a first step in distancing Avram from the false beliefs of his immediate ancestors.

Divine Providence caused the idol-worshiping Terach to stop at the city of Charan, so that he, too, would not follow Avram to Eretz Yisrael and impede Avram's spiritual progress.

# פרשת לך לך
# PARASHAS LECH LECHA

## Avram's Triple Challenge

וַיֹּאמֶר ה' אֶל־אַבְרָם לֶךְ־לְךָ מֵאַרְצְךָ וּמִמּוֹלַדְתְּךָ וּמִבֵּית אָבִיךָ
אֶל־הָאָרֶץ אֲשֶׁר אַרְאֶךָּ: וְאֶעֶשְׂךָ לְגוֹי גָּדוֹל וַאֲבָרֶכְךָ וַאֲגַדְּלָה
שְׁמֶךָ וֶהְיֵה בְּרָכָה: וַאֲבָרְכָה מְבָרְכֶיךָ וּמְקַלֶּלְךָ אָאֹר וְנִבְרְכוּ בְךָ
כֹּל מִשְׁפְּחֹת הָאֲדָמָה:
וַיֵּלֶךְ אַבְרָם כַּאֲשֶׁר דִּבֶּר אֵלָיו ה'

*God said to Avram, "Go for yourself from your land,*
*from your birthplace, and from your father's house*
*to the land that I will show you. And I will make*
*of you a great nation, I will bless you, and make*
*your name great, and you will be a blessing. I will*
*bless those who bless you, and him who curses you I*
*will curse; and all the families of the earth shall be*
*blessed through you."*
*And Avram went as God had spoken to him ....*
*(Bereishis 12:1-4)*

God's intent in sending Avram on a lonely journey away from his familiar surroundings was to distance him in every possible way from the negative influences that could hamper his growth. For this reason, he was told to leave all three potential sources of negativity: his land, his place, and his family. The land by its very climate and spiritual "atmosphere" could retard him in his great aspirations; even more so was this true of the social influence of the people and his close relatives. He was commanded in ascending order of difficulty (land, society, family) to leave these three facets of his background and "lech lecha," "go for yourself," from now on concentrate solely on your own development that will eventually provide the foundation for the Jewish people.

The effect of Avram's following of this instruction would be in proportion to the difficulty of the task, and in proportion to his own personal investment in it. For that reason, God did not reveal to him that He was sending him to Eretz Yisrael, the place to which he and his father had already intended to go. Now he set out without any sense of security or certainty, and it was clear that he was doing this with his whole heart and with pure motivations.

Furthermore, the act of leaving had to be an independent act that stood on its own, apart from the goal of arriving elsewhere, so that it could have its maximum effect in distancing Avram from the negative as a preparation for pursuit of the positive.

The Torah teaches us here more than just the specific story of Avram himself, as important as that is. From this we learn a general principle: When a person puts in the necessary effort to improve himself and to come to know God, he is given more direct awareness of God and guidance in reaching higher goals than he could have ever achieved on his own.

At the same time that God made the test difficult, He also gave reassurance to Avram that eventually the hardships he would suffer would be compensated: Leaving his land would separate him from that nation and make him a lone figure; for this, God promised him that he would become a "great nation" himself. When he would be among strangers rather than in his own place, he would be the object of jealousy for any blessing that came to him; this was offset by the promise that God would "bless him" and cause others to be happy with that blessing. Finally, upon separating himself from his family, he would feel the loss of his ancestry and history; the assurance that "I will make your name great" replaced this with a proud family line beginning from Avram himself.

In addition to all these promises that served as compensation for his loss, God also told him, "You will be a blessing," that through you all good will flow to the land where you will be, and that the Divine Providence will operate for everyone in accordance with your actions.

Avram's influence would extend to the point that "I will bless those who bless you." Vast numbers of people (indicated by the use of the plural "m'varchecha") would acknowledge Avram's greatness and therefore accept his ideas, while only a small minority, "him who curses you" (in the singular), would deny his message. As a result, "all the families of the earth shall be blessed through you," gaining knowledge of God and receiving reward and prosperity for pursuing that knowledge.

# Avram's Departure

וַיֵּלֶךְ אַבְרָם כַּאֲשֶׁר דִּבֶּר אֵלָיו ה' וַיֵּלֶךְ אִתּוֹ לוֹט וְאַבְרָם בֶּן־חָמֵשׁ
שָׁנִים וְשִׁבְעִים שָׁנָה בְּצֵאתוֹ מֵחָרָן: וַיִּקַּח אַבְרָם אֶת־שָׂרַי אִשְׁתּוֹ
וְאֶת־לוֹט בֶּן־אָחִיו וְאֶת־כָּל־רְכוּשָׁם אֲשֶׁר רָכָשׁוּ וְאֶת־הַנֶּפֶשׁ אֲשֶׁר־
עָשׂוּ בְחָרָן וַיֵּצְאוּ לָלֶכֶת אַרְצָה כְּנַעַן וַיָּבֹאוּ אַרְצָה כְּנָעַן:
וַיַּעֲבֹר אַבְרָם בָּאָרֶץ עַד מְקוֹם שְׁכֶם עַד אֵלוֹן מוֹרֶה וְהַכְּנַעֲנִי אָז
בָּאָרֶץ: וַיֵּרָא ה' אֶל־אַבְרָם וַיֹּאמֶר לְזַרְעֲךָ אֶתֵּן אֶת־הָאָרֶץ הַזֹּאת
וַיִּבֶן שָׁם מִזְבֵּחַ לַה' הַנִּרְאֶה אֵלָיו:
וַיַּעְתֵּק מִשָּׁם הָהָרָה מִקֶּדֶם לְבֵית־אֵל וַיֵּט אָהֳלֹה בֵּית־אֵל מִיָּם
וְהָעַי מִקֶּדֶם וַיִּבֶן־שָׁם מִזְבֵּחַ לַה' וַיִּקְרָא בְּשֵׁם ה'

*And Avram went as God had spoken to him; and
Lot went with him. Avram was seventy-five years
old when he left Charan. Avram took his wife Sarai
and Lot, his nephew, all their belongings that they
had acquired, and the people they had acquired in
Charan, and they left to the land of Canaan, and
they came to the land of Canaan.*

*Avram traversed into the land as far as the location
of Shechem, until Elon Moreh; and the Canaanites
were then in the land. God appeared to Avram and
said, "To your descendants I will give this land," and
he built there an altar to God who appeared to him.*

*From there, he relocated to the mountain east of
Beth-el and pitched his tent ... he built there an
altar to God and called out in the Name of God.*
*(Bereishis 12:4-8)*

The thoughts of truly great people have a reality and solid-
ity to them that gives them the worth of concrete actions.
Once Avram came to the decision to follow God's command
to leave his home for an unspecified destination, the Torah can
already state, "And Avram went," adding, "as God had spoken,"

that he did so only to fulfill God's instructions, without interest in the rewards that he had been promised.

The Torah contrasts Avram's intentions with those of Lot, who merely "went with him" (using the form "*ito*" which indicates a subordinate status), following along without his own initiative. Further recognition is given to the greatness of this decision with the mention of the fact that Avram was already "seventy-five years old," comfortable in his place and his role in society.

After this description of Avram's resolve to go, the Torah tells of his actual departure on the journey. Rather than make an initial exploratory trip by himself, Avram immediately set out with his wife, nephew, and "all the belongings and the people they had acquired in Charan," i.e., servants, and, according to our Sages,[1] converts to the beliefs of Avram. This act demonstrated visibly Avram's enthusiasm to fulfill God's will.

They went directly to the land of Canaan, and Avram waited there for further instructions from God. When no such orders were forthcoming, he continued throughout Canaan "as far as Shechem," despite the fact that "the Canaanites were then in the land," conquering it from the descendants of Shem. This made the way dangerous, and disappointed Avram's hope to find a more elevated society there. Nonetheless, he did not question God's plan and continued on his way.

> **The Canaanites were then in the land, conquering it from the descendants of Shem.**

In this merit, Avram received a new, higher level of prophecy: God "appeared to him" in a clear manner and revealed that what had seemed to him to be a loss was actually a gain in the long run. God said, "To your descendants I will give this land," and they would conquer it from the Canaanites, who were subject to Noach's curse, rather than have to take it from their fellow sons of Shem.

Avram responded by "building an altar to God" to demonstrate

---

1. *Bereishis Rabbah* 39:14.

his gratitude for this great revelation. He did this even though he was still in a state of danger and subjugation, and not yet able to engage in spreading knowledge of God. To accomplish that, Avram would subsequently build public altars "to call out in the Name of God."

# Avram and His "Sister"

אִמְרִי־נָא אֲחֹתִי אָתְּ לְמַעַן יִיטַב־לִי בַעֲבוּרֵךְ וְחָיְתָה נַפְשִׁי בִּגְלָלֵךְ

*"Please say you are my sister, in order that they should be good to me for your sake, and that I may live on account of you."*
*(Bereishis 12:13)*

When Avram and Sarai went to Egypt to escape the famine in Eretz Yisrael, he instructed her to say that she was his sister, giving as the reason "in order that they should be good to me for your sake."

At first glance, Avram's behavior seems quite peculiar and even dishonest, and definitely requires a clear explanation. Certainly his goal was a good one, to protect Sarai and himself from danger, but how was this an effective and a proper means to go about this?

One possible answer to this problem is that Avram was aware of the practice of the times that one seeking a wife had to pay a relative, either the woman's father or her brother, whatever price he demanded in order to acquiesce to the marriage. Avram planned to set such a high price that no one would be able to afford it, and thereby succeeding in protecting her. The false statement that she was his sister would not be real deception, since no actual deal would ever be made.

This plan was effective with regard to the ordinary Egyptian men, none of whom could pay the exorbitant amount that Avram demanded, but matters became difficult when "the officers of Pharaoh praised her to Pharaoh," who paid the money and took her into his house, an outcome that Avram had not anticipated. At this point, it was necessary for God to save her miraculously by afflicting Pharaoh and his house with disease.

A second explanation of Avram's actions is that in ancient times, a very beautiful woman was considered to be a Divine being, and was forbidden in marriage to anyone but royalty. Avram feared that if he told the truth that she was his wife, he would be accused of violating the honor of a goddess. Therefore, he said that she was his sister, in order

> *In ancient times, a very beautiful woman was considered to be a Divine being.*

to prevent anyone from taking her. Contrary to his expectations, however, Pharaoh became interested in her and Avram was powerless to resist, leaving it to God to save her in a supernatural way.

# The Fall of Lot

וְגַם־לְלוֹט הַהֹלֵךְ אֶת־אַבְרָם הָיָה צֹאן־וּבָקָר וְאֹהָלִים: וְלֹא־נָשָׂא אֹתָם הָאָרֶץ לָשֶׁבֶת יַחְדָּו כִּי־הָיָה רְכוּשָׁם רָב וְלֹא יָכְלוּ לָשֶׁבֶת יַחְדָּו: וַיְהִי־רִיב בֵּין רֹעֵי מִקְנֵה־אַבְרָם וּבֵין רֹעֵי מִקְנֵה־לוֹט . . .

וַיֹּאמֶר אַבְרָם אֶל־לוֹט אַל־נָא תְהִי מְרִיבָה בֵּינִי וּבֵינֶךָ וּבֵין רֹעַי וּבֵין רֹעֶיךָ . . .

וַיִּשָּׂא־לוֹט אֶת־עֵינָיו וַיַּרְא אֶת־כָּל־כִּכַּר הַיַּרְדֵּן כִּי כֻלָּהּ מַשְׁקֶה לִפְנֵי שַׁחֵת ה׳ אֶת־סְדֹם וְאֶת־עֲמֹרָה כְּגַן־ה׳ כְּאֶרֶץ מִצְרַיִם . . . וַיִּבְחַר־לוֹ לוֹט אֵת כָּל־כִּכַּר הַיַּרְדֵּן . . . אַבְרָם יָשַׁב בְּאֶרֶץ־כְּנַעַן וְלוֹט יָשַׁב בְּעָרֵי הַכִּכָּר וַיֶּאֱהַל עַד־סְדֹם: וְאַנְשֵׁי סְדֹם רָעִים וְחַטָּאִים לַה׳ מְאֹד:

וַה׳ אָמַר אֶל־אַבְרָם אַחֲרֵי הִפָּרֶד־לוֹט מֵעִמּוֹ שָׂא־נָא עֵינֶיךָ וּרְאֵה . . . צָפֹנָה וָנֶגְבָּה וָקֵדְמָה וָיָמָּה . . . כִּי אֶת־כָּל־הָאָרֶץ אֲשֶׁר־אַתָּה רֹאֶה לְךָ אֶתְּנֶנָּה וּלְזַרְעֲךָ עַד־עוֹלָם: וְשַׂמְתִּי אֶת־זַרְעֲךָ כַּעֲפַר הָאָרֶץ אֲשֶׁר אִם־יוּכַל אִישׁ לִמְנוֹת אֶת־עֲפַר הָאָרֶץ גַּם־זַרְעֲךָ יִמָּנֶה: קוּם הִתְהַלֵּךְ בָּאָרֶץ לְאָרְכָּהּ וּלְרָחְבָּהּ כִּי לְךָ אֶתְּנֶנָּה

*Lot, too, who went with Avram, had flocks, cattle,
and tents. And the land did not support them dwelling together for their possessions were abundant,
and they were unable to dwell together. And there
was quarreling [riv] between Avram's shepherds and
Lot's shepherds ....*

*And Avram said to Lot, "Please let there not be a
dispute [merivah] between me and you, or between
my shepherds and your shepherds ...."*

*So Lot lifted his eyes and saw the entire Jordan
plain; that it was totally lush — before God
destroyed Sodom and Gomorrah — like the garden
of God, like the land of Egypt .... And Lot chose for
himself the entire Jordan plain .... Avram dwelled in
the land of Canaan, and Lot dwelled in the cities of
the plain, and he pitched his tents as far as Sodom;
and the people of Sodom were wicked and sinners
toward God exceedingly.*

*God said to Avram after Lot had parted from him,
"Raise now your eyes and look ... north, south, east
and west ... For the entire land that you see, to you
will I give it, and to your descendants forever. And I
will make your descendants as the dust of the earth,
so that if one can count the dust of the earth, so,
too, will your descendants be counted. Arise and
walk about the land through its length and breadth!
For to you I will give it."*

*(Bereishis 13:5-17)*

The Torah reveals to us that Lot acquired a fortune in the
merit of following along "with Avram." Lot himself, however, seems to have been unaware of this; he began to regard
himself as "independently wealthy."

As a result, Lot began to differ with Avram in his ideas and
behaviors, and this led to a more open split between them.

"Their possessions were abundant" for them to dwell in close proximity only because "they were unable to dwell together" in personal harmony. People who agree on principles can find a way to stay together even in cramped circumstances, but those who have fundamental differences in outlook will be much quicker to notice the lack of physical "breathing space."

> **People who agree on principles can find a way to stay together.**

The conflict between Avram and Lot became more pronounced when even their servants and shepherds began to dispute with each other as a result of the general lack of peace between their masters. At this point, Avram told Lot that the "*merivah*" — the cause of the dispute — as opposed to the "*riv*" — the dispute itself — was the very fact that "we are brothers" and we are trying to live too closely together.

Before the destruction of Sodom and Gomorrah, the Jordan River used to flood the surrounding plain in a manner similar to the Nile in Egypt, making the area lush like "the garden of God and like the land of Egypt." Our Sages tell us that the trees there were like those in the Garden of Eden, and the plants were like those in the most fertile part of Egypt. The temptation of the pleasant life in this region led Lot to leave his uncle completely and abandon his ideals. First, Lot went into the general location of the evil cities of the plain, but eventually became a citizen of Sodom itself.

Avram, on the other hand, remained in "the land of Canaan," far from the harmful influence of any city, and certainly avoiding the proximity of Sodom, where the people were both "wicked" in their interpersonal behavior, and "sinners" toward God.

Now that Lot had departed and Avram was alone, God revealed to him the extent of His promise of a land that would belong only to Avram's descendants. Avram had thought that only the small area in which he had been residing would be his, but now God told him to look to all directions and, with a miraculous expansion of his vision, he saw all of Eretz Yisrael.

This was the appropriate time to inform him that he would have children as numerous as "the dust of the earth" who would succeed in conquering this entire land, and to give him permission to traverse the entire land.

# The Blessing of Malkizedek

וּמַלְכִּי־צֶדֶק מֶלֶךְ שָׁלֵם הוֹצִיא לֶחֶם וָיָיִן וְהוּא כֹהֵן לְקֵל עֶלְיוֹן: וַיְבָרְכֵהוּ וַיֹּאמַר בָּרוּךְ אַבְרָם לְקֵל עֶלְיוֹן קֹנֵה שָׁמַיִם וָאָרֶץ: וּבָרוּךְ קֵל עֶלְיוֹן אֲשֶׁר־מִגֵּן צָרֶיךָ בְּיָדֶךָ

*Malkizedek, king of Shalem [Jerusalem], brought out bread and wine; he was a priest of the Most High God. He blessed him, saying, "Blessed is Avram to the Most High God, Owner of heaven and earth; and blessed is the Most High God, Who has delivered your enemies into your hand ...."*
*(Bereishis 14:18-20)*

After Avram's miraculous victory over the four kings, Malkizedek, king of Shalem (Jerusalem), came out to meet Avram with food, and he blessed Avram. This blessing typified the unique role of Avram and his descendants in world history.

Superficially, it seemed that Avram had been on a mission of saving his relative, Lot, and Lot's property from captivity. The net result, however, was a spectacular revelation of God's special Providence over the righteous. By granting Avram and his small band a victory over the armies of superpowers, God demonstrated that wars between mighty empires were insignificant compared to the personal needs of someone who was only distantly connected to the great Avram, even one such as Lot who had diverged from the straight path of his uncle. The *tzaddik*, the person who devotes his entire self to the pursuit of good, is of

> *The tzaddik, the person who devotes his entire self to the pursuit of good, is of far-greater importance to God than huge and powerful nations.*

far-greater importance to God than huge and powerful nations.

This was the content of Malkizedek's blessing: First he blessed Avram himself, "Blessed is Avram to the Most High God," emphasizing that he was worshiping only the Source of all Creation and not any other power. He refers to God as "He Who owns the heavens and the earth"; God not only created everything and is above all the systems of nature that He set in motion, He is the "Owner" and total Controller of the world. The Hebrew word used for "owner" is "*koneh*" (literally "is owning"), the present tense, indicating that God constantly exercises His control, paying attention to each detail. This was Avram's chosen task in life, to make this aspect of God known to people. As a reward and a necessary consequence, Avram became the means for exhibiting this reality via a miracle done specifically for him.

This is the real meaning of a *berachah*, a blessing to a person, that the person should be a channel for bringing blessing into the world from God Who is "Most High" and does not reveal Himself directly. The person who serves in this role of "helping" God to evidence Himself in the world automatically gains blessing for himself; therefore, "Blessed is Avram."

The continuation of the blessing, though, is "Blessed is the Most High God;" God Himself "gains," so to speak, through the blessing to the *tzaddik*, in that He has now a means of giving kindness to the world.

When there is a truly righteous person present, everyone else profits since he brings God's blessing upon them. This was the first public demonstration of the promise God made to Avram, "You shall be a blessing," and the prototype for all the great *tzaddikim* of the Jewish people who were always concerned with bringing God's goodness to the whole world.

Malkizedek, who according to our Sages[2] was Shem, son of Noach, was himself a righteous servant of God. But here, Malkizedek recognizes the new aspect of Avram's approach, making oneself a tool for God's revelation to the world.

# Avram's Oath

וַיֹּאמֶר אַבְרָם אֶל־מֶלֶךְ סְדֹם הֲרִמֹתִי יָדִי אֶל־ה׳ אֵל עֶלְיוֹן קֹנֵה
שָׁמַיִם וָאָרֶץ: אִם־מִחוּט וְעַד שְׂרוֹךְ־נַעַל וְאִם־אֶקַּח מִכָּל־אֲשֶׁר־לָךְ.

*Avram said to the king of Sodom, "I have raised my hand in oath to Hashem, the Most High God, Owner of heaven and earth, if so much as a thread or a shoelace, if I shall take anything that belongs to you ...."*
*(Bereishis 14:22-23)*

One of the most important criteria by which good actions are judged is the purity of intent of the individual doing the actions. If a person tries to purify his motivations by simple force of will, he may face a difficult struggle against his nature. If, on the other hand, he acquires a genuine deep appreciation of the value of the good deed itself, he will automatically be unwilling to "trade" that value for some material reward or ulterior motive.

This was the method that Avram used in reaching his high level of devotion to God, and which he demonstrated when refusing to take even "a shoelace" of the spoils of the war that were rightfully his. To Avram, the *Kiddush Hashem* of demonstrating God's kindness to His servants was the greatest reward possible, and it was unthinkable for him to consider exchanging that for anything else.

---

2. *Nedarim* 32b, *Avos d'Rabbi Nosson* 2, etc.

This is what Avram meant when he said, "I have raised my hand," the strength that gave me victory, "to the Most High God." I dedicate that strength and the triumph itself to the cause of publicizing God's Providence for the righteous; this is my payment for the effort of the war. As a result, "If I took so much as a thread or a shoelace, it would be as if I took it from you," the king of Sodom.

*I dedicate that strength and the triumph itself to the cause of publicizing God's Providence for the righteous; this is my payment for the effort of the war!*

A parallel concept expressed by this oath is that Avram did not see the victory itself as his own doing, but rather as God's power acting through him. "I have raised my hand ... to Hashem, the Most High God," admitting that my hand and strength themselves belong to and come only from Him; therefore, anything I would take would be an undeserved reward.

# Avram's Shield

אַחַר הַדְּבָרִים הָאֵלֶּה הָיָה דְבַר־ה' אֶל־אַבְרָם בַּמַּחֲזֶה לֵאמֹר אַל־תִּירָא אַבְרָם אָנֹכִי מָגֵן לָךְ שְׂכָרְךָ הַרְבֵּה מְאֹד: וַיֹּאמֶר אַבְרָם ה' אֱלֹקִים מַה־תִּתֶּן־לִי וְאָנֹכִי הוֹלֵךְ עֲרִירִי

*After these events, the word of God came to Avram in a vision, saying: "Fear not, Avram, I am your Shield; your reward is very great." And Avram said, "My Lord, Hashem Elokim, what can You give me, seeing that I go childless?"*
*(Bereishis 15:1-2)*

After Avram left the scene of the war with the four kings, "the word of God" came to him, a phrase that often indicates an answer from God to an unspoken question in a person's heart.

Avram experienced fear after the war, fear that expressed itself on three levels. God informed Avram that his fear was not justified at any of these levels.

First, Avram was simply afraid of reprisal by the kings or their allies. To calm this fear, God told him, "I am your Shield." At a deeper level, Avram was concerned that perhaps he deserved Divine punishment for killing, and also that his success in the war may have come at the expense of his merits. To these two fears, God said, "your reward is very great." Not only do you not deserve to be punished for the deaths you brought about, this is precisely what God had desired, the destruction of these evil people. Your reward will not be diminished but rather increased as a result.

Avram was pleased with this revelation, but puzzled as to the way in which it could be fulfilled. He asked, "What can You give me, seeing that I go childless?"

The question is raised as to how Avram knew that God was promising him great reward in *this* world, which would only make sense in the context of a physical continuation of his line. Perhaps God was referring only to the reward in *Olam Haba*, the World to Come?

This question, however, is based on a misunderstanding of the nature of *Olam Haba*. The reward of *Olam Haba* is actually not a reward or payment in the conventional sense, but rather a direct outcome of the good action, an aspect of the mitzvah itself. Just as one does not

> **The spiritual pleasure of Olam Haba is not an external reward for mitzvos; it is the essence of the mitzvos themselves.**

promise a student that if he applies himself to his studies, he will be "rewarded" with knowledge, so the spiritual pleasure of *Olam Haba* is not an external reward for mitzvos, but instead is the *essence* of the mitzvos, now eternally available for the sustained joy of purifying the soul and drawing near to God.

[This also explains the fact that this eternal spiritual reward is not mentioned in the Torah openly, since it is not something separate from the mitzvos themselves and therefore there is no need to discuss this separately.]

Since God used the term "reward," Avram knew that God was speaking about giving him reward in this world, over and above what he would receive in the next world. Therefore, Avram expressed his difficulty in understanding how that could come about.

# Avram's Question

וְהֶאֱמִן בַּה׳ וַיַּחְשְׁבֶהָ לוֹ צְדָקָה: וַיֹּאמֶר אֵלָיו אֲנִי ה׳ אֲשֶׁר
הוֹצֵאתִיךָ מֵאוּר כַּשְׂדִּים לָתֶת לְךָ אֶת־הָאָרֶץ הַזֹּאת
לְרִשְׁתָּהּ: וַיֹּאמַר אֲדֹ־נָי ה׳ אֱלוֹקִים בַּמָּה אֵדַע כִּי אִירָשֶׁנָּה:
וַיֹּאמֶר אֵלָיו קְחָה לִי עֶגְלָה מְשֻׁלֶּשֶׁת

*And he believed in God, and he considered it as a
kindness. He said to him, "I am God, Who brought
you out of Ur Kasdim to give you this land to inherit
it." And he said, "My Lord, Hashem/Elokim, with
what, I wish to know, I will inherit it?"
He said to him, "Take for Me three heifers ...."*
*(Bereishis 15:6-9)*

God promised Avram that he would have a son and that an entire nation would come from him. Yet, Avram wondered how this could be, in light of his knowledge of astrological predestination[3] that seemed to dictate against such a possibility.

God answered that Avram was above these sorts of forces, and that the system that influenced the rest of the world would not withhold from Avram that which he deserved. Avram accepted this promise, "he believed in God," but he considered this

---

3. The parphysical system of influence programmed into the heavenly bodies at the time of creation.

"exemption" itself to be a special favor from God not in line with what he deserved — "he considered it as a kindness."

There is a practical difference between that which God gives according to a person's merit and that which He gives as a pure kindness. When God follows the way of "*mishpat*," giving because the recipient was judged worthy, the gift can be taken back in the event the merit for which it was given is no longerextant. If, however, the gift was given as "*tzedakah*," then it has a permanence that puts it beyond the range of constant re-evaluation. Avram first saw God's changing his natural fate to be without children as a pure gift, and therefore one that would persist despite the subsequent behavior of his descendants.

God informed him that this was in fact an error, and that actually he did deserve this special treat-

> *If God gives "tzedakah," then the gift has a permanence that puts it beyond the range of constant re-evaluation.*

ment. This was told to him by way of a recounting of the past, "I am God, Who brought you out of Ur Kasdim." Avram's overwhelming self-sacrifice for God's honor in Ur Kasdim was sufficient to make him worthy of a miraculous suspension of the rules of nature.

Knowing this, Avram was now unsure whether the gift would always remain in the hands of his children. He asked, "With what [merit] I wish to know will I inherit it" (reading "*bamah eida*" as if it said "*eida bamah*")? In what way will my descendants be able to continue the same behavior that gained me this promise originally?

God answered Avram with instructions to do precisely the act which the Jews in later generations would be expected to do, the bringing of symbolic offerings. Avram's original readiness to give up his life for *Kiddush Hashem* created in him and in his descendants the characteristic of self-sacrifice; the animal offerings brought in the Temple are intended to provide an opportunity for a person to express this characteristic in a figurative way. A person is supposed to see the animal brought on the Altar as if it were himself, as if he were being slaughtered and burnt for God.

These symbolic offerings would create the opportunity for Avram's progeny to always connect to Avram's intense devotion to God, the devotion that made him deserving of acquiring the Land.

# Prediction of Exile

וַיֹּאמֶר לְאַבְרָם יָדֹעַ תֵּדַע כִּי־גֵר יִהְיֶה זַרְעֲךָ בְּאֶרֶץ לֹא לָהֶם
וַעֲבָדוּם וְעִנּוּ אֹתָם אַרְבַּע מֵאוֹת שָׁנָה

*And He said to Avram, "Know with certainty that your children will be strangers in a land which is not theirs — they will serve them, and they will afflict them — four hundred years."*
*(Bereishis 15:13)*

The "Covenant Between the Pieces" between God and Avram demonstrated the power of offerings, brought with proper intent, to keep the Jewish people on the level at which they would deserve to retain control over Eretz Yisrael. The climax of this covenant was God's announcement to Avram that, nonetheless, before his descendants would be able to enter the Land, they would first have to go through a purifying process of exile to bring them up to the necessary level. This would have three distinct stages, each one more difficult than the one before:

First, "Your children will be strangers in a land which is not theirs," without specific suffering, but subject to the whims of the local rulers. This stage would begin with Yitzchak Avinu himself, who had strife with the Philistine king and his people; something that never happened to Avraham. The experience of being strangers would take away something of their sense of freedom, prompting them to turn their minds toward awareness of God, since they would perceive the limits of their own power.

Next, "They will serve them." After the deaths of the sons of Yaakov, the Jews in Egypt began to work for Pharaoh, first willingly as part of a general work tax imposed by the government, and afterward through coercion. Slavery would weaken their tendency to pursue material possessions as an end, and make them more spiritual in that aspect of themselves.

*Slavery would weaken their tendency to pursue material possessions.*

The last stage would be, "They will afflict them," this time phrased in terms of what the Egyptians would do to them, since it would be imposed on them involuntarily. This suffering would help them to conquer the desire for physical pleasures, reaching the level of true sacrifice for God.

# A Preparation for Yitzchak

וְשָׂרַי אֵשֶׁת אַבְרָם לֹא יָלְדָה לוֹ וְלָהּ שִׁפְחָה מִצְרִית וּשְׁמָהּ הָגָר

*Sarai the wife of Avram had not borne him children; and she had an Egyptian maidservant whose name was Hagar.*
*(Bereishis 16:1)*

Many years were to pass from the time that Avram had been promised children until the birth of Yitzchak.

A child's nature is related to his father's state at the time the child is conceived; God wanted Avram to reach the pure spirituality of old age and to undergo the elevating transformation of *bris milah* prior to Yitzchak's conception.

In addition, our Sages tell us that a certain lower aspect was still present in Avram, an aspect that needed to "come out" in the form of a child before he could produce a totally pure son like Yitzchak. This side of Avram manifested itself in the form of his first son, Yishmael.

Immediately after the promise at the "Covenant Between the Pieces," the Torah tells us that "Sarai, the wife of Avram, had not borne him children." By beginning the sentence with Sarai's name and juxtaposing her name to the previous section, the Torah emphasizes that the fulfillment of the promise — via the birth of a son to "the wife of Avram" — was being delayed for the reasons mentioned above. The process of extracting the lower side of Avram was to be catalyzed by Sarai herself, through her "Egyptian maidservant, Hagar."

> *The process of extracting the lower side of Avram was to be catalyzed by Sarai herself.*

Hagar was fit for this purpose because of her lowly station as an Egyptian and as a maidservant, and by the fact that she still retained her non-Jewish name, Hagar, indicating that she had not accepted the mitzvos that Avram and his followers were keeping voluntarily.

# Completing Creation

וַיְהִי אַבְרָם בֶּן־תִּשְׁעִים שָׁנָה וְתֵשַׁע שָׁנִים וַיֵּרָא ה' אֶל־אַבְרָם וַיֹּאמֶר אֵלָיו אֲנִי־קֵל שַׁקַּי הִתְהַלֵּךְ לְפָנַי וֶהְיֵה תָמִים: וְאֶתְּנָה בְרִיתִי בֵּינִי וּבֵינֶךָ וְאַרְבֶּה אוֹתְךָ בִּמְאֹד מְאֹד

*When Avram was ninety-nine years old, God appeared to Avram and said to him, "I am Keil Shakkai, walk before Me and be complete. I will set My covenant between Me and you, and I will increase you most exceedingly."*
*(Bereishis 17:1-2)*

When God came to Avram to command him to perform *bris milah*, He introduced Himself using a new Name, "*Keil Shakkai.*"

Early commentators give two interpretations of the Name "*Shakkai.*" One relates it to the root "*shadah*" meaning to throw, indicating that God can "throw" the laws of nature in any direction He pleases. According to the other interpretation, this Name derives from the word "*dai,*" "enough," alluding to God's completion of the world and deciding that it was "enough."

According to each of these approaches, this Name is especially appropriate in the context of this mitzvah: *Bris milah* both goes against the natural state in which a man is born, and it also completes his body, a task that God left for man to accomplish.

This act of *bris milah* symbolizes the goal to which Avram and his descendants would be devoted, that of controlling the physical desires rather than simply following the "natural" path of pursuit of pleasure, and working to perfect the world that God gave to man in its raw state.

In this connection, it is clear why God said about this covenant, "I will set my covenant between Me and you," a two-sided agreement. The earlier covenant God made with Avram, the "Covenant Between the Pieces," was one sided. About it the Torah states: "God contracted a covenant with Avram," without naming Avram as an active party. The covenant of *bris milah*, on the other hand, was an agreement binding Avram and his progeny to contribute their input into the completion of God's world, and guaranteeing them the reward they merit for that behavior.

> *Bris milah was an agreement binding Avram and his progeny to contribute their input into the completion of God's world.*

God gave Avram the mission of "walking before Me" on a constant path of spiritual progress and improvement of the world. The first step on this path was to "be complete," to remove the negativity that had been made a part of his body and that was a blemish on his perfection.

# A New Level of Prophecy

וַיִּפֹּל אַבְרָם עַל־פָּנָיו וַיְדַבֵּר אִתּוֹ אֱלֹקִים לֵאמֹר: אֲנִי הִנֵּה בְרִיתִי
אִתָּךְ וְהָיִיתָ לְאַב הֲמוֹן גּוֹיִם: וְלֹא־יִקָּרֵא עוֹד אֶת־שִׁמְךָ אַבְרָם
וְהָיָה שִׁמְךָ אַבְרָהָם כִּי אַב־הֲמוֹן גּוֹיִם נְתַתִּיךָ

*Avram fell on his face, and God [Elokim] spoke
with him, saying: "As for Me, this is My covenant
with you: You shall be as father to a multitude
of nations. Your name shall no longer be called
'Avram.' Your name shall be 'Avraham,' for I have
made you the father of a multitude of nations."
(Bereishis 17:3-5)*

The covenant of *bris milah* between God and Avraham Avinu was much more than the giving of one specific mitzvah; it was a total transformation and change of Avraham as an individual and the initiation of an entirely new way of serving God.

The most explicit sign of this was the change of his name from Avram to Avraham, the added letter "*hei*" coming from the word "*hamon*," meaning a multitude. This signified that from now on Avraham's influence would extend to all nations despite his new obligation to separate and to elevate himself above the other peoples. Even though *bris milah* would make him physically different from others, it would provide him with the power to teach and guide all mankind in the way of God.

Symbolically, the sign of the covenant in the organ of reproduction, which concentrates all of a man's essence to produce a child in his own image, indicates an involvement of the entire person in his relationship with God; the control of the desire that is a central part of that process of reproduction is a key to control of the entire body and to the ability to rule benevolently over others. Avraham was now beginning the mission of the Jewish people to lead humanity toward the fulfillment of its purpose, and this necessitated a huge shift from his emphasis on himself as an individual to a focus on the multitude. This was what was being conveyed in the covenant of *bris milah*.

On hearing the revelation of this commandment, "Avram fell on his face." He was unable to stand upright in a manner that expressed his strength as an isolated person as long as he had not actualized the directive being given him. Then, "God spoke with him"; for the first time, the name "*Elokim*" is used for God in a prophecy to Avram, and has great significance in this context.

The four-letter Name is God's "proper Name" so to speak, but "*Elokim*" indicates God's relationship to the world. For this reason, it is the only Holy Name that can appear in the possessive form, "*Elokei*." God is "*Elokei haOlam*," the God of the universe, in the sense that He reveals Himself through the wisdom and power evident in His creations.

From this point, God would be called the God of specific individuals, "*Elokei Avraham*," "*Elokei Yisrael*," etc. This is a much deeper and more personal revelation of God as He deals with those close to Him, guiding their lives in hidden ways to make Himself intimately known to mankind. "God spoke *with* him" rather than "to" him, to emphasize this new relationship. From now on, intimacy and cooperation between man and God would be the hallmark of the new way of relating to the Divine, as inaugurated by this unique covenant.

> *This is a much deeper and more personal revelation of God as He deals with those close to Him, guiding their lives in hidden ways.*

# The Reward of the Covenant

וְהִפְרֵתִי אֹתְךָ בִּמְאֹד מְאֹד וּנְתַתִּיךָ לְגוֹיִם וּמְלָכִים מִמְּךָ
יֵצֵאוּ: וַהֲקִמֹתִי אֶת־בְּרִיתִי בֵּינִי וּבֵינֶךָ וּבֵין זַרְעֲךָ אַחֲרֶיךָ לְדֹרֹתָם
לִבְרִית עוֹלָם לִהְיוֹת לְךָ לֵאלֹקִים וּלְזַרְעֲךָ אַחֲרֶיךָ: וְנָתַתִּי לְךָ
וּלְזַרְעֲךָ אַחֲרֶיךָ אֵת אֶרֶץ מְגֻרֶיךָ אֵת כָּל־אֶרֶץ כְּנַעַן לַאֲחֻזַּת עוֹלָם
וְהָיִיתִי לָהֶם לֵאלֹקִים

*"I will make you very, very fruitful; I will make you
into nations, and kings will issue from you. I will
establish My covenant between Me and you and
between your descendants after you, throughout
their generations, as a bris olam, an eternal covenant, to be a God to you and to your descendants
after you. And I will give you and your descendants
after you the land of your sojourning — the whole
land of Canaan — as an eternal inheritance; and I
will be their God."*
*(Bereishis 17:6-8)*

The new approach to serving God that was initiated with
Avraham's *bris milah* was to be in its very essence a fruitful
one, expressed in tangible results and achievements. This
is symbolized in the sign of the *bris* on the procreative organ.
But to insure that Avraham would not take this symbolism in the
opposite, superficial sense, as an injury to the reproductive powers, God promised him that as a result of the *bris*, "I will make you
very, very fruitful." The repetition of "very" indicates a blessing
beyond the natural.

Not only would this increase occur in the number of individuals, but "I will make you into nations," God added. The twelve
tribes of Israel would be equivalent to twelve separate nations in
their size, and also by virtue of their different characteristics, as
expressed through their leaders, the "kings" who will "issue from
you."

This fruitful aspect of the covenant leads directly to the fact that it will endure forever. The phrase "*bris olam*" indicates that this covenant is both eternal and eternally entwined with the fate of the world. The world continues to exist as a result of the covenant between God and

*The phrase "bris olam" indicates that this covenant is both eternal and eternally entwined with the fate of the world.*

Avraham's descendants symbolized by *bris milah*; the laws of nature only remain in force in order to facilitate God's being the God of Avraham, as He promised, "To be a God to you." God's presence would now rest on Avraham and on "his seed after him," from the time of the forefathers until the giving of the Torah, in Avraham's merit.

The next stage would be that God would "give the whole land of Canaan as an eternal inheritance" to Avraham's children, the word used for "inheritance" being "*achuzah*" (from "*ochez*," "hold"), which denotes actual possession and control over the land. From the time that the Jews would enter the land after going out of Egypt and receiving the Torah, God would be "their God" *in their own merit*, in addition to the merit of the forefathers.

# Bris Milah: Symbol and Reality

זֹאת בְּרִיתִי אֲשֶׁר תִּשְׁמְרוּ בֵּינִי וּבֵינֵיכֶם וּבֵין זַרְעֲךָ אַחֲרֶיךָ הִמּוֹל
לָכֶם כָּל־זָכָר: וּנְמַלְתֶּם אֵת בְּשַׂר עָרְלַתְכֶם וְהָיָה לְאוֹת בְּרִית בֵּינִי
וּבֵינֵיכֶם

*"This is My covenant which you shall observe,*
*between Me and you and your descendants after*
*you; you shall circumcise all males. You shall cir-*
*cumcise the flesh of your foreskin, and this will be a*
*sign of the covenant between Me and you."*
*(Bereishis 17:10)*

After God described to Avraham the promises He was making in the covenant of *bris milah*, He told him Avraham's side of the pact: the act of circumcision itself. The role of this act in the covenant was to be a double one, making this covenant different from that of Noach in a significant sense.

When God declared the rainbow to be a symbol of His promise not to repeat the Flood, the content of the covenant was separate from the sign that represented it. With *bris milah*, however, the physical sign is also the essential content of the human part

> **With bris milah, the physical sign is also the essential content of the covenant.**

of the covenant. God says, "This is my covenant," not "the sign of my covenant." Removing the *orlah* itself has an effect on the thoughts, emotions, and actions of the person, and makes him more spiritual and less likely to be swayed by material desires. Here it says, "You shall circumcise all males," meaning the entire male person is "circumcised" in his heart and mind as well as his externality.

God continues to tell Avraham the details of how this is to be done: "You shall circumcise the flesh," actually physically creating the "sign of the covenant between Me and you." This sign has practical value as a reminder to the Jew of his special connection to God, and of uniting Jews and setting them apart from the rest of the world for their particular mission. This mitzvah that changes the nature of a Jew also records and expresses that change in a perceptible, permanent fashion.

# Sarah's Son

וַיֹּאמֶר אֱלֹקִים אֶל־אַבְרָהָם שָׂרַי אִשְׁתְּךָ לֹא־תִקְרָא אֶת־שְׁמָהּ שָׂרָי כִּי שָׂרָה שְׁמָהּ: וּבֵרַכְתִּי אֹתָהּ וְגַם נָתַתִּי מִמֶּנָּה לְךָ בֵּן וּבֵרַכְתִּיהָ וְהָיְתָה לְגוֹיִם מַלְכֵי עַמִּים מִמֶּנָּה יִהְיוּ: וַיִּפֹּל אַבְרָהָם עַל־פָּנָיו וַיִּצְחָק וַיֹּאמֶר בְּלִבּוֹ הַלְּבֶן מֵאָה־שָׁנָה יִוָּלֵד וְאִם־שָׂרָה הֲבַת־תִּשְׁעִים שָׁנָה תֵּלֵד: וַיֹּאמֶר אַבְרָהָם אֶל־הָאֱלֹקִים לוּ יִשְׁמָעֵאל יִחְיֶה לְפָנֶיךָ

*And God said to Avraham, "As for Sarai, your wife — do not call her name Sarai, for Sarah is her name. I will bless her, indeed I will give you a son through her. I will bless her, and she will produce peoples [goyim]; kings of nations [amim] will issue from her."*

*And Avraham fell upon his face and laughed, and he said to himself, "Will a hundred-year-old man have a child? And will Sarah, who is ninety years old, give birth?"*

*And Avraham said to God, "May Yishmael live before You!"*

*(Bereishis 17:15-18)*

From the onset of Avraham Avinu's journey toward greatness and the founding of the Jewish people, he was accompanied by his wife, Sarai, who was an indispensable partner in his quest.

Our Sages tell us that originally her name was Yiskah,[4] but

---

4.*Megillah* 14a.

Avraham gave her the "nickname" Sarai, from the word "*sar*," meaning a leader or noble person. As long as Avraham was a lone individual in his unique path of serving God, the name Sarai remained a private matter between the two of them, and it could be understood as meaning "*my* noblewoman."

Once God commanded Avraham about *bris milah* and made a covenant with him concerning the nation that was to issue from him, Sarai's status also changed. The name of nobility was no longer a personal matter between husband and wife, but rather the expression of her public and essential character. At this juncture, God decreed that she would be called Sarah, "*a noble-woman*," whose nobility would be seen by all.

Thereupon, God revealed the details of the beginning of *Am Yisrael* with the imminent birth of Avraham's son. Avraham had already been promised that he would have descendants, but now God told him, "I will bless her," including Sarah in the earlier blessing to Avraham, "indeed I will give you a son through her," who will be the fulfillment of the promise. From that son will come "*goyim*," large groups of people, and kings of "*amim*," organized nations. These refer to the Tribes of Israel, all of whom would issue from Sarah in fulfillment of her being blessed.

In reaction to this, "Avraham fell upon his face," prostrating himself in a show of gratitude to Hashem, and he laughed with joyous amazement combined with puzzlement. A threefold miracle would be necessary to bring about the realization of God's word in this case. First, "Can a man of a hundred years have a child?" even with a young woman. Second, "Can Sarah, who was barren, have a child at all?" Finally, Sarah herself was no longer young at all, and "Can a woman of ninety years give birth?"

> **A threefold miracle would be necessary to bring about the realization of God's promise.**

Avraham was very familiar with God's ways of dealing with the world, and one of His central rules is that He does not produce a miracle when there is no necessity to do so. Avraham reasoned, therefore, that his older son, Yishmael, whom he had considered until now to be his heir apparent, was somehow destined to be unfit for that role or to die young. Therefore he prayed, "May Yishmael live before You!" — may he live physically, and may he behave in a manner acceptable "before You" as a son of Avraham.

God replied that Avraham was not aware of the outstanding difference between Yishmael and the sort of son who could issue from Sarah. Sara was not only Avraham's wife and partner in his revolutionary spiritual approach to life, she was from the blessed family of Shem as well, and from its foremost descendants. This would justify the outright suspension of natural laws to bring about this miracle. The very name of this son, Yitzchak, would commemorate the laughter and astonishment that everyone would show at his miraculous birth.

Yitzchak alone would be the continuation of God's covenant with Avraham; although God heard Avraham's prayers for Yishmael and blessed Yishmael with great numbers, only Yitzchak, son of Sarah, would be fit to carry on with Avraham's mission in the world.

# An Urgent Mitzvah

וַיְכַל לְדַבֵּר אִתּוֹ וַיַּעַל אֱלֹקִים מֵעַל אַבְרָהָם: וַיִּקַּח אַבְרָהָם אֶת־
יִשְׁמָעֵאל בְּנוֹ וְאֵת כָּל־יְלִידֵי בֵיתוֹ וְאֵת כָּל־מִקְנַת כַּסְפּוֹ כָּל־זָכָר
בְּאַנְשֵׁי בֵּית אַבְרָהָם וַיָּמָל אֶת־בְּשַׂר עָרְלָתָם בְּעֶצֶם הַיּוֹם הַזֶּה
כַּאֲשֶׁר דִּבֶּר אִתּוֹ אֱלֹקִים

*When He finished speaking with him, God ascended
from upon Avraham. And Avraham took his son
Yishmael, all the servants born in his household,
and all those he had purchased — every male of
Avraham's household — and he circumcised the
flesh of their foreskin that very day, as God had spoken to him.*
*(Bereishis 17:22-23)*

The phenomenon of prophecy has not been with us for thousands of years; yet, we have traditions as to its nature. One
of these is that it is not limited to actual words heard by the
prophet, but includes also a general heightened state of awareness of God that precedes those words and persists for some time
afterward.[5] In the case of the prophecy whereby God commanded
Avraham about the mitzvah of *bris milah*, though, an exception
was made, and the Divine Presence was removed immediately:
"God ascended from upon Avraham."

The reason for this was that there was to be no delay between
the actual performance of the mitzvah and the commandment to
do so. Even the great level of
spirituality involved in Avraham's
prophecy was not as important
as the immediate completion of
the physical act of the mitzvah,
and this set a basic precedent for the *primacy of action* in the
Torah's outlook.

> **This set a basic precedent
> for the primacy of action
> in the Torah's outlook.**

---

5. *Derashos HaRan.*

Once Avraham saw the urgency of doing the mitzvah, he understood that no compromises of any sort were to be made, even if they seemed absolutely necessary. He went and "circumcised that very day every male in Avraham's household," even though the infirmity that they would all suffer following this operation would leave them open to attack by marauders. Avraham was able to grasp the message not only in the prophecy itself, but even in its sudden removal that indicated a higher priority. From this, Avraham knew that God would protect him in the merit of the swift and complete performance of the mitzvah.

# פרשת וירא
# PARASHAS VAYEIRA

---

# A New Level

וַיֵּרָא אֵלָיו ה׳ בְּאֵלֹנֵי מַמְרֵא וְהוּא יֹשֵׁב פֶּתַח־הָאֹהֶל כְּחֹם
הַיּוֹם: וַיִּשָּׂא עֵינָיו וַיַּרְא וְהִנֵּה שְׁלֹשָׁה אֲנָשִׁים נִצָּבִים עָלָיו

*God appeared to him [vayeira eilav Hashem] in
Eilonei Mamrei while he was sitting at the entrance
of the tent in the heat of the day. He lifted his eyes
and he saw: And behold! three men were standing
over him ....*

*(Bereishis 18:1-2)*

The first prophecy that Avraham Avinu received after his *bris
milah* was a combination of the direct word of God and
a vision of angels, all for the purpose of bringing him the
good news of the imminent birth of Yitzchak. In addition to the

actual message of this revelation, God demonstrated to Avraham the higher perception of prophecy that he now merited as a result of the *bris.* This exhibited itself in six different ways:

- This prophecy came to Avraham as a result of his own preparation, rather than as a special gift from God. This is indicated in the use of the phrase *"Vaiyeira eilav Hashem."* Literally, this means "Appeared to him God," with the words "to him" placed before "God," indicating that Avraham *himself* merited this appearance of God.

- The prophecy came in Eilonei Mamrei, a place far from any particularly holy spot, such as the altars that Avraham had previously erected.

- "He was sitting," in a relaxed manner, rather than having to fall down and receive the prophecy in a very passive position.

- Avraham was "at the entrance of the tent," among numerous other individuals who would normally disturb his meditative concentration; nonetheless, he was able to reach the level of prophecy.

- It was "the heat of the day," an added source of potential distraction.

- Avraham first had a full experience of the Divine Presence, "God appeared to him," and then, "He lifted his eyes and he saw three men," the angels. In other instances, prophets were shown angels first, as an introduction and preparation for the actual prophecy.

*In other instances, prophets were shown angels first, as an introduction and preparation for the actual prophecy.*

All of these signified to Avraham how deeply God loved him and how the fulfillment of his mitzvah of *bris milah* opened new horizons of spiritual awareness.

# Special Guests

וַיֹּאמַר אֲדֹנָי אִם־נָא מָצָאתִי חֵן בְּעֵינֶיךָ אַל־נָא תַעֲבֹר מֵעַל עַבְדֶּךָ

**And he said, "My masters [adonai], if I find favor in**
**your eyes, please do not pass by your servant."**
**(Bereishis 18:3)**

Avraham's overriding characteristic trait was that of kindness, providing for both the physical and spiritual welfare of everyone he met, feeding his guests and teaching
them to offer their thanks not to him but to God. When three
angels, therefore, appeared to Avraham in the form of wayfarers,
his instinct to invite them in for a meal was almost irresistible.

Avraham's goal throughout his life was to do kindness for
people, thereby emulating God's kindness and drawing people's
attention to the constant benefits they received from God. After
so many years of this behavior, he had incorporated it completely
in his nature to the extent that even when he noticed people
rushing on a journey who did not seem especially needy, he
was overcome with the desire to give to them and to make their
lives more pleasant. He "ran to them and bowed down on the
ground," and addressed them as "my masters" even though, to
all appearances, they were ordinary people.

Our Sages[1] reveal to us an even greater aspect to Avraham's
display of respect for his guests and his intense devotion to serving God in all his actions:

The word "*Adonai*," meaning "my masters," with which
Avraham addressed the visitors, is treated in the *halachos*[2] of the
*Sefer Torah* as a Name of God. There are two ways of understanding this, both of which are expressions of the same concept
that Avraham incorporated into all his dealings:

First, he spoke to God, asking permission, so to speak, to

---

1. *Shavuos 35b b'shem R'Elazar HaModai.*

2. *Rambam, Yesodei HaTorah 6:9.*

interrupt the prophetic vision he was experiencing in order to welcome the guests.

At a different level, though, Avraham actually was speaking to the *guests* as "my masters," relating to his efforts of kindness for them as the most direct way of being in contact with God; therefore, he addressed them with a Divine Name.

We find the same concept with regard to Nechemiah's speech to the king of Persia. When Nechemiah said, "if it please the king,"[3] although he was talking to the human king, his intention was to pray to the King of the universe. He had a constant awareness that every request he made of a person was actually a prayer to God, Who is the only One Who can grant requests. Yet, at the same time, he was able to show respect for the Persian king.

> *Avraham had a constant awareness that every request he made of a person was actually a prayer to God.*

Similarly, Avraham was expressing his respect for God and his desire to do "kindness" for Him, so to speak, by spreading knowledge of God to people. Avraham did this in a way that came across, and genuinely so, as a show of respect to human beings, who are created in God's image.

Avraham literally begged the travelers to be his guests; he treated them with such honor that it seemed as though they were doing him a favor. He had fresh bread baked for them and cattle slaughtered especially for their benefit. The Torah relates to us that as a result of Avraham's intense devotion to this mitzvah, it was as if he gave life to the angels. Angels do not need physical food, yet the Torah states, "they ate."

This is understandable in light of the fact that the Hebrew root "*ochel*" means not only eating in the simple sense, but also any act which gives something continued existence, such as a fire that "eats" wood and thereby continues to burn. Here, the

---

3. *Nechemiah* 2:4. The previous verse implied that this was a prayer to God.

angels, who had come to do the kindness of announcing Sara's pregnancy and of saving Lot (and even of destroying Sodom, which epitomized the opposite of kindness), received their spiritual sustenance from Avraham's pure intentions in doing physical kindness.

# Sodom and Avraham

וה׳ אָמָר הַמְכַסֶּה אֲנִי מֵאַבְרָהָם אֲשֶׁר אֲנִי עֹשֶׂה: וְאַבְרָהָם הָיוֹ
יִהְיֶה לְגוֹי גָּדוֹל וְעָצוּם וְנִבְרְכוּ־בוֹ כֹּל גּוֹיֵי הָאָרֶץ: כִּי יְדַעְתִּיו
לְמַעַן אֲשֶׁר יְצַוֶּה אֶת־בָּנָיו וְאֶת־בֵּיתוֹ אַחֲרָיו וְשָׁמְרוּ דֶּרֶךְ ה׳
לַעֲשׂוֹת צְדָקָה וּמִשְׁפָּט לְמַעַן הָבִיא ה׳ עַל־אַבְרָהָם אֵת
אֲשֶׁר־דִּבֶּר עָלָיו

*God said, "Shall I conceal from Avraham what I am about to do? Avraham will certainly become a great and mighty nation, and all the nations of the earth will be blessed because of him, since I have known him; and, he will command his children and family after him to keep the way of God, to do charity and justice; [and] in order that Hashem bring upon Avraham that which He spoke to him."*
*(Bereishis 18:17-19)*

When God sent the angels to destroy Sodom, He did so only in the context of His focus on Avraham:

On the one hand, the level of Avraham's kindness to guests contrasted intensely with the cruelty and selfishness of Sodom, and thereby made the Divine judgment on Sodom that much more strict. The angels "looked out upon Sodom" just after leaving Avraham's tent, and

*Avraham's kindness to guests contrasted intensely with the cruelty and selfishness of Sodom, and thereby made the Divine judgment on Sodom that much more strict.*

saw how their behavior was the diametric opposite of Avraham's.

On the other hand, God had several reasons to inform Avraham of the impending destruction and to provide him with the opportunity to pray for the people of Sodom and its neighbors. These reasons God revealed to the angels: "God said, 'Shall I conceal from Avraham what I am about to do?'"

The first reason to tell Avraham about the punishment of Sodom was that "the nations of the earth shall be blessed because of him, since I have known him." God "knew" Avraham in the sense of paying special attention to him and applying close Divine Providence to him. This attention extended to the entire world in Avraham's merit. As a result of the existence of this righteous man, God dealt with everyone around him in a manner that transcended nature, relating to them according to their actions rather than simply according to physical law.

Thus, Sodom was only being punished for its actions because Avraham had created the spiritual environment where God operated in terms of reward and punishment. It was only fitting, then, that Avraham be informed of what was about to happen and be permitted to pray for the people who should be blessed for his sake.

Secondly, no matter what would actually happen, Avraham was a person who was capable of utilizing the event as a lesson for himself and for his descendants. "He will command his children and family after him to keep the way of God." The punishment of Sodom, if it had to take place, would serve well as an example of how evil behavior was recompensed, and of how, in the big picture, this seeming destruction was actually a benefit for the world.

Finally, God was showing His concern for the promise He had made to Avraham to give him the entire land of Canaan. The scope of this promise would be reduced through the annihilation of the Sodom region and its relegation to a salty sea. God therefore told Avraham about His plan "in order (to make it possible) that Hashem bring upon Avraham that which He spoke to him."

Through Avraham's prayers, God might spare the cities and leave that area untouched, available for Avraham's future children.

# The Nature of Divine Judgment

וַיֹּאמֶר ה' זַעֲקַת סְדֹם וַעֲמֹרָה כִּי־רָבָּה וְחַטָּאתָם כִּי כָבְדָה
מְאֹד: אֵרְדָה־נָּא וְאֶרְאֶה הַכְּצַעֲקָתָהּ הַבָּאָה אֵלַי עָשׂוּ
כָּלָה וְאִם־לֹא אֵדָעָה:

*God said, "Because the outcry of Sodom and Gomorroh has become great, and although their sin is extremely weighty, I will go down to see; if what they did is equal to the cry I heard, I will bring destruction! And if not, I will know."*
*(Bereishis 18:20-22)*

Certainly God was aware of the magnitude of the sins of Sodom. In the area of interpersonal behavior, God said that "the outcry" of the oppressed people in Sodom "has become great" in number, even if each individual sin seems minor; in the area of their relationship to God, their sins were "weighty" and serious.

Nevertheless, God's mercy required a "closer investigation." He said to the angels sent to destroy the cities, "I will go down to see," i.e., I will look at *all* aspects of the situation and of the people involved, rather than seeing simply the acts that were performed as a human judge is wont to do.

*The human court can only see the crime, but it can never come to a complete understanding of the person who committed the crime.*

In *Koheles* it states, "I saw that under the sun, in the place of justice there is [seen] the crime."[4] The human court can only see the crime, but it

4. *Koheles* 3:16.

can never come to a complete understanding of the person who committed the crime, and therefore all instances of the same transgression need to be punished more or less in the same way. God, on the other hand, takes all factors into account, relating to the person and the situation as a whole, as *Koheles* continues, "the righteous and the wicked will be judged by God." God looks at the big picture: the act itself, its context, and its consequences.

In the case of Sodom, their extreme inhospitality and cruelty to outsiders and to the poor, if evaluated from the point of view of the damage done to the victims, would seem to demand strict punishment. However, God considered their actions in their overall context and with attention to the nature of the perpetrators. If there would have been an inordinate number of poor who demanded help and who as a result would have depleted all the resources of Sodom, or if the personality of the rich would have been naturally miserly, or if the times would have been ones of war or disaster, the retribution coming to the people of Sodom would have been lessened.

In fact, though, the people of Sodom were lavish spenders on themselves; they lived in times of peace and tranquility; visits from strangers were rare, and there were few needy people. Rather, they did their sins from a sense of arrogance and rebelliousness against God.

God told the angels: "If what they did is equal to the cry I heard," I will punish them with the most extreme strictness, but otherwise, "I will know," I will take all mitigating circumstances into account.

In fact, there were no reasons to lighten their sentence, and the angels were told to carry out a complete destruction.

# In Defense of Sodom

וְאַבְרָהָם עוֹדֶנּוּ עֹמֵד לִפְנֵי ה': וַיִּגַּשׁ אַבְרָהָם וַיֹּאמַר הַאַף תִּסְפֶּה
צַדִּיק עִם־רָשָׁע: אוּלַי יֵשׁ חֲמִשִּׁים צַדִּיקִם בְּתוֹךְ הָעִיר הַאַף תִּסְפֶּה
וְלֹא־תִשָּׂא לַמָּקוֹם לְמַעַן חֲמִשִּׁים הַצַּדִּיקִם אֲשֶׁר בְּקִרְבָּהּ: חָלִלָה
לְּךָ מֵעֲשֹׂת כַּדָּבָר הַזֶּה לְהָמִית צַדִּיק עִם־רָשָׁע וְהָיָה כַצַּדִּיק כָּרָשָׁע
חָלִלָה לָּךְ הֲשֹׁפֵט כָּל־הָאָרֶץ לֹא יַעֲשֶׂה מִשְׁפָּט:
וַיֹּאמֶר ה' אִם־אֶמְצָא בִסְדֹם חֲמִשִּׁים צַדִּיקִם בְּתוֹךְ הָעִיר וְנָשָׂאתִי
לְכָל־הַמָּקוֹם בַּעֲבוּרָם: וַיַּעַן אַבְרָהָם וַיֹּאמַר הִנֵּה־נָא הוֹאַלְתִּי
לְדַבֵּר אֶל־אֲדֹ־נָי וְאָנֹכִי עָפָר וָאֵפֶר: אוּלַי יַחְסְרוּן חֲמִשִּׁים
הַצַּדִּיקִם חֲמִשָּׁה הֲתַשְׁחִית בַּחֲמִשָּׁה אֶת־כָּל־הָעִיר וַיֹּאמֶר לֹא
אַשְׁחִית אִם־אֶמְצָא שָׁם אַרְבָּעִים וַחֲמִשָּׁה:
וַיֹּסֶף עוֹד לְדַבֵּר אֵלָיו וַיֹּאמַר אוּלַי יִמָּצְאוּן שָׁם אַרְבָּעִים וַיֹּאמֶר
לֹא אֶעֱשֶׂה בַּעֲבוּר הָאַרְבָּעִים:
וַיֹּאמֶר אַל־נָא יִחַר לַאדֹנָי וַאֲדַבֵּרָה אוּלַי יִמָּצְאוּן שָׁם שְׁלֹשִׁים
וַיֹּאמֶר לֹא אֶעֱשֶׂה אִם־אֶמְצָא שָׁם שְׁלֹשִׁים:
וַיֹּאמֶר הִנֵּה־נָא הוֹאַלְתִּי לְדַבֵּר אֶל־אֲדֹ־נָי אוּלַי יִמָּצְאוּן שָׁם
עֶשְׂרִים וַיֹּאמֶר לֹא אַשְׁחִית בַּעֲבוּר הָעֶשְׂרִים:
וַיֹּאמֶר אַל־נָא יִחַר לַאדֹ־נָי וַאֲדַבְּרָה אַךְ־הַפַּעַם אוּלַי יִמָּצְאוּן שָׁם
עֲשָׂרָה וַיֹּאמֶר לֹא אַשְׁחִית בַּעֲבוּר הָעֲשָׂרָה:

*... And Avraham still stood before God. Avraham
approached and said, "Will You even wipe out the
righteous along with the wicked? What if there
should be fifty righteous people within the city? Will
You wipe out and not forgive the place for the sake
of the fifty righteous ones within it? It would be
sacrilege for You to do such a thing, to kill the righteous with the wicked — even if the righteous are
like the wicked — a profane thing for You; will the
Judge of the whole world not do justice?"
And God said, "If I find in Sodom fifty righteous
people within the city, I will forgive the entire place
for them." Avraham responded and said, "Behold,*

*now, I began to speak to God; although I am but
dust and ash. What if the fifty righteous shall lack
five? Would you destroy the whole city because of
five?" And He said, "I will not destroy if I find there
forty-five."*

*He added to speak to Him and said, "What if forty
would be found there?" And He said, "I will not do
it for the sake of the forty."*

*And he said, "Let not God be angry that I speak:
What if thirty would be found there?" And He said,
"I will not act if I find there thirty."*

*And he said, "Here, I have begun to speak to God:
What if twenty would be found there?" And He said,
"I will not destroy for the sake of the twenty."*

*And he said, "Let not God be angry, and I will speak
but this once: What if ten would be found there?"
And He said, "I will not destroy for the sake of the
ten."*

*(Bereishis 18:22-32)*

God informed Avraham of the catastrophe that was about
to befall Sodom and its sister cities in order to give
Avraham the opportunity to pray for them, to exercise
his trait of kindness even toward those who epitomized cruelty.
For us, this is a priceless lesson in the true meaning and technique
of prayer:

When Avraham prayed, he did not merely ask for what he
wanted, he gave clear reasoning why it would be in God's "interest" to grant the request and why it made sense to do so. The
Torah gives us a unique glimpse of Avraham's precisely thought-
out yet intensely emotional dialogue with God in his plea for
mercy for Sodom.

Upon hearing the directive that God gave to the angels to
destroy Sodom, Avraham perceived a Divine allusion that there
was room for negotiation when he realized that, despite the

angels' departure, God's Presence was still with him. "And Avraham still stood before God." God had not "gone with" the angels, so to speak, but had "remained," waiting for Avraham's response.

Avraham understood this as a signal that the angels had been granted the power to destroy indiscriminately, the righteous together with the wicked, since when God means to select only the guilty for punishment, He does so by revealing Himself and His clear Providence, as He would at the time of the Exodus from Egypt. It was on this release of unmitigated destructive power that Avraham focused his protest.

This concept that God sometimes gives free rein to an angel of destruction[5] has its limits,[6] as our Sages explain. A "perfect *tzaddik*" who has no faults at all to speak of cannot be harmed even when the "destroyer" is given power by God. These individuals would have had no need for Avraham's prayers even though they were in Sodom, and they would have survived. Avraham, though, begged God to recognize the merit of those who were relatively righteous compared to their neighbors in the evil cities, the "righteous people within the city."

His first request of God was to judge these people by a subjective rather than a strictly objective standard, and to give them credit for at least rising above the low level of their surroundings. He asked, "Will You wipe out and not forgive the place for the sake of the fifty righteous ones within it?" Avraham said, "It cannot be that You would do such a thing, to kill the righteous with the wicked," that is, the righteous who lived with the wicked and were influenced by them. Rather, they should be judged relative to the wicked people who constituted their entire frame of reference. "It cannot be that the Judge of the whole world," Who sees things in their universal context, would look at these individuals in such a narrow fashion as to ignore the environment that shaped them. Even if "the righteous are like the wicked" to

---

5. *Bava Kamma* 60a.

6. *Ramban, Bereishis* 6:9; *Mishlei* 12:21 according to *Berachos* 7a.

a great extent, justice should require a differentiation between them in proportion to whatever the righteous person succeeded in achieving.

God accepted this logic and told Avraham, "If I find in Sodom fifty righteous people," even though they are "in Sodom" and a part of its culture, "I will forgive the entire place for them," completely canceling the decree in order to prevent these people being harmed by the general destruction.

With this granted, Avraham added a mild modification of his request. He had mentioned fifty people originally because that would mean ten for each city, ten being a minimum number for a "congregation"[7] and therefore enough to be considered a significant entity within the city. Now he asked, perhaps this standard could be slightly relaxed:

"I began to speak," said Avraham, admitting that — as the initiator of the discussion — perhaps his first estimate as to the required number of righteous people was too high; after all, he said, "I am but dust and ash," and in no way capable of fathoming the rules of Divine justice. "Perhaps the fifty shall lack five," who will not be quite on the same level as the other forty-five, although still superior to their evil neighbors. "Would you destroy the whole city because of five," a seemingly small difference? God agreed to this as well and said, "I will not destroy," in that case.

> **As the initiator of the discussion, perhaps Avraham's first estimate as to the required number of righteous people was too high.**

Avraham took this reasoning a step farther: "He added," and said that if forty-five would be sufficient, it should follow that forty should also be enough, since the five additional people did not constitute a full "congregation," and could be disregarded. In this case, the forty righteous would be divided into four congregations and would have enough merit to save four cities, the fifth being spared according to the rule of "following the majority."

---

7. *Megillah* 23b.

God accepted this, saying, "I will not do it," that is, I will not do anything to any of the cities.

Avraham immediately took the obvious logical step of extending the majority rule to the case of only thirty righteous people, first asking God's pardon for seeming to bargain: "Let not God be angry that I speak ...." God granted this as well.

Now, Avraham began a new claim, one that seemed to contradict his previous one:

Even if this number of people would not be found, and the rule of following the majority, upon which Avraham had based his previous claims, would apply[8] — making it impossible to prevent the entire catastrophe — perhaps there would be room to spare individual cities that did have the requisite number of righteous people. "Here, I have begun to speak," said Avraham, introducing this new approach that would disregard his own concept of going according to the majority.

Avraham understood that God's mercy could be relevant even in these two contradictory cases, since each one indicated in its own way that some group of people deserved to be saved, whether it was the entire population of all five cities or whether that of the specific city where the ten righteous were found. Thus, Avraham asked God if perhaps there was room to spare individual cities that did have the requisite number of righteous people.

God answered this time by saying, "I will not destroy" (and not, "I will not do it," as above). This meant that God would not destroy that particular city, although He would punish the others, making it inaccurate to say, "I will not do it."

Finally, Avraham took this idea to its next logical step and said, "Let not God be angry," that I am pursuing this matter further, but should it not follow that even ten people be enough to save

---

8. Explanation: Twenty people would be enough to justify saving only two of the five cities. Because the doomed cities would be the majority, the rule of following the majority would now apply in the reverse, condemning all five cities.

one city? God again answered, "I will not destroy."

With this, Avraham's requests came to an end. He had asked for whatever he could, based on his deep understanding of the ways of God's mercy; and God had granted his requests, not only as a result of the emotional fervor with which they were made, but also and perhaps primarily because of the compelling reasoning that Avraham presented.

# A Clearly Thought-Out Sin

וַיָּבֹאוּ שְׁנֵי הַמַּלְאָכִים סְדֹמָה בָּעֶרֶב וְלוֹט יֹשֵׁב בְּשַׁעַר־סְדֹם
וַיַּרְא־לוֹט וַיָּקָם לִקְרָאתָם וַיִּשְׁתַּחוּ אַפַּיִם אָרְצָה: וַיֹּאמֶר הִנֶּה נָּא־
אֲדֹנַי סוּרוּ נָא אֶל־בֵּית עַבְדְּכֶם וְלִינוּ וְרַחֲצוּ רַגְלֵיכֶם וְהִשְׁכַּמְתֶּם
וַהֲלַכְתֶּם לְדַרְכְּכֶם וַיֹּאמְרוּ לֹא כִּי בָרְחוֹב נָלִין:
וַיִּפְצַר־בָּם מְאֹד וַיָּסֻרוּ אֵלָיו וַיָּבֹאוּ אֶל־בֵּיתוֹ וַיַּעַשׂ לָהֶם מִשְׁתֶּה
... טֶרֶם יִשְׁכָּבוּ וְאַנְשֵׁי הָעִיר אַנְשֵׁי סְדֹם נָסַבּוּ עַל־הַבַּיִת מִנַּעַר
וְעַד־זָקֵן כָּל־הָעָם מִקָּצֶה

*And the two angels came to Sodom in the evening; and Lot was sitting at the gate of Sodom. Lot saw and stood up to go toward them, and he bowed, face to the ground. And he said, "Behold, now, my lords, come aside please to the house of your servant, stay overnight, wash your feet, and rise early and go on your way." And they said, "No, rather we will sleep in the street."*

*But he pressured them greatly, so they turned toward him and came to his house, and he made a feast for them .... They had not yet lain down when the townspeople, Sodomites, surrounded the house, from young to old, all the people from the city limits.*

**(Bereishis 19:1-4)**

**P**eople are not robots or machines, and the quality of their actions cannot be meaningfully assessed in a simple mechanical way. Only by taking account of a person's internal state before and during an act can that act be judged. That is why the true judgment is only that of God, Who knows people's inner feelings, motivations, and capabilities.

An act that is done in a state of mental clarity, after serious deliberation, is considered more closely associated with the one who performed it than one that flows from some fleeting emotions or reactions to circumstances.

When planning the destruction of Sodom and its neighboring cities, God gave them an opportunity to act properly in the easiest possible circumstances. If they would have simply left the wayfarers alone in this case, they would have been exonerated from the severe punishment that God had decreed for them; but if they failed this test, it would be obvious that their evil behavior was a conscious, consistent philosophy of life and they could claim no excuses for their actions: There was no hope for improvement.

*If they failed this test, they could claim no excuses.*

In describing the arrival of the angels who appeared as travelers in Sodom, the Torah details no less than seven reasons why the dwellers in Sodom should have been expected to refrain from harming them:

- The guests arrived "in the evening," so they could not be faulted for having to stay rather than to travel at night.
- Lot, who would welcome them in, was "sitting at the gate," an expression that alludes to his status as a judge in Sodom, which would seem to be a reason for the mob to let his guests stay in peace.
- Furthermore, Lot had initiated the invitation. He "stood up and went toward them," so the guests were not responsible for the "sin" of taking hospitality.

- Lot did not take them around the city, but rather told them, "Come aside to the house of your servant," making sure not to cause a public scene with his invitation to the guests.

- He asked them to remain with their feet dirty, and only to wash in the morning before leaving, to make it clear to the residents of Sodom that they were not planning on an extended stay.

- He invited them with the explicit condition that they stay only until the morning, at which time they would be expected to "rise early and go."

- Even after hearing Lot's invitation, they initially refused and said, "We will sleep in the street," instead, finally agreeing only after he "pressured them greatly." Even then, they did not request food, but ate only because he prepared a meal for them.

Although the people of Sodom had all these factors turning them away from violent action against the wayfarers, they found it imperative to follow their selfish beliefs, and they "surrounded the house" as in a siege (as emphasized by the use of the word "al" rather than "es"). The presence in the mob of all elements of society, "from young to old, all the people," underscored the universal acceptance of this evil way of life in Sodom. This behavior under such circumstances sealed their fate and left no avenue to judge them leniently.

# An Irrevocable and
# Precise Judgment

כִּי־מַשְׁחִתִים אֲנַחְנוּ אֶת־הַמָּקוֹם הַזֶּה כִּי־גָדְלָה צַעֲקָתָם אֶת־פְּנֵי ה'
וַיְשַׁלְּחֵנוּ ה' לְשַׁחֲתָהּ:

... וַיִּתְמַהְמָהּ וַיַּחֲזִקוּ הָאֲנָשִׁים בְּיָדוֹ ... וַיֹּאמֶר הִמָּלֵט עַל־נַפְשֶׁךָ
אַל־תַּבִּיט אַחֲרֶיךָ וְאַל־תַּעֲמֹד בְּכָל־הַכִּכָּר הָהָרָה הִמָּלֵט פֶּן־
תִּסָּפֶה:

... אַל־נָא אֲדֹנָי: הִנֵּה־נָא מָצָא עַבְדְּךָ חֵן בְּעֵינֶיךָ וַתַּגְדֵּל חַסְדְּךָ
אֲשֶׁר עָשִׂיתָ עִמָּדִי לְהַחֲיוֹת אֶת־נַפְשִׁי וְאָנֹכִי לֹא אוּכַל לְהִמָּלֵט
הָהָרָה פֶּן־תִּדְבָּקַנִי הָרָעָה וָמַתִּי: הִנֵּה־נָא הָעִיר הַזֹּאת קְרֹבָה לָנוּס
שָׁמָּה וְהִוא מִצְעָר אִמָּלְטָה נָּא שָׁמָּה הֲלֹא מִצְעָר הִוא וּתְחִי נַפְשִׁי:
וַיֹּאמֶר אֵלָיו ... מַהֵר הִמָּלֵט שָׁמָּה כִּי לֹא אוּכַל לַעֲשׂוֹת דָּבָר
עַד־בֹּאֲךָ שָׁמָּה ...

... וַיַּשְׁכֵּם אַבְרָהָם בַּבֹּקֶר אֶל־הַמָּקוֹם אֲשֶׁר־עָמַד שָׁם ... וַיַּשְׁקֵף ...
וְהִנֵּה עָלָה קִיטֹר הָאָרֶץ כְּקִיטֹר הַכִּבְשָׁן:

[The angels said to Lot:] "For we are destroying this
place; since their cry is great before God, and God
sent us to destroy it."

... Yet he hesitated, so the [angels] grasped his
hand. ... And [the angel] said, "Flee for your life; do
not look behind you; do not stop anywhere in all
the plain; escape to the mountain, lest you be swept
away."

... [Lot said]: "Please, no, my Lord. Behold, now,
Your servant has found favor in Your eyes, and Your
kindness was great which You did for me, to keep
my soul alive. Yet, I cannot escape to the mountain;
perhaps the harm will catch up with me and I will
die. Here, please, this city is near enough to flee
there, and it is small; please may I flee there — is it
not small? — and my soul shall live."

And [the angel] said: "... Escape there quickly, for I

*cannot do a thing until you arrive there."*
*… Avraham got up early in the morning [and went]*
*to the place where he had stood … and he gazed*
*down … and, behold! the smoke of the land began*
*to rise like the smoke of a kiln.*
*(Bereishis 19:13,16,17,18,19,20,22,27,28)*

Until the angels actually informed Lot that they were ready to carry out their mission to destroy Sodom, the fate of the cities was still uncertain. At that point, though, they announced the ruling of the Heavenly Court by saying, "We are destroying this place."

By speaking in the present tense, they indicated that it was as though they were already involved in the destruction, which was therefore inevitable; and they gave the reason for this state of affairs: "Since their cry is great before God, and God sent us to destroy."

A negative decree from God can be changed as long as it has not yet been "sealed" and labeled as an absolute decision. Even after that point, there is room for repentance to have an effect as long as there are no victims of a crime calling out to God for revenge. But when the suffering of those who were hurt is not addressed, repentance is meaningless and unacceptable.

In the case of Sodom, the fact that God had already sent the angels to destroy the cities was an expression of the fact that the decree was sealed, and the "great cry" of the innocent who were harmed by the people of Sodom made any attempt at repentance hopeless.

The angels said, "We are destroying this place," even though one of the two angels was sent to save

**Thus the irony: The final sealing of the decree was done through an angel of mercy.**

Lot, not to destroy. They used the plural because saving Lot and removing him from Sodom took away the city's last merit. Thus the irony: The final sealing of the decree was done through the action of this angel of mercy, the one who saved Lot. The lack of kindness and mercy in Sodom was so total that even an angel of mercy could only bring destruction to such a place.

As the Torah describes the actual occurrence of events after dawn, the fire from above followed Lot and burnt each spot as he left it, making it clear that he was being saved miraculously and that his leaving a place caused the destruction to arrive there.

Despite this special protection that Lot was receiving, he also was warned, "Do not stop anywhere in all the plain," since he was only guaranteed survival as long as he was proceeding at a reasonable pace. He did not have sufficient merit to survive in the midst of the fire, and he had to have as his goal "escaping to the mountain," where there would be no destruction.

Lot found this ordeal of keeping a step ahead of the disaster to be too taxing for his strength. He therefore prayed to God: "Since I have found favor in Your eyes, and You have done kindness for me to keep my soul alive" — since You are in any case giving me more than I rightfully deserve — therefore take into account the fact that "I cannot escape to the mountain" due to my weakness, and "perhaps the harm will catch up with me."

Lot asked for a further kindness, the sparing of the smallest of the five cities, originally named Bela, so that he could go there instead. Since it was a small, recently built town, with relatively few sins, Lot's merit would be sufficient to spare it. The angel charged with rescuing Lot told him that this request was granted, but with the condition that he "escape there quickly," since the progress of the fire was along a straight path, and the city was located off the direct path and would necessitate a diagonal detour. Lot would therefore need to proceed more rapidly[9] to stay ahead of the destruction. The exact nature of God's judgment combined with His mercy is seen here down to the smallest detail.

-----

9. Relative to "forward" motion, a person moving at a diagonal is moving slower than a person moving straight ahead. In order to flee diagonally and escape the fire's wide path, Lot needed to go faster than if he were to run straight ahead of the fire.

All of these miracles that occurred to save Lot were actually beyond his personal merit; only because of his connection with Avraham did he receive such unusual treatment. The Torah tells us this when it relates Avraham's reaction to the events: "Avraham got up early and [went to] the place where he had stood," and began to pray at dawn, before his usual time for prayer at sunrise. "The smoke of the land began to rise," and the main cities of Sodom and Gomorroh were destroyed immediately, but Avraham's prayers gave Lot the opportunity to escape with open miracles in the time between dawn and sunrise.

Lot could have been saved in his own merit had he listened to the warning of the angels and begun to leave in the middle of the night; but since he waited until dawn when the actual destruction began — evidently due to his lack of faith that it would really happen — he was spared only as a result of Avraham's special prayers.

# Beyond Punishment

וַיַּהֲפֹךְ אֶת־הֶעָרִים הָאֵל וְאֵת כָּל־הַכִּכָּר וְאֵת כָּל־יֹשְׁבֵי הֶעָרִים וְצֶמַח הָאֲדָמָה

*And [God] overturned [vayahafoch] these cities and the entire plain, all the dwellers of the cities, and the plants of the earth.*

*(Bereishis 19:25)*

The destruction of the cities of Sodom and Gomorroh and their region that the Torah describes as having been extremely fertile "like the garden of God, like the land of Egypt,"[10] had an aspect that went beyond Divine retribution for sins.

---

10. *Bereishis* 13:10.

Besides raining down upon the cities fire and brimstone, God also "overturned" (*vayahafoch*) the area by means of an earthquake that caused the formation of a huge crater; this crater then filled with salt from the depths and became the uninhabitable Dead Sea. This event, occurring in the spring when the Jordan River was at its height and the blessing of the land at its greatest, demonstrated clearly the fact that the great potential for good in that area, when not properly utilized, became its opposite (*vayahafoch*).

This aspect of the punishment extended far beyond the people of the cities to include even the animals, plants, and inanimate objects there, as the Torah states "the cities, dwellers of the cities, and the plants of the earth" were destroyed, demonstrating the law of the Creation that opportunity for good can never be neutral; if not utilized, it becomes evil.

> ***Opportunity for good can never be neutral; if not utilized, it becomes evil.***

# Clearing Sarah's Name

וּלְשָׂרָה אָמַר הִנֵּה נָתַתִּי אֶלֶף כֶּסֶף לְאָחִיךְ הִנֵּה הוּא־לָךְ כְּסוּת
עֵינַיִם לְכֹל אֲשֶׁר אִתָּךְ וְאֶת־כֹּל וְנֹכָחַת

*And to Sarah he said, "Behold I have given a thousand silver pieces to your brother; behold, let it be your 'covering of the eyes' for all who are with you; and to all, you will be vindicated."*
***(Bereishis 20:16)***

Repentance is a process that has many components. In particular, the rectification of an offense to another person often requires much more than simply reinstating the situation that existed prior to the sin. If the transgression caused embarrassment, it may be necessary to find a clever means of rebuilding the reputation of the victim in the eyes of others.

This was the case after Avimelech returned Sarah to Avraham, when there was a need to eradicate the suspicions of the public that he had violated her. Avimelech found a way to do this by presenting Avraham with a large gift, and he explained to Sarah that this gift would be effective in clearing her name among all of those who had heard about the event.

The gift would serve two purposes: It would serve as a "cover-up" ("k'sus einaiyim") that would distract the attention of the simple people and give them a counterpoint to the degradation Sarah had suffered by being forcibly taken into Avimelech's house. In addition, it would provide a rational proof ("v'nochachas") that nothing had been done to her, which would convince those of a more intellectual temperament. They would understand that if a powerful king felt the need not only to return the woman he had taken but also to shower her "brother" with wealth, it could only mean that Avraham's God had performed miracles to save her and to put Avimelech in a state of fear and submission to Avraham.

> *If the transgression caused embarrassment, it may be necessary to find a clever means of rebuilding the reputation of the victim in the eyes of others.*

While Avimelech may have repented only out of fear, he certainly took his repentance seriously; and we can learn from him the proper technique to follow when trying to right the wrongs we have done.

# Attention to Detail

וַה׳ פָּקַד אֶת־שָׂרָה כַּאֲשֶׁר אָמָר וַיַּעַשׂ ה׳ לְשָׂרָה כַּאֲשֶׁר
דִּבֵּר: וַתַּהַר וַתֵּלֶד שָׂרָה לְאַבְרָהָם בֵּן לִזְקֻנָיו לַמּוֹעֵד אֲשֶׁר־דִּבֶּר
אֹתוֹ אֱלֹקִים

*And God remembered Sarah as He had said, and*
*God did for Sarah as He had spoken. Sarah con-*
*ceived and bore a son to Avraham in his old age, at*
*the appointed time of which God **had spoken**.*
*(Bereishis 21:1-2)*

God's promise to Avraham and Sarah to grant them a son
in their old age had two aspects to it: first, the miracle of
such a birth itself, and second, the way in which the event
came about just as predicted, at a certain specified time, demonstrating explicitly God's personal attention to them.

Armed with this knowledge, we can understand what would
otherwise seem to be unnecessary wordiness in the Torah's
description of this occurrence:

The Torah states, "And God remembered Sarah as He had
said, and God did for Sarah as He had spoken." The verb
"*dibeir,*" "spoke," denotes a detailed discussion of a subject, as
opposed to "*amar,*" "said," which indicates a more concise utter-
ance. God had "said" to Avraham that He would give him a son
through Sarah. Later, God "spoke" through the angels to both of
them, promising that Yitzchak would be born a year later.

Now the Torah relates that both of these aspects of the promise
were fulfilled. The next verse
makes this more explicit when
it mentions the two parts of the
miracle: "Sarah conceived and
bore a son," as God had *said,*
and furthermore, it happened precisely "at the appointed time of
which God *had spoken.*" God's kindness went beyond promising

> **God's kindness went**
> **beyond promising a miracle**
> **and keeping the promise.**

a miracle and keeping the promise; it also included details of when to expect the fulfillment of the prediction.

# The Naming of Yitzchak

וַיִּקְרָא אַבְרָהָם אֶת־שֶׁם־בְּנוֹ הַנּוֹלַד־לוֹ אֲשֶׁר־יָלְדָה־לּוֹ שָׂרָה
יִצְחָק: וַיָּמָל אַבְרָהָם אֶת־יִצְחָק בְּנוֹ בֶּן־שְׁמֹנַת יָמִים כַּאֲשֶׁר צִוָּה
אֹתוֹ אֱלֹקִים: וְאַבְרָהָם בֶּן־מְאַת שָׁנָה בְּהִוָּלֶד לוֹ אֵת יִצְחָק בְּנוֹ:
וַתֹּאמֶר שָׂרָה צְחֹק עָשָׂה לִי אֱלֹקִים כָּל־הַשֹּׁמֵעַ יִצְחַק־לִי:
וַתֹּאמֶר מִי מִלֵּל לְאַבְרָהָם הֵינִיקָה בָנִים שָׂרָה כִּי־יָלַדְתִּי בֵן לִזְקֻנָיו

*And Avraham called the name of his son who was born to him, whom Sarah bore to him, Yitzchak. And Avraham circumcised his son Yitzchak at the age of eight days, as God had commanded him. Avraham was one hundred years old when his son Yitzchak was born to him.*

*Sarah said, "God brought laughter to me; all who will hear will laugh for me." And she said, "Who is the One Who said to Avraham that Sarah would nurse children? For I have borne him a son in his old age."*

*(Bereishis 21:3-7)*

The custom of all Jews is to give a boy his name at the time of his *bris milah*, and therefore it is puzzling that at the very first *bris* of a baby, the name was given earlier. Yitzchak Avinu received his name as soon as he was born.

The key to understanding this is the last phrase in the verse about the *bris*, "as God had commanded him," which applies to both verses, the one regarding the name and the one regarding the *bris*. Once we recall that Avraham Avinu was specifically commanded to give the name "Yitzchak," it is clear that he would wish to do this mitzvah as soon as possible — that is, as soon as the child was born — while the mitzvah of *bris milah* could not be performed before the eighth day. We, however, who give any name we wish, have no reason to rush to give the name. Therefore, we combine the naming with the *bris*.

Furthermore, the Torah stresses that Yitzchak was the son "whom Sarah bore to him." This reminds us that, unlike Yishmael, Yitzchak was Avraham's son from his wife Sarah, herself a Divinely inspired prophet. In the merit of being the child of these two great people, Yitzchak would be the one to carry on Avraham's goals and ideals. For this reason, even the giving of his name was a mitzvah in itself that could not wait for even eight days.

What was the tremendous significance of this name that God Himself chose? The name Yitzchak served as a reminder of the miraculous circumstances of his birth and of the joyous faith that his parents-to-be had far in advance of the actual fulfillment of God's promise. By pointing out that Avraham was 100 years old at the time of Yitzchak's birth, the Torah connects the naming of Yitzchak with Avraham's happy laughter at the time when God told him of the gift he was to be granted. Avraham rejoiced in advance over the fact that he would have a child at such an old age, even though he himself would remain in the same physical state as he had been, that of a 100-year-old man. Now, when that came to pass, the name Yitzchak forever commemorated that laughter.

Sarah, though, had a different kind and degree of laughter, since God performed the miracle for her in a different sort of way. She was returned to her youthful state at the time of the angels' visit, and she was full of joy at that moment. This caused her to laugh about what had already occurred rather than the future actualization of a prophecy.

The period of gestation and birth were in a sense "natural" since she was now physically a young woman; but overall, this itself constituted an even greater miracle and kindness than the one granted to Avraham. Therefore, Sarah said now, "God brought laughter to me," in a way that not only brought about the desired outcome, but also gave me the personal pleasure of being young; and therefore, "all who will hear will laugh for me," for my miracle that was beyond that of Avraham's.

The biggest demonstration of this level of God's kindness was that Sarah's youthful state continued even after Yitzchak's birth, allowing her to nurse him. This miracle was not strictly necessary, since she could have hired a young woman to nurse the baby. For this, Sarah gave thanks to God and said, "Who is the One Who said to Avraham that Sarah will nurse children?" This benefit had not been predicted in any of the prophecies about Yitzchak; it was there only to illustrate God's personal love for Sarah herself, granting her a permanent new youthfulness which transcended what was "necessary" for the practical aspects of having a child. Even though "I have borne him a son in his old age," and the purpose of the miracle was achieved, the miracle of youth remained in order to provide the maximum joy and laughter of deep happiness.

> **This benefit had not been predicted in any of the prophecies about Yitzchak.**

# Avraham's Greatest Test

וַיְהִי אַחַר הַדְּבָרִים הָאֵלֶּה וְהָאֱלֹקִים נִסָּה אֶת־אַבְרָהָם וַיֹּאמֶר
אֵלָיו אַבְרָהָם וַיֹּאמֶר הִנֵּנִי

*And it was after these things that God tested*
*Avraham and said to him, "Avraham,"*
*and he said, "Here I am."*
*(Bereishis 22:1)*

The Hebrew language has two words denoting a test of an object or a person, signifying two totally different levels of testing.

The root *"bachan"* connotes testing something or someone to see if they have the qualities expected of them, a sort of "quality control" directed to finding faults or problems. The root *"nasah,"* on the other hand, describes an attempt to determine if a person or thing is exceptional and able to withstand unusual circumstances or challenges.

God tests everyone constantly to ascertain if they are following His ways to the extent they should. The great people, like Avraham Avinu, though, are put through tests that bring out their ability to go *beyond* the limits of human nature to do God's will. Since such behavior is by definition past a person's normal capabilities, there is therefore no limit to the amount that it is possible to test someone in this way. Avraham passed ten such tests, and each of them was more difficult than the previous one.

The Torah introduces Avraham's greatest transcendence of human limitations, the commandment to bring his son Yitzchak as an offering, by stating that "after [all] these things," the previous nine tests that "God had tested (*'nisah'*) Avraham," He told him to bring Yitzchak as an offering. With this introduction the Torah reveals to us that this commandment was never intended to be carried out per se but was given only for the purpose of testing and evidencing Avraham's superhuman ability to obey God's wishes.

In general, a test can be (a) for the benefit of the one giving the test, (b) for the one undergoing the test, or (c) for the edification of those who observe the event. In this case, all three of these motivations were present. The Midrash[11] gives three analogies to the *Akeidah* that express these three aspects of the purpose of this test:

- A producer of flax applies strenuous processing techniques to the best flax, since he knows that it can withstand the strain and will thereby be improved.

- A farmer who knows that his ox is strong puts the yoke on it and uses it to pull the plow, benefiting the one giving the test.

- A dealer in pottery knocks on the strongest pots to demonstrate their resilience to prospective customers.

The *Akeidah* revealed Avraham's greatness to God Who gave him the test. The question is asked, of course, why does God need any proof of a person's level, since God knows everything about the person?

We can deal with this problem once we remember that the very fact of human free-will is beyond our comprehension since God knows the entire future. God has put into the fabric of Creation the possibility of looking at the world as unfolding according to human choice, and it is from this point of view that the Torah always speaks, presenting each event in time as if it were new to God just as much as it is to Man. Despite our lack of full understanding of how this is possible, it is clear that we are intended to live our lives solely with the understanding that our choices are ours and those choices trigger "responses" from God, just as they would from another person.

> *The question is asked: Why does God need any proof of a person's level, since God knows everything about the person?*

11. *Midrash Rabbah* 32:3.

David HaMelech says in *Tehillim,*[12] "God, You have examined me and You know," "*chakartani va'teida.*" This verse speaks of these two aspects of God's knowledge about Man: His continuous "examination" of Man, recording and judging each new action, and His "knowing" of the essence of a person and all his future behavior from the start. Just as we are to see all of the events of the Torah and of our own lives from our human point of view that presents them in temporal order, one after the next, so the Torah provides the picture of the *Akeidah* as a test that revealed *to God* a new height of Avraham Avinu's potential.

Throughout the Torah, we find God initiating contact with great people such as the *Avos* and Moshe Rabbeinu by calling their names twice, as a sign of His great closeness to them, but in this instance He called to Avraham only once.

According to the Midrash,[13] the reason for this change was to make it clear to everyone that Avraham performed this deed with a calm mind, free of any modicum of an emotional reaction, even that engendered by the extra allusion to his special relationship to God implicit in God's repeating his name.

On another level of understanding, the fact that Avraham's name was not repeated is actually indicative of his being in a state where he was already prepared and purified physically for any act that God would demand of him. God's calling a person's name twice represents His giving the person a chance to first divest himself from mundane concerns and then to hear the second, higher "call" to his soul. Avraham had no need of this preparation, and even after hearing his name only once, he responded immediately, "Here I am," ready to do Your will with no trace of material distractions.

---

12. *Tehillim* 139:1.

13. See *Yalkut Shimoni Bereishis* 22:96.

# A Mistake of Love

וַיֹּאמֶר קַח־נָא אֶת־בִּנְךָ אֶת־יְחִידְךָ אֲשֶׁר־אָהַבְתָּ אֶת־יִצְחָק וְלֶךְ־
לְךָ אֶל־אֶרֶץ הַמֹּרִיָּה וְהַעֲלֵהוּ שָׁם לְעֹלָה עַל אַחַד הֶהָרִים אֲשֶׁר
אֹמַר אֵלֶיךָ

*"Please take your son, your only one, whom you*
*love, Yitzchak, and go to the land of Moriah and*
*bring him up there as a burnt-offering upon one of*
*the mountains which I will tell you."*
*(Bereishis 22:2)*

The *Akeidah*, the binding of Yitzchak by his father Avraham, has always puzzled anyone who ponders its meaning:

God seemingly issues a cruel commandment to bring the precious son of his beloved Avraham as an offering, evidently destroying the whole future of the great nation that was to issue from him. Then at the last moment, He "changes His mind," something that appears contradictory to everything we understand about God. Our Sages[14] quote the prophet who describes the *Akeidah* as an act that God "did not command."[15] This is a curious statement, since the Torah seems to tell us that God did command it explicitly. What were Avraham's thoughts during all this, and what was achieved through this entire sequence of events?

If we simply shift our point of view from the mere mechanical analysis of the exchange of words between God and Avraham to a look at the inner emotional world of our great forefather, the whole scenario suddenly becomes clear:

First, we must take note that the directive from God to perform the *Akeidah* was given in anything but a purely technical manner. Avraham is told, "Please take your son, your only

---

14. *Tanchuma Bechukosai* 5; see *Taanis* 4a.
15. *Yirmiyahu* 7:31.

one, whom you love, Yitzchak." Avraham's feelings are being addressed here more than his mind or his limbs.

Savage pagans have performed human sacrifice in a wholesale manner by numbing their natural mercy and making themselves callous. Is this a great spiritual achievement? God is asking of Avraham the exact opposite, to remember and awaken his tremendous love for his son, his "only one," whose potential far surpassed that of his half-brother Yishmael, for "Yitzchak" (who was 37 years old at the time, according to our Sages[16]) who had already attained unequaled greatness in wisdom and righteousness.

> *Savage pagans have performed human sacrifice in a wholesale manner by numbing their natural mercy and making themselves callous. Is this a great spiritual achievement?*

In this state of intense emotional attachment to his son, he was expected to demonstrate that his love of God exceeded this incomparably powerful love for another person. The objective here was not simply obedience; it was to show the greatest display of love for God in the clearest possible manner, through comparison with the greatest possible love for a human being.

In this context, we can begin to grasp God's plan for giving Avraham the opportunity to express his love for God. In order to make this possible without actually taking a human life, God presented His commandment in a way that was cryptic and allowed for misinterpretation. The verb "ha'aleihu," "bring him up," is never used in the Torah to refer to the bringing of offering, and the prefix in the word "l'olah" is also unusual. A precise understanding of the words would seem to be "set him aside for the possibility of becoming an offering." If Avraham had been in a state where he was dissecting the precise wording with which he had been commanded, he could have realized that all that was being asked of him was to place Yitzchak on the altar and then take him down, as actually happened in the end.

---

16. *Bereishis Rabbah* 56:8.

In addition, God's implied promise to tell Avraham on which mountain to carry out the commandment was never fulfilled. If Avraham could have grasped from this fact that what God actually meant by "which I will tell you" was not that He would reveal the identity of the mountain, but that He would tell Avraham *what* to offer, the ram rather than his son.

Avraham, in his enthusiasm to follow God's orders, did not detect these nuances, and took the commandment at its face value, hastening to literally bring Yitzchak as an offering. This provided the clearest demonstration of his deep love for God, and when God revealed to him the real meaning of His words, there was no change of mind involved, only clarification of what had originally been said. The story of the *Akeidah* thus becomes an example of how God sometimes uses human frailty and fallibility as one more tool for enabling a person's greatness to shine through and lead to *Kiddush Shem Shamayim*.

# Avraham's Intuition

וַיֹּאמֶר אַבְרָהָם אֶל־נְעָרָיו שְׁבוּ־לָכֶם פֹּה עִם־הַחֲמוֹר
וַאֲנִי וְהַנַּעַר נֵלְכָה עַד־כֹּה וְנִשְׁתַּחֲוֶה וְנָשׁוּבָה אֲלֵיכֶם

**And Avraham said to his servants,**
**"Stay here by yourselves with the donkey;**
**while I and the lad will go yonder,**
**we will worship, and we will return to you."**
**(Bereishis 22:5)**

As an outcome of his pure devotion to God, Avraham Avinu was privileged to have an inner perception of the truth, a perception from within his own soul, and as a result was able to keep the mitzvos of the Torah despite not having been explicitly commanded to do so. In addition to this knowledge, he was also able to perform the mitzvos without opposition from the evil inclination, since the motivation for their performance came from within. All the acts that Avraham did in serving God resonated with his understanding and his instinct for good.

The commandment to sacrifice his son Yitzchak was a glaring exception to this rule. Avraham sensed deep in his heart that this was something that went against everything he had been teaching throughout his life, and he suddenly perceived a strong resistance to this act from within his soul.

> **Avraham sensed deep in his heart that this was something that went against everything he had been teaching throughout his life.**

In actuality, the source of this resistance was the fact that killing Yitzchak was truly a horrific act, and that God never meant for it to be carried out. Therefore, Avraham's healthy moral instinct made it abhorrent for him to do so.

As a result of this feeling, he could not bring himself to do, in public, an act that would contradict all of his own doctrine of many years' standing. He told his two servants, who were his greatest disciples, to stay behind while he and Yitzchak went to bring an offering.

In the end, Avraham received reward for intending to fulfill the commandment even though it was so against his own judgment. At the same time, God revealed that Avraham's instinct was in fact accurate, and that the act itself was an intrinsically repugnant one. As an overall outcome of the entire episode, God's rejection of the concept of human sacrifice became all the more clear, while Avraham demonstrated his ability to overcome even his spiritual nature when commanded to do so by God Himself.

# The New Yitzchak

*... וַיַּעֲקֹד אֶת־יִצְחָק בְּנוֹ וַיָּשֶׂם אֹתוֹ עַל־הַמִּזְבֵּחַ מִמַּעַל לָעֵצִים*

*... He bound Yitzchak, his son, and he placed him
on the altar, on top of the wood.*

*(Bereishis 22:9)*

T he *Akeidah*, the binding of Yitzchak, is generally referred to as a test for Avraham Avinu. This test served all of the three purposes for which an individual can be tested: to help that person himself grow in character by bringing out his potential into reality; to let the tester ascertain the true nature of the one being tested; and to demonstrate to the world at large the greatness of that person. This last goal in particular was achieved by the *Akeidah*: It showed all the nations what Avraham's special merit was, and impressed upon them the clarity of his prophecy and the depth of his belief in the Afterlife which afforded him the certainty to do such a deed.

Still, it is impossible to ignore the fact that the *Akeidah* involved two people, especially in light of our Sages' statement[17] that Yitzchak was already 37 years old at the time. He could have refused to cooperate with a commandment that had not been given directly to him and from which he could claim to be exempt. His aged father could not have forced him to comply; his own consent was needed for the act to be carried out, and he gave it willingly, allowing himself to be bound upon the altar without resisting. If so, we must understand why the *Akeidah* is not looked at as a supreme test for Yitzchak, perhaps even more than for Avraham.

A deeper look into Yitzchak's role in the development of the Jewish people provides the key to this question. Yitzchak's very existence was the result of an overwhelming miracle, a demonstration of the supernatural quality that *Am Yisrael* would always

---

17. Ibid.

possess. Not only was his birth a physical miracle, with his parents being over 90 years old, but from a more spiritual point of view, he had not been destined to come into being.

*Yitzchak's very existence was the result of an overwhelming miracle, a demonstration of the supernatural quality that Am Yisrael would always possess.*

Avraham had been able to see that the "standard" system of spiritual cause and effect dictated that he would be without children. Only a total disruption of the normal order of things could have brought Yitzchak into the world, and this fact created a serious weakness in the ability of the Jewish people to endure.

A miracle that is done for the benefit of a person can only continue as long as the beneficiary merits to be treated in a miraculous fashion. The existence of the Jewish people, therefore, would always be fragile, since as soon as they lapsed into behavior that was only on a level commensurate with a natural nation, they would lose their right to exist. The natural world in which God hides His hand behind human cause and effect would leave no place for such a nation, and they would be destroyed, God forbid. Somehow, Yitzchak's miraculous status had to be sustained in a way that would not require a constant "input" of merit from his descendants.

This was the role of the *Akeidah* from Yitzchak's point of view. He willingly put himself in the position where he was to be brought as an offering and burnt to ashes, marking an end to the precarious existence that had begun at his supernatural conception. This readiness for self-sacrifice would be considered as a fulfillment *in advance* of the punishment that would otherwise have been visited on Yitzchak's children when they did not meet the high standards expected of them.

Yitzchak descended from the altar as if a different person, a person sanctified with the holiness of an offering and no longer subject to the scrutiny he had been under previously as to whether he merited continued existence. For Yitzchak, the significance of the *Akeidah* was not as a test per se to show his capabilities, but as an actual change in his essence that gave him a new source of the right to survive.

This change is reflected in two ways in the Torah's narrative of the events immediately following the *Akeidah*:

First of all, the angel now gave a blessing that Yitzchak's descendants would be as numerous as the stars and as the sand on the seashore. This blessing was appropriate now that the spiritual opposition to Yitzchak's continued existence had been removed.

In addition, with the angel's call to Avraham to refrain from killing Yitzchak, the Torah begins to use the Tetragrammaton, the four-letter Name of God, instead of the Name *Elokim* that had been used previously in this episode. The Name *Elokim* is the one that appears throughout the description of the Creation, as it denotes God evidencing Himself through the natural order of things, whether physical or spiritual. This natural order was what necessitated the *Akeidah*, since Yitzchak had no right to a guaranteed place within it. Following the *Akeidah*, God reveals Himself through His special, "personal" Name, indicating that now He would deal with Yitzchak on a close personal level, watching over him and sustaining him and his children throughout their spiritual ups and downs.

This change in God's relationship to Yitzchak is parallel to the "change of mind" that our Sages[18] attribute to Him at the time of the Creation. He "added" the quality of mercy, represented by the four-letter Name, to the "original" plan to rule the world through pure strict justice that does not allow for the existence of fragile, fallible human beings. Here the same idea is expressed in the life of Yitzchak: Until the *Akeidah*, Yitzchak personified the perfection necessary to survive with God's Attribute of Justice; but afterward, armed with the merit of his readiness for

18. *Pesikta Rabbasi* 40; *Shemos Rabbah* 30:13, etc.; see *Rashi, Bereishis* 1:1.

self-sacrifice, he acquired for himself and his descendants the privilege to be treated with mercy and patience for their faults.

# The Voice of a Mitzvah

וַיִּקְרָא אֵלָיו מַלְאַךְ ה׳ מִן־הַשָּׁמַיִם וַיֹּאמֶר אַבְרָהָם אַבְרָהָם וַיֹּאמֶר הִנֵּנִי:

וַיֹּאמֶר אַל־תִּשְׁלַח יָדְךָ אֶל־הַנַּעַר וְאַל־תַּעַשׂ לוֹ מְאוּמָה כִּי עַתָּה יָדַעְתִּי כִּי־יְרֵא אֱלֹקִים אַתָּה וְלֹא חָשַׂכְתָּ אֶת־בִּנְךָ אֶת־יְחִידְךָ מִמֶּנִּי

*And an angel of God called to him from heaven and said, "Avraham, Avraham!" And he said, "Here I am."*

*And he said, "Do not stretch out your hand against the lad; do not do anything to him; for now I know that you are a God-fearing person, as you have not withheld your son, your only one, from Me [mimeni]."*
*(Bereishis 22:11-12)*

The episode of the *Akeidah* begins with God Himself commanding Avraham to bring his son as an offering, providing him with the level of certainty necessary to even contemplate such an act. It therefore seems peculiar that when this commandment was "rescinded," that message was conveyed by a mere angel rather than by a second prophecy from God Himself. Perhaps Avraham should have had reason to doubt or question the authority of the angel to contradict the instructions he had received from God. What is behind this change?

Our Sages[19] tell us that every mitzvah act is one with creative powers, and beyond the physical action involved in fulfilling the commandment, the mitzvah brings into being an angel that is a permanent product of the person's good act. This angel is

---

19. *Avos* 4:11.

then entrusted with the task of giving reward to the person who created it, a concept hinted at in the statement in *Pirkei Avos*,[20] "the reward of a mitzvah is a mitzvah." The angel that is a concrete representation of the mitzvah provides the reward for the mitzvah act.

The angel resulting from a mitzvah is created at the moment at which the mitzvah is completed. In the case of the *Akeidah*, God's objective was only to have Yitzchak placed on the altar as a demonstration of Avraham's devotion to Him, and so, at that point, an angel was already created. If Avraham would have continued and actually sacrificed his son, the entire mitzvah would have been transformed into a horrific act of bloodshed, and the angel previously created would have been destroyed. When that angel called to Avraham, it was begging for its own survival.

> **When that angel called to Avraham, it was begging for its own survival.**

This was no mere conveyance of information that had been sent by God through the seemingly inferior channel of an angel's speech rather than through prophecy. Avraham was hearing direct evidence of the spiritual consequences of his actions; there was no need for a new directive from God Himself when Avraham perceived firsthand what was happening in a spiritual sense.

This concept leads us to a reading of the words of the angel that is somewhat different than the conventional understanding:

Ordinarily, the verse is interpreted to mean that when the angel said, "you did not withhold your only son *from Me*," this was said as a quote from God. According to the explanation given here, however, the word "*mimeni*," "from me," could be read as the angel's giving *the source* of its knowledge that the mitzvah had been fulfilled: "I know this," it said to Avraham, "*mimeni*," "from myself," from the very fact that I exist as a complete being resulting from a complete mitzvah; therefore, the whole purpose of the mitzvah was only to show that "you are one who fears

---

20. *Pirkei Avos* 4:2.

God," but not to actually have Yitzchak brought as an offering.

Avraham was granted solid evidence of the repercussions of his actions: What to him had seemed as merely a stage of preparation was in fact an entire mitzvah, but one that was in danger of being turned into an act of murder. Avraham could not argue with the angel or disobey it; it was revealing its own source of life, and therefore represented the ultimate level of knowledge needed in the situation.

# The Hardest Part of the Akeidah

אַל־תִּשְׁלַח יָדְךָ אֶל־הַנַּעַר וְאַל־תַּעַשׂ לוֹ מְאוּמָה
*"Do not stretch your hand against the lad;*
*do not do anything to him ...."*
*(Bereishis 22:12)*

The greatest demonstration possible of Avraham's single-mindedness in his service of God came *after* the *Akeidah*.

Of course, it was supremely difficult to do something that went against his instincts and his professed beliefs, but one aspect of the *Akeidah* was easy for Avraham: At least he did not have the internal struggle against ulterior motives for his action. He had nothing to gain materially or socially from offering his son, so in this respect, his test was simple.

But when Avraham was commanded to *desist* from slaughtering Yitzchak, the temptation to obey for selfish motivations was almost irresistible. What greater personal pleasure could there be than to remove his beloved son from the altar and return home with him?

*What greater personal pleasure could there be than to remove his beloved son from the altar and return home with him?*

Only God, Who knows the innermost secrets of a person's heart, could see that Avraham removed Yitzchak from the altar with the same unselfish and uncomplicated desire to follow God's directive as he had when placing him on the altar.

In fact, Avraham had to be told, "do not do anything to him," in order to ensure that Avraham would not injure Yitzchak even minimally to serve as a symbolic fulfillment of the initial commandment to bring him as an offering. This warning, put in the mouth of the angel by God, to refrain from any harm to Yitzchak, served as a testimony to Avraham's absolutely pure intentions and to the lack of any self-serving component to his actions.

# The Heavenly Altar

וַיִּשָּׂא אַבְרָהָם אֶת־עֵינָיו וַיַּרְא וְהִנֵּה־אַיִל אַחַר נֶאֱחַז בַּסְּבַךְ בְּקַרְנָיו
וַיֵּלֶךְ אַבְרָהָם וַיִּקַּח אֶת־הָאַיִל וַיַּעֲלֵהוּ לְעֹלָה תַּחַת בְּנוֹ

*Avraham raised his eyes and saw, and here was*
*a ram — afterward entangled by its horns in the*
*branches. And Avraham went and took the ram, and*
*offered it up as a burnt-offering in place of his son.*
*(Bereishis 22:13)*

When Avraham Avinu was told to desist before actually carrying out *Akeidas Yitzchak,* he remained puzzled. The initial commandment he had received was to "offer him up as a burnt-offering." Knowing that God does not change His mind, Avraham felt the need to understand what God had intended. His was no mere intellectual curiosity; Avraham had an intense awareness that God's commandment still obligated him, and he felt a powerful need to determine how to satisfy that obligation.

This need led him to a deeper analysis of God's words: God had not said explicitly who the "him" or "it" was that was to be offered; therefore, it stood to reason that something else could be substituted for Yitzchak, if only there would be some clear indication what that something was. God's use of the pronoun "him" or "it" implied that the identity of the offering would be obvious and would fit into the category of that "which I shall tell you" in some implicit sense.

Avraham was immediately prepared to look for the new object of God's command, and his search was quickly crowned with success. He saw that "here was a ram" that had just appeared, and immediately "afterward" it became "entangled by its horns in the branches." To Avraham's keen perception of Divine Providence, it was clear that this ram was what God intended him to bring as an offering.

When Avraham offered the ram, he kept in mind that this was intended to take the place of his son, and by doing so, he inaugurated a new form of sacrificial worship. This offering was not a mere symbolic gift to God, but rather it was considered as if he had brought Yitzchak as an offering.

A person whose very existence comes from God's kindness should feel obligated to offer his whole life to God in gratitude; in his heart he should be willing to sacrifice himself on the altar. Certainly this is true when a person has sinned and needs to bring an offering as an atonement. God, in His mercy, allows a person to substitute the body of an animal, since physically it is similar to a human body. In place of the sacrifice of his soul, God accepts the mental image that he conjures up of himself being slaughtered, since this thought emanates from the soul and affects it. This was the new concept

> **This was the new concept that came into being when Avraham brought the ram: that a person could sacrifice himself mentally, through the image that the physical sacrifice of an animal produced in his mind.**

that came into being when Avraham brought the ram: that a person could sacrifice himself (or in this case, his son) mentally, through the image that the physical sacrifice of an animal produced in his mind.

Our Sages in the Midrash[21] give a concrete picture of this concept in the form of the angel Michael offering the souls of the righteous on a Heavenly altar. The righteous person who imagines himself being offered instead of the animal which he brings is presenting his soul to be offered on a level far above that of the physical slaughter of an animal. The first time this level of devotion was achieved was at the *Akeidah*. From then on, every actual offering — and every act of studying about the offering — recalls the *Akeidah*, the model for this manner of mental service of God; it brings the merit of Avraham to his children, who inherited from him this ability to give themselves over fully to God.

Paradoxically, this sort of thinking, which might seem almost brutal and violent at first glance, actually has the opposite effect on a person's soul, refining it and distancing it from coarseness. The thought of giving up one's physical life for God's honor, a thought so powerfully stimulated by seeing an animal slaughtered as an offering, serves to raise a person beyond the material world into a purely spiritual perception of reality.

This is the heritage that Avraham and Yitzchak gave to all Jews after them through their pure intentions at the *Akeidah*, and this is what our Sages meant to convey to us through the imagery of souls being "offered on the Heavenly altar."

Avraham, with the clear perception of the eternal significance of his actions, commemorated them by renaming the place where he stood. (This procedure is repeated many times throughout the Torah when the great potential of an important event is preserved forever in the name and holiness of a place.) The mountain of Moriah would ultimately be the site of the *Beis HaMikdash*, the Holy Temple, a place of absolutely unique sanc-

---

21. *Midrash Hane'elam Lech Lecha, Ma'amar B, see Zevachim 62a.*

tity. Avraham gave it the additional Name of "*Hashem Yireh,*" meaning "God will *see*"; He will look at every offering brought in that Temple as if the one who brought it offered his own life with the same purity of intention as Yitzchak was prepared to do.

The Torah adds, "This is what is said today," that even future generations who will not be privileged to have the unparalleled spiritual awareness of Avraham will still be given this understanding of the depth of meaning in their sacrificial service. Avraham knew that God's command to "offer him up as a burnt-offering" could not possibly be for naught. This appreciation of the power of God's word gave him the ability to put all the energy that he had ready for the offering of Yitzchak into offering the ram. The Torah itself, by making Avraham's renaming of the mountain into an immutable spiritual reality, "what is said today," gives all of Avraham's descendants the capability of achieving the same heights he reached at the *Akeidah*.

# פרשת חיי שרה
# PARASHAS CHAYEI SARAH

## Holy Business

וַיָּקָם אַבְרָהָם מֵעַל פְּנֵי מֵתוֹ וַיְדַבֵּר אֶל־בְּנֵי־חֵת לֵאמֹר: גֵּר־וְתוֹשָׁב
אָנֹכִי עִמָּכֶם תְּנוּ לִי אֲחֻזַּת־קֶבֶר עִמָּכֶם וְאֶקְבְּרָה מֵתִי מִלְּפָנָי

*Avraham rose up from the presence of his dead*
*and spoke to the Hittites, saying: "I am a stranger*
*and sojourner among you; grant me burial-property*
*among you, that I may bury my dead from*
*before me."*
*(Bereishis 23:3-4)*

The Torah devotes twenty verses to Avraham Avinu's negotiations with the Hittites — who ruled in Chevron — regarding the purchase of a burial place for Sarah, more space than it gives to many sections of mitzvos that would seem more significant than this narrative. In addition, the Hittites,

"*B'nei Chet,*" are mentioned *ten times* in this section, seemingly far too much attention to these people who should be considered minor characters in the story of Avraham. The Midrash[1] addresses these issues and states that these ten repetitions of this phrase indicate that this section is in some manner equated in importance to the Ten Commandments, a concept that obviously requires an in-depth examination.

Avraham's goal in life was not only his own personal spiritual growth, but also the dissemination of the essentials of the true beliefs and practices to everyone he could reach. In particular, he wanted to convey the precept of life after death and revivification of the dead to the Hittites and other peoples of Canaan who were deeply mired in a materialistic view of the world.

When his wife Sarah died and Avraham had difficulties finding a burial place for her, he did not become wrapped up in his own suffering. Instead, he saw this as an opportunity to make a clear presentation of his outlook to the people among whom he dwelled:

Even though the Hittites had burial customs, Avraham was able to discern from the details of their practices that they looked at burial as simply a practical necessity; perhaps it was a symbolic honoring of the dead, as well as a way of protecting the living from the detrimental effects to physical and emotional health that could come from contact with the dead.

The Hittites buried their dead in temporary graves until the body had decayed, and then moved the bones to a different place. They intentionally refrained from having family burial plots, "*achuzas kever,*" and therefore initially refused Avraham's request to sell him land for such a purpose. To them, death was the absolute end, and the thought of remaining with one's family after death made no sense.

*To them, death was the absolute end, and the thought of remaining with one's family after death made no sense.*

---

1. *Bereishis Rabbah* 58:8.

This is the concept that Avraham wanted to combat, and he truly desired to influence them to change their laws in this regard.

Avraham introduced his view of death at the very outset of his request to make the purchase: "I am a stranger and sojourner among you," he told them, emphasizing not only his status relative to the citizens of the land, but also the fact that he, like all mortal people, was intrinsically a sojourner in this world. It served Avraham's purpose to offer a large sum of money and to ask for a special legal dispensation to have a small piece of land for a family burial plot, since from the viewpoint of eternity, this is all a person has in this world.

To Avraham, it was deeply meaningful to have his family share a burial place, so that at the time of the Revivification of the Dead they would stand together as a unit, separate from those who did not share their beliefs and goals. The Hittites offered Avraham the right to bury his dead in "our best graves," but without a permanent and specified area of his own, but he demanded "*achuzas kever*" in protest against their degraded beliefs about the nature of man.

Avraham's strength and persistence in this test, especially at a time of deep personal sorrow, merited that even the Hittites, sunk as they were in their this-worldly outlook, were influenced toward his beliefs. For this reason, the ten repetitions of the phrase "*B'nei Chet*" have a similar centrality in the Torah to that of the Ten Commandments. Just as the Ten Commandments include all the concepts of the Torah philosophy of life in a concentrated form, so do these ten phrases include Avraham's methodology of communicating the fundamental tenets of Judaism in a tangible form, accessible even to those whose current way of life is farthest removed from them.

# The Lesser of Two Evils

וְאַשְׁבִּיעֲךָ בַּה' אֱלֹקֵי הַשָּׁמַיִם וֵאלֹקֵי הָאָרֶץ אֲשֶׁר לֹא־תִקַּח אִשָּׁה
לִבְנִי מִבְּנוֹת הַכְּנַעֲנִי אֲשֶׁר אָנֹכִי יוֹשֵׁב בְּקִרְבּוֹ

*"And I will have you swear by Hashem, God of the*
*heavens and God of the earth, that you will not*
*take a wife for my son from the daughters of the*
*Canaanites among whom I dwell."*
*(Bereishis 24:3)*

Avraham Avinu's unique position as the lone proponent of the true faith compelled him to make an exceedingly difficult choice: to perpertuate his beliefs, and to fulfill the blessing to be the founder of a great nation that would serve God, Avraham needed to choose a wife for his son Yitzchak. Unfortunately, the world was replete with individuals who did not follow in the ways of Avraham. Where would he find a suitable woman?

The possibilities seemed reducible to two basic options: either finding someone from the land in which Avraham had been dwelling, or to try to make a match with someone from his former homeland, Aram Naharaim. Each of these choices had its advantages and disadvantages:

The people of Canaan were deeply sunk in degraded character traits such as cruelty and promiscuity, while those of Aram Naharaim were more attached to idolatrous beliefs, although their character was more elevated than the Canaanites. The future of the Jewish people would depend greatly on the nature of their progenitors. Who would serve better as the second mother of *Am Yisrael?*

*Who would serve better as the second mother of Am Yisrael?*

Rabbeinu Nissim,[2] the great Jewish thinker and Talmudist of

---

2. *Derashos HaRan, Drush 5.*

the 1400's, provides us with an insight that gives the key to Avraham's decision. He divides the mitzvos of the Torah into two general groups: those that influence a person's character and even the nature of his body, and those whose effect is limited to the area of the mind.

Rabbeinu Nissim asserts that a person's behavior in the first area, those mitzvos that mold his personality, can continue to have influence on his descendants in a way that transcends the power of mere education or social pressure. As we know from many classic Jewish sources, *Sefer HaChinuch*[3] foremost among them, repeated actions shape a person's essence to fit those actions. Rabbeinu Nissim takes this a step further to say that one's new nature is passed on, presumably in a nonphysical manner, to one's children.

The mitzvos that deal only with the mind, important and central as they may be, do not in themselves change anything about a person, but only constitute a guide to correct thinking and outlook. Since the person himself is not changed, certainly his descendants will not have the results of his actions, good or bad, imprinted on their nature.

Avraham knew the people of Canaan well, and was familiar with their low character. He had spent most of his life working to get them to improve in any way possible, a task that he saw as Divinely appointed. It was not with hatred or disdain that he decided to reject them as a possible source for a wife for Yitzchak, but only with concern for the future generations of *Am Yisrael* who would always carry the traits of their progenitors with them.

He told his servant, "Swear that you will not take a wife for my son . . . from the Canaanites *among whom I dwell.*" The fact that Avraham had *dwelled among them* and put so much effort into elevating their level clued him in to their unsuitability as a match for Yitzchak. Better to go to Aram Naharaim, where the level of character was superior, and educate Yitzchak's wife in the principles of Avraham's belief. This would be a far easier

---

3. *Sefer HaChinuch Mitzvah* 16, etc.

challenge than trying to change personality traits ingrained by generations of degraded Canaanite behavior.

# Eliezer's Test

וַיֹּאמַר ה' אֱלֹקֵי אֲדֹנִי אַבְרָהָם הַקְרֵה־נָא לְפָנַי הַיּוֹם וַעֲשֵׂה־חֶסֶד עִם אֲדֹנִי אַבְרָהָם: הִנֵּה אָנֹכִי נִצָּב עַל־עֵין הַמָּיִם וּבְנוֹת אַנְשֵׁי הָעִיר יֹצְאֹת לִשְׁאֹב מָיִם: וְהָיָה הַנַּעֲרָ אֲשֶׁר אֹמַר אֵלֶיהָ הַטִּי־ נָא כַדֵּךְ וְאֶשְׁתֶּה וְאָמְרָה שְׁתֵה וְגַם־גְּמַלֶּיךָ אַשְׁקֶה אֹתָהּ הֹכַחְתָּ לְעַבְדְּךָ לְיִצְחָק וּבָהּ אֵדַע כִּי־עָשִׂיתָ חֶסֶד עִם־אֲדֹנִי

*And he said, "Hashem, God of my master Avraham,*
*create a happenstance before me this day that You*
*do kindness with my master Avraham. Behold, I am*
*standing by the spring of water, and the daughters*
*of the townsmen come out to draw water. Let it be*
*that the maiden to whom I shall say, 'Tip, please,*
*your jug so I may drink,' who replies, 'Drink, and I*
*will even water your camels,' her will You have*
*designated for Your servant, for Yitzchak,*
*and through her I will know that You have*
*done kindness with my master."*
*(Bereishis 24:12-14)*

Avraham Avinu had given his servant Eliezer only one restriction on his choice of a wife for Yitzchak, but Eliezer himself went further in his criteria. Avraham had made the servant swear not to take a daughter of the Canaanites, whose character was so depraved. From this, Eliezer realized that good personality traits were uppermost in Avraham's mind. Therefore, he devised a test to find a girl who would most exemplify the qualities appropriate for one who would join Avraham's household.

Eliezer realized, though, that such a one-time test would not be fool proof. He therefore asked God for special assistance to guarantee that this test would provide evidence of her general character. The word "*hakrei,*" "create a happenstance," in his prayer indicates that he was asking for an *unusual event*, one that would occur "before him" and "this day," to assure him that this was in fact the proper match for Yitzchak.

He devised the test in such a way that only a girl who was truly filled with kindness and concern for others would do what he expected. According to what he asked for, there were four challenges that the girl had to meet in order to demonstrate her innate good character:

First of all, Eliezer was "standing by the spring of water," where he seemingly should have no trouble taking a drink by himself; any girl not eager to do a favor would have a ready-made excuse for ignoring his request.

Secondly, it was a time of day when there were many girls from the city going out to draw water, and so each one could say to herself, *Let him ask someone else who is not as busy as I am, and who has not yet filled up her pitcher and who is not ready to leave.*

> *It was a time of day when there were many girls going out to draw water, so each one could say to herself, "Let him ask someone else."*

Third, Eliezer planned to ask her to pour the water for him from the pitcher on her shoulder, tempting her to get angry at his refusal to take the pitcher himself.

Finally, he expected her to extrapolate from his seeming laziness that he must have incurred an injury to his hands, and to follow this up by doing *more* than she had been asked to do, that is, giving water also to the camels, since she would assume that he was incapable of doing so. A truly kind person would apply thought to the practice of kindness in addition to physical action, and this would demonstrate the depth of her commitment to giving to others.

Eliezer's prayer was immediately answered with special Divine Providence: Rivkah, the daughter of the wealthy family of Besuel, Avraham's relative, went out at that moment with a pitcher to draw water, despite the fact that she would ordinarily have left such a task to a servant. This was God's way of arranging a match for Yitzchak with his cousin, a girl of unparalleled good character.

Eliezer ran to her, made his request, and watched carefully as all the details of his test were fulfilled. However, even after she had quickly and energetically drawn water for the camels, he still waited quietly to make sure that her motivations were pure. It was always possible that after she finished, she would ask for payment for her work, showing that she was not interested in doing a kindness for a stranger after all. Only after she had given water to all the camels without asking for anything in return was he sure that God had given him the sign he had requested.

He immediately gave her the jewelry he had brought as a present for the girl whom he would select. The fulfillment of his test was enough evidence that this was the proper girl for Yitzchak, and he only asked the name of her father as a formality.

When he found out that she was the daughter of Avraham's nephew Besuel, he gave extra thanks to God for granting him something he had not even requested. This was additional confirmation of the fact that God had sent this girl to be Yitzchak's wife and the future mother of the Jewish people.

# The Betrothal of Rivkah

וַיַּעַן לָבָן וּבְתוּאֵל וַיֹּאמְרוּ מֵה׳ יָצָא הַדָּבָר לֹא נוּכַל דַּבֵּר אֵלֶיךָ רַע
אוֹ־טוֹב: הִנֵּה־רִבְקָה לְפָנֶיךָ קַח וָלֵךְ וּתְהִי אִשָּׁה לְבֶן־אֲדֹנֶיךָ כַּאֲשֶׁר
דִּבֶּר ה׳

*And Lavan and Besuel answered and said,*
*"This is from God. We can not say to you neither*
*bad or good. Here is Rivkah before you;*
*take her and go, and let her be a wife to your*
*master's son, as God has spoken."*
*(Bereishis 24:50-51)*

Once Eliezer had related the details of his test of Rivkah to her family, even these idolaters could recognize the miraculous nature of the events that brought Rivkah together with the servant of their relative Avraham. They saw that this was beyond the ordinary,

> *Even these idolaters could see the miraculous nature of the events.*

and realized that their free will had no power over the will of God that was so evident here. Besuel, Rivkah's father, and even her brother Lavan, who was so steeped in idol-worship as the Torah describes later in *Parashas Vayeitzei,*[4] could only say, "This is from God." Since they "could say nothing bad" to prevent the match, therefore they felt powerless even to "say good," to agree to it, so they gave their consent without any expression of choice. They merely said, "Here is Rivkah before you," allowing Eliezer to take her with him as the betrothed wife of Yitzchak.

Upon hearing this, Eliezer took their words at face value, not even thanking them or offering them presents as would ordinarily be expected in accordance with the custom of the time. Instead he immediately bowed and thanked God for His Providential intervention and prepared to depart with Rivkah.

---

4. *Bereishis* 31:30.

This, however, was too much for Rivkah's family, and they began to resist. They made excuses about needing more time for her to prepare for the wedding, but Eliezer made himself clear, reminding them of the miraculous nature of the events that were unfolding. "Do not slow me down," he said to them, using the word "*t'acharu*" which denotes being late for an appointed time. God had done a miracle for him at the exact time at which he had requested it, indicating that the time was ripe for this match to be made. They should not interfere with the proper *time* of the match, just as they had agreed not to disrupt the match itself, which had been decreed by God in such a clear manner.

# A Complete Life

וְאֵלֶּה יְמֵי שְׁנֵי־חַיֵּי אַבְרָהָם אֲשֶׁר־חָי מְאַת שָׁנָה וְשִׁבְעִים שָׁנָה
וְחָמֵשׁ שָׁנִים: וַיִּגְוַע וַיָּמָת אַבְרָהָם בְּשֵׂיבָה טוֹבָה זָקֵן וְשָׂבֵעַ וַיֵּאָסֶף
אֶל־עַמָּיו

*And these are the days of the years of Avraham's*
*life which he lived: one hundred years, seventy*
*years, and five years. And Avraham expired and*
*died at a good old age, mature and content, and he*
*was gathered unto his people.*
*(Bereishis 25:7-8)*

When the Torah comes to summarize the life of Avraham Avinu after his passing, it uses the seemingly redundant phrase, "the years of Avraham *which he lived*." A person's life cannot be described in simply quantitative terms, as the number of years he or she existed; only the time that was used properly for serving God can really be termed the time that was "lived."

Even though there were other righteous people before

Avraham, his uniqueness was in the great tests he had passed and the extraordinary challenges with which he had dealt. The first of these challenges was the environment he was born into: the house of Terach and the idolatrous community in which he

> *Only the time that was used properly for serving God can really be termed the time that was "lived."*

lived. Avraham's greatness was that not only was he able to rise above the level of his family and surroundings and move on to a different sort of life, he succeeded also in redeeming those early years of his life and making them part of a seamless whole devoted only to the One true God.

This is the Torah's message here in the words "*which he lived,*" that all of Avraham's 175 years were "lived" in the deepest spiritual sense, and even his childhood that had begun in a milieu of falsehood had served him as a springboard toward truth.

This same phrase is found concerning Adam as well,[5] who through repentance repaired the damage wrought by his sin and thereby made his life a complete unity of devotion to God.

The Torah continues, describing Avraham's death in a way unlike that used for most others, with three different words for death: "*Vayigva*" (expired), "*vayamas*" (died), "*vayei'asef el amav*" (was gathered unto his people).

The first of these, "*vayigva*," denotes the demise of the body itself; "*vayamas*" indicates the separation of the soul from the now-lifeless body; and "*vayei'asef el amav*" refers to the soul's return to the spiritual realm from whence it came and to its eternal reward.

Our Sages[6] note that the words "*vayigva*" and "*vayei'asef*" are only used in connection with the righteous, since only their souls return to the pure spiritual state from where they initiated, and only the demise of their holy bodies is worthy of mention. For all ordinary people, the basic word "*vayamas*" is sufficient, since

---

5. *Bereishis* 5:5.

6. *Bava Basra* 16b.

it denotes the significant event that occurred at their death, the separation of soul from body.

Only for great people like Avraham, and even for those like Yishmael who repented from his earlier errors, does the Torah go into detail about the return of the body to a state of lifeless matter and the restoration of the soul to an eternal Heavenly state.

# פרשת תולדות
# PARASHAS TOLDOS

---

## The Next Generation

וַיְהִי יִצְחָק בֶּן־אַרְבָּעִים שָׁנָה בְּקַחְתּוֹ אֶת־רִבְקָה בַּת־בְּתוּאֵל
הָאֲרַמִּי מִפַּדַּן אֲרָם אֲחוֹת לָבָן הָאֲרַמִּי לוֹ לְאִשָּׁה

*And Yitzchak was forty years old when*
*he married Rivkah, daughter of Besuel*
*the Aramean from Padan Aram,*
*sister of Lavan the Aramean, as his wife.*
**(Bereishis 25:20)**

The world is full of crab-apple trees and trees that bear no fruit at all; they spring up everywhere without any human effort. By contrast, cultivating choice trees which bear luscious fruit requires lots of work and preparation, the right location and the right season.

So, too, in order for God's "Chosen Fruit," Yaakov and his twelve sons, to come into existence, it was necessary that Yitzchak wait until age 40 to marry. Only then, with the boiling urges of youth subsided and his intellect ripened, was Yitzchak fit to produce children "in his image," children who would spring from his now-perfected spiritual aspect. Thus, "*And Yitzchak was forty years old when he married ....*"

Now the Torah tells us God's kindness in preparing a match so well suited for Yitzchak:

"*He married Rivkah,*" the benevolent one who drew water for Eliezer and all of his camels, proving herself worthy of Yitzchak in her own right.

Moreover, she was "*daughter of Besuel,*" Yitzchak's cousin, and "*from Padan Aram,*" Yitzchak's ancestral homeland. Being from his family and homeland, Rivkah was suitable for Yitzchak by nature, just as a sprig taken from one apple tree is suitable to be grafted onto another apple tree without effecting a change in its essence.

> *A sprig taken from one apple tree is suitable to be grafted onto another apple tree without effecting a change in its essence.*

Finally, she was "*sister of Lavan,*" another stroke of Divine Providence. Lavan's house would one day serve Yaakov both as a refuge from his murderous brother Esav, as well as the home of Yaakov's own future wife.

# The Symbolism of
# Yaakov and Esav's Birth

וַיִּתְרֹצֲצוּ הַבָּנִים בְּקִרְבָּהּ וַתֹּאמֶר אִם־כֵּן לָמָּה זֶּה אָנֹכִי וַתֵּלֶךְ
לִדְרֹשׁ אֶת־ה': וַיֹּאמֶר ה' לָהּ שְׁנֵי גיים [גוֹיִם] בְּבִטְנֵךְ וּשְׁנֵי לְאֻמִּים
מִמֵּעַיִךְ יִפָּרֵדוּ וּלְאֹם מִלְאֹם יֶאֱמָץ וְרַב יַעֲבֹד צָעִיר:
וַיִּמְלְאוּ יָמֶיהָ לָלֶדֶת וְהִנֵּה תוֹמִם בְּבִטְנָהּ: וַיֵּצֵא הָרִאשׁוֹן אַדְמוֹנִי
כֻּלּוֹ כְּאַדֶּרֶת שֵׂעָר וַיִּקְרְאוּ שְׁמוֹ עֵשָׂו: וְאַחֲרֵי־כֵן יָצָא אָחִיו
וְיָדוֹ אֹחֶזֶת בַּעֲקֵב עֵשָׂו וַיִּקְרָא שְׁמוֹ יַעֲקֹב ....
וַיִּגְדְּלוּ הַנְּעָרִים וַיְהִי עֵשָׂו אִישׁ יֹדֵעַ צַיִד אִישׁ שָׂדֶה
וְיַעֲקֹב אִישׁ תָּם יֹשֵׁב אֹהָלִים

*And the children struggled within her, and she said,
"If so, why am I thus?" and she went to inquire from
Hashem. And Hashem said to her, "Two nations are
in your womb, and two kingdoms from your insides
shall be separated, and the kingdoms will struggle
with each other for power, and the elder shall serve
the younger."
Her term to bear was completed, and,
behold, there were twins in her womb.
The first one emerged ruddy, entirely like a hairy
mantle, so they called his name Esav. After that his
brother emerged, with his hand gripping Esav's heel,
so he called his name Yaakov ....
And the youths grew up, and Esav was one who
knows trapping, a man of the field, while Yaakov
was a man of perfection and truth, abiding in tents.*
**(Bereishis 25:22-27)**

Man was created as a soul grafted onto a body.

Mankind, too, is comprised of two elements. There
are the holy, godly people, those who so elevate themselves to the point where they are vehicles fit for prophecy, and
then there are the masses.

The first group is Creation's plan and purpose, its *tsurah*, while the latter serves as its *chomer*, the "stuff" of which it consists.

This *tsurah/chomer* paradigm finds symbolic expression in the manner of Yaakov and Esav's birth.

Just as *tsurah* dictates the confines of *chomer*, so, too, "*Rav ya'avod tza'ir,*" the elder, Esav, must serve the younger, Yaakov. The mundane "man of the field" can find purposeful expression only through submission to "*Yaakov, ish tam,*" the person who elevates himself by constantly striving toward spiritual perfection.

> **The mundane "man of the field" can find purposeful expression only through submission to "Yaakov, ish tam," the person who elevates himself by constantly striving toward spiritual perfection.**

Moreover, a person starts life as a baby ruled solely by instincts and desires; only later does the higher faculty of the soul begin to hold sway. Thus, the unbridled Esav appears first on the scene; only afterward does the virtuous Yaakov emerge, holding Esav's heel. Yaakov's grip upon Esav's heel symbolizes that he will prevail in the end, just as the heel is the endmost extremity of the body.

Throughout life, a man's soul and body are in constant conflict. The soul prevails in the virtuous man, while the wicked are ruled by their bodies. So too, "*And the children struggled within her*" — Yaakov and Esav, like soul versus body, were at odds from the very beginning. When Yaakov is righteous, he controls Esav. Otherwise, Esav rules.

Yet, Yaakov and Esav's struggle within the womb did not last forever … rather, "*her term to bear was completed, and, behold, there were twins in her womb.*" Thus, too, the historical strife between the Jews and the nations of the world will eventually disappear with the "birth" of the Messianic age.

# Honest Dealings

וַיָּזֶד יַעֲקֹב נָזִיד וַיָּבֹא עֵשָׂו מִן־הַשָּׂדֶה וְהוּא עָיֵף: וַיֹּאמֶר עֵשָׂו אֶל־
יַעֲקֹב הַלְעִיטֵנִי נָא מִן־הָאָדֹם הָאָדֹם הַזֶּה כִּי עָיֵף אָנֹכִי עַל־כֵּן
קָרָא־שְׁמוֹ אֱדוֹם:
וַיֹּאמֶר יַעֲקֹב מִכְרָה כַיּוֹם אֶת־בְּכֹרָתְךָ לִי:
וַיֹּאמֶר עֵשָׂו הִנֵּה אָנֹכִי הוֹלֵךְ לָמוּת וְלָמָּה־זֶּה לִי בְּכֹרָה:
וַיֹּאמֶר יַעֲקֹב הִשָּׁבְעָה לִּי כַּיּוֹם וַיִּשָּׁבַע לוֹ וַיִּמְכֹּר אֶת־בְּכֹרָתוֹ
לְיַעֲקֹב:
וְיַעֲקֹב נָתַן לְעֵשָׂו לֶחֶם וּנְזִיד עֲדָשִׁים וַיֹּאכַל וַיֵּשְׁתְּ
וַיָּקָם וַיֵּלַךְ וַיִּבֶז עֵשָׂו אֶת הַבְּכֹרָה

*Yaakov was cooking a stew, and Esav
came in from the field, and he was weary.
And Esav said to Yaakov, "Pour into me,
now, some of the red [stuff] to this red [man],
for I am weary"; because of this he called
his name "Edom" [Red].
And Yaakov said, "Sell me, as this day,
your birthright."
And Esav said, "Behold, I am going to die,
so of what use to me is a birthright!"
Yaakov said, "Swear to me, as this day."
He swore to him and he sold Yaakov his birthright.
Yaakov gave Esav bread and lentil stew,
and he ate, and he drank, and he got up and left;
and thus, Esav disdained the birthright.
(Bereishis 25:29-34)*

The concept of the birthright was that the firstborn be separated for Divine service, while the other brothers would engage in mundane worldly matters. Furthermore, upon the firstborn was incumbent managing the estate[1] and seeing

---

1. See *Rashi* to *Bereishis* 15:2 ד״ה וּבֶן מֶשֶׁק בֵּיתִי.

to all the needs of the father, mother, and the members of the household, as the Ran writes.

Now Yaakov's desire for the birthright was not motivated by honor, nor in order to inherit the double portion to which the firstborn is entitled. Rather, Yaakov desired the birthright for its spiritual aspect, the Divine blessings of the soul that accompanied it, as well as the inheritance of the Holy Land. Yaakov saw how utterly unfit Esav was for these things, and he therefore deisired them for himself..

The extent to which Esav had despised his birthright and had distanced himself from his obligations as firstborn are illustrated here in the Torah's description of the sale of that birthright:

First, we find that *"Yaakov was cooking a stew"* to provide food for the family. Overseeing and providing for the needs of the household was Esav's responsibility, but one which he shirked, choosing instead to be a *"man of the field."* In light of our Sages' statement[2] that this was no ordinary stew, but rather the mourner's meal prepared for Yitzchak upon the death of Avraham, Esav's negligence here was particularly reprehensible. Instead of taking the helm during his father's time of crisis, *"Esav came in from the field"* where he had gone for a hunt.

Next, the Torah tells us that Esav was *"weary,"* which our Sages[3] equate with a spiritual weariness, resulting from Esav's criminal activities of murder and plunder.

*"Haliteini, na* — Pour it into me, now!" says Esav as he bursts in from the field, without so much as stopping to catch his breath. His gluttony doesn't even allow him to recognize what type of food it is; rather, he demands *"some of the red"* stuff.

---

2. *Bereishis Rabbah* 63:11, *Yalkut Shimoni Bereishis* 25:110.

3. *Bava Basra* 16b.

Esav tells Yaakov to feed "*some of the red [stuff] to this red [man],*" referring to *himself* as "*this red*" one. With this unabashed portrayal of himself as "the red man who loves red food," Esav shows that he *identifies* with his hot-blooded, impetuous temperament so much so that he takes pride in the fact that he loves everything that is the color of blood. Therefore, "*he*" — Esav himself — "*called his name 'Edom' [Red].*" Rather than feel shame at his criminal exploits, Esav revels in and boasts of his unbridled, bloodthirsty nature that brings him to murder and to all other forms of immorality.

The clearest indication of Esav's unworthiness of the birthright is in his own repudiation of it: "*Behold, I am going to die, so of what use to me is a birthright?*" Esav said: "The birthright's only value is the spiritual reward it brings in the afterlife; if so, I don't need it, because I don't believe in the afterlife," thereby rejecting the basic principle of *emunah*.

Even after eating and drinking his fill, "*Esav disdained the birthright.*" With this the Torah informs us that Esav did not sell the birthright out of hunger, or out of desire for this particular food; for if that had been the case, then he would have regretted his decision immediately upon eating and drinking, once his cravings had been satisfied. Rather, the birthright was something that Esav regarded as a worthless burden, and he was only too glad to have Yaakov take it off his hands.

# Sustained in Famine

וַיְהִי רָעָב בָּאָרֶץ מִלְּבַד הָרָעָב הָרִאשׁוֹן אֲשֶׁר הָיָה בִּימֵי
אַבְרָהָם וַיֵּלֶךְ יִצְחָק אֶל־אֲבִימֶלֶךְ מֶלֶךְ־פְּלִשְׁתִּים גְּרָרָה׃
וַיֵּרָא אֵלָיו ה' וַיֹּאמֶר אַל־תֵּרֵד מִצְרָיְמָה שְׁכֹן בָּאָרֶץ
אֲשֶׁר אֹמַר אֵלֶיךָ׃ גּוּר בָּאָרֶץ הַזֹּאת וְאֶהְיֶה עִמְּךָ וַאֲבָרְכֶךָ

*And there was a famine in the land, apart from the*
*first famine that was in the days of Avraham;*
*and Yitzchak went to Avimelech, king of Philistine,*
*to Gerar. And Hashem appeared to him and said,*
*"Do not descend to Mitzrayim; dwell in the land*
*that I will indicate to you. Sojourn in this land,*
*and I will be with you and I will bless you ...."*
*(Bereishis 26:1-3)*

The difference between Avraham and Yitzchak in regard to the level of Divine Providence each one experienced is remarkable. During the first famine, Avraham needed to leave the Land of Israel and migrate to Mitzrayim to find food; Hashem did not single him out from the rest of the Canaanite population for unique or miraculous kindness. Yitzchak, on the other hand, merits a prophetic revelation in which Hashem tells him: *"Do not descend to Mitzrayim,"* but rather *"Sojourn in this land, and I will be with you and I will bless you ..."* In other words, "Despite the severe famine that plagues everybody else, you, Yitzchak, will enjoy special Divine protection and prosperity."

There are several reasons for this difference:

The first reason is that the famine served as one of the "ten tests" with which Hashem tested Avraham Avinu, as our Sages[4] tell us. Avraham originally came to his recognition of the Creator through philosophical investigation and inquiry. Hashem, however, wanted Avraham to go beyond this level, to believe

---

4. *Pirkei Avos* 5:4.

in Him with a complete and total faith, *emunah* unbounded by "proofs of God's existence." Through the "ten tests," Avraham's true mettle would be brought out into the open: Would he follow Hashem no matter what, or would he begin having doubts? Avraham's "exile" to Mitzrayim was one of these tests.

Yitzchak, on the other hand, had no need for such tests, because he was already strong and steady in his *emunah*, having received it as a tradition from his father. Thus, he is promised special protection and blessing.

To make this point, the Torah notes that this famine was *"apart from the first famine that was in the days of Avraham,"* an otherwise obvious assertion. Rather, the Torah means that this famine was altogether different from the first famine in its nature and purpose: Whereas the first famine served as a test for Avraham, the second famine served as an opportunity for Heaven to single out Yitzchak for unique and miraculous Providence, protecting him from kings and prospering him *"a hundredfold"* while the rest of the land searched for bread.

A second reason Avraham did not merit the same level of Divine Providence afforded Yitzchak was that Avraham had not yet achieved the perfection to be worthy of such. When the first famine struck, Avraham himself had not yet undergone *bris milah*, nor had Hashem yet made the *Bris Bein Habesarim*, the "Covenant Between the Parts," with Avraham.

The Land, too, for its part, had not yet achieved the holiness required for it to serve as host for the kind of miraculous prosperity that Yitzchak was granted. True, God had already promised to give the Land to Avraham and to his offspring; however, Avraham had not actually acquired it yet.

Only after Avraham's return from Mitzrayim, and after Lot's separation from him, did Hashem tell Avraham, "Arise and walk about the land, through its length and breadth." By doing so, say our Sages,[5] Avraham thereby acquired the Land through "*chaza-kah*," a legal demonstration of ownership. With this act, the Land was elevated to a new status, a level of sanctity whereby seemingly "natural" events such as famine would now be directed from above by special *hashgachah pratis*.

Under this new order, the *tzaddik* could be miraculously exempted from the fallout of a national catastrophe, his fields blooming while all others withered. Outside the Land of Israel — or even in it but before Avraham acquired it — the *tzaddik* would be included in the general decree; or, if spared, spared through hidden miracles via "nature."

> **Under this new order, the tzaddik could be miraculously exempted from the fallout of a national catastrophe, his fields blooming while all others withered.**

For all these reasons, this famine was altogether "*apart from the first famine*," both in its purpose, in regard to the spiritual level of those whom it affected, and in regard to the holiness of the Land in which it occurred.

# Two Types of Exile

וַיְהִי רָעָב בָּאָרֶץ ... וַיֵּלֶךְ יִצְחָק אֶל־אֲבִימֶלֶךְ מֶלֶךְ־פְּלִשְׁתִּים גְּרָרָה: וַיֵּרָא אֵלָיו ה' וַיֹּאמֶר אַל־תֵּרֵד מִצְרָיְמָה ... גּוּר בָּאָרֶץ הַזֹּאת

*And there was a famine in the land ... and Yitzchak went to Avimelech, king of Philistine, to Gerar. And Hashem appeared to him and said, "Do not descend to Mitzrayim .... Sojourn in this land ...."*
**(Bereishis 26:1-3)**

---

5. *Bava Basra* 100a.

I f there is famine in the city," our Sages state,[6] "get yourself out of there"; and "If one has it bad in this city, he should go to a different city,"[7] We see this rule illustrated by the example of Yitzchak who, in order to avoid the famine, went to Gerar. Finding the famine there as well, he considered going to Mitzrayim, as Avraham had during the first famine.

The question may be asked: How can a person think to avoid a decree from Heaven simply by relocating? You can't "run away" from God! This question was asked to the Rashba,[8] and he gave two answers:

One answer is that when a Divine decree is visited upon a certain place, all those in that place — even individuals not specifically deserving of that decree — are included by virtue of their being part of the general populace. Thus, by relocating, the righteous individual excludes himself from the decree.

*How can a person think to avoid a decree from Heaven simply by relocating?*

The second answer is that, even if the decree *was* directed specifically at this particular person, perhaps its purpose was to force him into "exile," the subsequent hardships of travel and disorientation atoning for whatever brought about the decree in the first place.

Now, exile can express itself in one of two ways: either through actual physical displacement and traveling from place to place, or through the alienation and estrangement of a person who considers himself as though he is in exile, even though he remains permanently in one location.

It was this second type of exile to which Yitzchak would be subject. At the *Bris Bein Habesarim*, Hashem said to Avraham: "... for your offspring will be *geirim* [sojourners] in a land not their own ...."[9] Here, in fulfillment of this prophecy, Hashem

---

6. *Bava Kamma* 60b.

7. *Bava Metzia* 75b.

8. *Teshuvas Rashba Chelek Alef, Siman* 19.

9. *Bereishis* 15:13.

tells Yitzchak, "*Sojourn [gur] in this land,*" using the word "*gur*" which implies the displaced existence of an outsider. Thus, the exile decreed upon the seed of Avraham, which began with the birth of Yitzchak, would continue "*in this land.*"

# Starring the Jewish People

וְהִרְבֵּיתִי אֶת־זַרְעֲךָ כְּכוֹכְבֵי הַשָּׁמַיִם וְנָתַתִּי לְזַרְעֲךָ אֵת כָּל־
הָאֲרָצֹת הָאֵל וְהִתְבָּרְכוּ בְזַרְעֲךָ כֹּל גּוֹיֵי הָאָרֶץ

*"And I will increase your offspring like the stars*
*of the heavens, and I will give to your offspring*
*all these lands, and through your offspring*
*all the peoples of the world will be blessed."*
*(Bereishis 26:4)*

The truly righteous person, the *tzaddik*, is like a pipeline via which Heaven showers its blessings upon the earth; as our Sages[10] say, "[All the nations are] blessed because of Israel."

In this vein, Hashem told Yitzchak that his offspring would eventually be like the "*stars of the heavens,*" not only in number, but in regard to the benevolent influence that they would bring to the world as well. For just as the stars channel blessing upon the earth, each country having its own specific heavenly body that serves as a conduit directing

*For just as the stars channel blessing upon the earth, each country having its own specific heavenly body that serves as a conduit directing toward that place energy and blessing derived from Above, so too the Jewish people would eventually bring a flow of blessing to mankind.*

10. *Yevamos* 63a.

toward that place energy and blessing derived from Above, so too the Jewish people would eventually bring a flow of blessing to mankind.

This, however, will occur only when "*I will give to your off-spring all these lands.*" Then, their own merit, when coupled with the special degree of godliness that they can only achieve by living in the Holy Land, will grow to the point that they become that pipeline of blessing for the entire world, at which point "*through your offspring all the peoples of the world will be blessed.*"

# Yitzchak's Wife

... וַיֹּאמֶר אֲחֹתִי הִוא כִּי יָרֵא לֵאמֹר אִשְׁתִּי פֶּן־יַהַרְגֻנִי אַנְשֵׁי
הַמָּקוֹם עַל־רִבְקָה כִּי־טוֹבַת מַרְאֶה הִוא: וַיְהִי כִּי־אָרְכוּ־לוֹ שָׁם
הַיָּמִים וַיַּשְׁקֵף אֲבִימֶלֶךְ מֶלֶךְ פְּלִשְׁתִּים בְּעַד הַחַלּוֹן וַיַּרְא וְהִנֵּה
יִצְחָק מְצַחֵק אֵת רִבְקָה אִשְׁתּוֹ

*... He said, "She is my sister," for he was afraid
to say, "My wife" — "lest the people of the place
kill me because of Rivkah, for she is beautiful to
behold." And it was, when he was there for many
days, that Avimelech, king of Philistine,
peered through the window and saw, and behold!
Yitzchak was sporting with Rivkah, his wife.*
**(Bereishis 26:7-8)**

Here again we see Hashem's Providential approach toward Yitzchak, noteworthy in its contrast to that experienced by Avraham (see "Sustained in Famine" to verses 26:1-3):[11] The *hashgachah* manifested itself here in two ways:

---

11. For the contrast to Avraham see "Avram and His Sister" to *Bereishis* 12:13.

The first is that, unlike Sarah, who was taken forcibly to the houses of both Pharaoh and Avimelech, Rivkah was spared such a fate. Although Avimelech certainly desired to take Rivkah for himself, yet Hashem put caution into his heart, so that he merely *"peered through the window"* to investigate her true marital status, but not daring to take actual measures to procure her as his wife.

Secondly, Avimelech had a perfect excuse here to execute Yitzchak in a way that would have been totally legal and that would have rendered Avimelech completely blameless, and yet Hashem saved Yitzchak from this danger as well:

> *Avimelech had a perfect excuse here to execute Yitzchak in a way that would have been totally legal and that would have rendered Avimelech completely blameless.*

Under the *"Sheva Mitzvos B'nei Noach,"* the "Noachide laws," a person is not allowed to marry his sister,[12] and he is liable to the death penalty for doing so. Yet here, with Avimelech as witness, *"Yitzchak was sporting with Rivkah,"* who was *"his wife"* in reality, but who for all legal purposes was his sister according to Yitzchak's own admission!

For Yitzchak had not made a mere *one-time* claim that Rivkah was his sister, a claim he could quickly recant; rather, *"he was there for many days"* under this assumed identity, and had thereby established his brotherly relationship as a legal reality. (According to Jewish[13] and Noachide laws alike, when a relationship such as this is claimed and then assumed for thirty days,[14] it becomes a *chazakah,* a halachically established presumption that the parties may no longer deny; and it is basis enough to subject the parties to the death penalty.)

---

12. From the same mother (Malbim).

13. *Tractate Kiddushin* 80a.

14. *B'derech melitzah,* one can say that the Torah hints to this by saying that Avimelech looked at the "חלון" ("window"), whose letters rearrange to spell חנו ל', meaning *"they dwelt for 30"* days [R.Subar].

Nevertheless, Hashem put it into Avimelech's heart to believe Yitzchak and to consider him righteous, and thus Hashem protected Yitzchak from yet another danger.

# Yitzchak's Calculation

וַיְהִי כִּי־זָקֵן יִצְחָק ... וַיִּקְרָא אֶת־עֵשָׂו בְּנוֹ הַגָּדֹל ... וַיֹּאמֶר הִנֵּה־נָא זָקַנְתִּי לֹא יָדַעְתִּי יוֹם מוֹתִי ... בַּעֲבוּר תְּבָרֶכְךָ נַפְשִׁי בְּטֶרֶם אָמוּת

*And it was when Yitzchak became old ... that he called to his elder son, Esav .... And he said, "Behold, now, I have become old; I do not know when I will die. ... so that my soul may bless you before I die."*
*(Bereishis 27:1,2,4)*

Among the many difficulties presented by this section of the Torah is the question why Yitzchak wanted to bless Esav over Yaakov. Didn't he realize that Yaakov was a righteous person and that Esav was not? And why couldn't he bless them both, just as we see that Yaakov blessed each of his sons?

The purpose of the entire Creation is that there exist a good and righteous person upon whom God's *hashgachah* can rest, a person who will serve as an abode for God's Divine presence to dwell here on earth. We see this from the verse in *Koheles*[15] "*...fear God and keep His commandments, for this is all the man,*" which the Sages explain to mean, "the entire world was created only for [the righteous person's] sake."[16]

Such a person, however, is very rare, very hard to come by; and because he can't be in the world all by himself, therefore all the multitude of humankind was created along with him in order to attend him and to see to all his needs, as the Sages

---

15. *Koheles* 12:13.
16. *Berachos* 6b.

say, "the entire world was created to attend to this person."[17]

By way of analogy, consider a tree. A tree has numerous roots, branches, bark, leaves, and peels, but the most important part of the tree is its fruit. Yet, the fruit is very small in quantity compared with the rest of the tree, with all its bark, branches, roots, etc.

Hashem desired that there be an entire nation who would cleave to the Divine idea, and from whom would emanate prophets, *tzaddikim,* princes of holiness, people who fear God. This nation would fulfill the purpose of the Creation and be God's "holy fruit."

It is not possible, though, for the entire nation to engage in Divine pursuits, for, who, then, would produce their food and provide all their needs? Therefore, God singled out the Tribe of Levi to be separate from all worldly things, designated solely for service of Hashem, and the rest of the Jewish nation would bear the burden of supplying their needs by giving the Levites *maaser,* ten percent of their produce. A Levite would have no portion or "inheritance of field or orchard," for "*Hashem is his inheritance*"[18] and he would be the one to draw close to God, as Moses said to the Levites: "*… that the God of Israel separated you from out of the congregation of Israel, to draw you close to Him.*"[19]

Through this arrangement, the rest of the Jewish people are able to take part in the reward that a Levite receives for his righteous acts and his service of God, since he is their agent for this Divine service, and they relieve him of his duty to labor in the field by providing him with his day-to-day needs. Thereby, both the Israelites and the Levites will be blessed in this world and the next.

The Israelites would thus serve as a kind of intermediate stage between the nations of the world and the Tribe of Levi, just as

---

17. Ibid.

18. *Devarim* 10:9, 18:2.

19. *Bamidbar* 16:9.

we find in the physical world that *almog* is a form of life midway between inert matter and vegetation, and *filif* is an intermediary stage between plant and animal life. So too, the Israelites were to be the intermediaries between the Tribe of Levi, who are holy to God, and the nations, who cleave to the mundane and the earthly.

Now, Hashem had blessed Avraham that a treasured nation would emerge from his offspring, a nation that would be God's chosen people and who would inherit the Land of Israel.

But Avraham did not give this blessing to Yitzchak, for no person has the power to bequeath this blessing to his child. Yitzchak, as well, did not intend to bless Yaakov with Avraham's blessing, for he knew that his blessing would not achieve anything; rather, whoever was fitting to receive this blessing would be blessed with it directly from Hashem.[20]

Thus you see that the blessing Yitzchak gives now to Yaakov and Esav was "*from the dew of the Heaven*" and "*abundant grain and wine,*"[21] but he makes no mention at all of inheriting the Land of Israel, nor about Hashem being their God, because this is a spiritual blessing, one that is not in Yitzchak's power to give over to his sons.[22]

What inspires Yitzchak now to bless Esav?

As stated in the previous verses,[23] Esav had married two women from the daughters of Canaan, and their evil ways brought bitter heartache to Yitzchak and Rivkah. Through this, Yitzchak realized that Esav was unsuitable for the "Blessings of

---

20. For this same reason, Yaakov did not bless his son Levi, because Yaakov saw prophetically that the tribe of Levi would be God's servants in the *Beis HaMikdash*, and this sort of blessing comes from God alone (*Malbim*).

21. *Bereishis* 27:28.

22. Later (*Bereishis* 28:3-4) when Yitzchak says, "*May God bless you [Yaakov] ... and give you the blessings of Avraham ... to inherit the Land ...,*" Yitzchak is not blessing Yaakov but praying that God do so, as the wording of the verse implies.

23. *Bereishis* 26:34-35.

Avraham," and that Yaakov alone was fitting to receive them. Seeing that Yaakov had acquired the birthright and the Divine service that goes along with it, and seeing that Yaakov, through his righteousness, had become a truly holy man of God, Yitzchak understood that Yaakov alone would be the one to inherit the blessings of Avraham, and that all Yaakov's offspring would be singled out to be servants of God.

Realizing all this, Yitzchak began to have troubling thoughts regarding *both* of his sons:

Yitzchak worried that Esav — who, due to his evil ways, had been rejected as the firstborn and excluded from Avraham's blessings — would become just like any one of the other families of the earth.

And he worried that Yaakov — because all his seed would be designated for Divine service — would be unable to work the soil or engage in other earthly matters. For such pursuits would cause them to cease their Divine service, as the Sages say: "Is it possible for a man to plow in the plowing season and plant in the planting season ...? When will his Torah study get done?"[24] And who would fight Yaakov's wars, to defend him against all enemies? Since the strong of soul are feeble of body, how could Yaakov defend himself against the mighty warriors who would rise to attack him and to conquer his land?

Thus, Yitzchak carefully considered what to do so that *neither* of his sons would be lost: neither Yaakov, in his humility and physical weakness, nor Esav, in having rejected the birthright and having become a "man of the field."

Yitzchak decided, therefore, that his two sons should become one nation, like the Israelites and the Levites. Esav would receive Yitzchak's blessing for abundant wealth, grain, wine, military might, and rulership. The seed of Yaakov, on the other hand, would be designated solely for Divine service, just as the Tribe of Levi was to be in the future. Under this arrangement, Yitzchak hoped that the children of Esav would serve as this intermediate

---

24. *Berachos* 35b.

stage between the Children of Israel and the gentiles, as actually occurred later to the Israelites in relation to the Tribe of Levi.

With this in mind, Yitzchak decides to bless Esav, hoping that through this blessing Esav will become worthy to receive the "fat of the land" and "abundant grain and wine," to rule nations and to command regimes. As for Yaakov, Yitzchak had no intention to bless him, because Yaakov's blessing would be a spiritual one, emanating directly from God alone.

And then, when the time would come for God to give the Torah, the seed of Yaakov would be chosen as God's servants, guardians of holiness, and the seed of Esav would provide their needs and protect them, just as the peel and the leaves protect the fruit.

> *Yitzchak decided, therefore, that his two sons should become one nation, like the Israelites and the Levites. Esav would receive Yitzchak's blessing for abundant wealth, grain, wine, military might, and rulership. The seed of Yaakov, on the other hand, would be designated solely for Divine service, just as the Tribe of Levi was to be in the future.*

# Food for Blessing

וַיִּקְרָא אֶת־עֵשָׂו בְּנוֹ הַגָּדֹל וַיֹּאמֶר אֵלָיו בְּנִי וַיֹּאמֶר אֵלָיו הִנֵּנִי׃ ...
וַיֹּאמֶר הִנֵּה־נָא זָקַנְתִּי לֹא יָדַעְתִּי יוֹם מוֹתִי׃ וְעַתָּה שָׂא־נָא
כֵלֶיךָ תֶּלְיְךָ וְקַשְׁתֶּךָ וְצֵא הַשָּׂדֶה וְצוּדָה לִּי צֵידה [צָיִד] ׃
וַעֲשֵׂה־לִי מַטְעַמִּים כַּאֲשֶׁר אָהַבְתִּי וְהָבִיאָה לִּי
וְאֹכֵלָה בַּעֲבוּר תְּבָרֶכְךָ נַפְשִׁי בְּטֶרֶם אָמוּת

*... He called his elder son Esav and said to him,*
*"My son," and he said to him, "Here I am."*

*He said, "Behold, now, I have become old;*
*I do not know when I will die. Now, therefore,*
*take up your equipment, your sword and your bow,*
*and go out to the field and hunt game for me.*
*Then make me delicacies such as I love and bring*
*it to me, and I will eat, in order that my*
*soul may bless you before I die."*
*(Bereishis 27:1-4)*

As a prelude to blessing Esav, Yitzchak commanded Esav to prepare him delicious food. The reason Yitzchak did this revolves around the very essence of what a blessing is.

Giving a blessing is a spiritual happening. The concept behind it is that the one giving the blessing uses spiritual strength to ascend and connect his soul with the Supernal Source of blessing, from the place in Heaven where the "waters of blessing" flow as if from a receptacle onto the recipient.

But the recipient must be a fitting vessel for this. If he is not up to par, the one giving the blessing, through his own spiritual elevation, can help prepare the recipient to receive the shower of blessing by establishing a spiritual connection with the recipient and by boosting him to a higher plane of spirituality.

Thus the Torah tells us that first, Yitzchak invokes his soul's connection to Esav by saying, "*My son*"; Esav answers, "*Here*

*I am*," reciprocating Yitzchak's call for spiritual fusion and thus showing his preparedness for the blessing.

To help elevate Esav, Yitzchak gives him an opportunity to fulfill the commandment to "honor your father," which is a particular mitzvah for which the Torah promises long life in this world.[25] Why did Yitzchak choose this particular commandment?

There are three partners in a person, his father, his mother, and Hashem: Hashem creating the *tzurah* (abstract form) and the father and mother preparing the *chomer* (physical form). Therefore, when someone fulfills Hashem's command to honor his parents, who created his *chomer*, he receives an extended life of his body in this world; and, since he honors Hashem as well Who created the soul, he will get the spiritual reward in the next world.

> *Someone who goes out to trap a few birds does not usually bring all his hunting gear with him. Yitzchak, however, commanded Esav to take all his equipment as though he were going on a major hunting expedition. "And go out to the field," he told him, "even if you have animals or birds at home that you have previously trapped ...."*

In order that Esav receive the blessings of this world, Yitzchak commanded him in the mitzvah of honoring his father. To add to the spiritual dimension of the mitzvah, that it be done in a full fashion, Yitzchak commanded that Esav perform it with the maximum activity, effort, and preparation. Therefore, Yitzchak said, "*Take up your equipment, your sword and your bow*"; even though someone who goes out to trap a few birds does not usually bring all his hunting gear with him, Yitzchak, however, commanded Esav to take all his equipment as though he were going on a major hunting expedition. "*And go out to the field*," he told him, "even if you have animals or birds at home that you have previously trapped; nevertheless, go out to the field and hunt '*for my sake*,' deliberately for the mitzvah of '*honor your father....*'"

---

25. *Shemos* 20:12, *Devarim* 5:16.

# Rivkah's Calculation

וְרִבְקָה שֹׁמַעַת בְּדַבֵּר יִצְחָק אֶל־עֵשָׂו ...

*And Rivkah heard Yitzchak speaking to Esav ....*
*(Bereishis 27:5)*

The verb "*li'shmoa*" can mean "to hear," or it can mean "to understand." Here, it takes on the second meaning:[26] Rivkah not only heard, but she understood Yitzchak's intentions to bind the two sons together into a "Yissachar/Zevulun" or "Levite/Israelite" type of relationship, whereby Yaakov would engage in Torah studies while Esav would support, shield, and protect him.

Rivkah understood all too well Esav's evil, wicked nature. Not only would Esav fail to shield and protect Yaakov as a peel protects a fruit, on the contrary, he would be the all-devouring insect, the devastating rot. Any wealth or power that Yitzchak would bestow upon Esav would be used not *for* Yaakov but against him; and this would be to the ultimate detriment of *both* of her children.

Therefore, Rivkah decided that it would be best if Yaakov received the "this-worldly" blessings of wealth and sovereignty, and that this would not necessarily present a contradiction to his spiritual pursuits.

Because, for the truly righteous person, spiritual and physical success can dwell side by side, provided he uses his wealth and power solely for his spiritual advancement. For this reason, too, the Levites in the future *are* destined to have a portion in the Land:[27] When "the land will be full of knowledge of Hashem"[28] and "the spirit of *tumah* I [Hashem] will wipe away from the

---

26. Malbim's cue for this insight may be the construction "*shoma'as b-*," she heard "into," i.e., understood, as opposed to simply "*shoma'as es*," "she heard."

27. *Bava Basra* 122a; *S'mag Lavin*, Mitzvah 277.

28. *Yeshayahu* 11:9.

earth,"[29] at that time wealth and dominion will no longer distract the Levites from their Divine service. Rather than individuals "winning the battles" against their evil inclination, the evil inclination will surrender altogether and join the side of good. No longer will the evil inclination desire anything physical, except that which the soul requires as a springboard toward spiritual success. This is to be the level of the Jewish people in the world of the future.

> **Rather than individuals "winning the battles" against their evil inclination, the evil inclination will surrender altogether and join the side of good.**

With this in mind, Rivkah calculated that *both* sons would be more successful via this arrangement: Yaakov would have the blessings of this world, while Esav would be the vassal over whom Yaakov would rule, with the spirit *and* the sword, as indeed occurred all the days of David HaMelech, Shlomo HaMelech, all the righteous kings of Israel,[30] and when the Israel conquered the Edomites in the time of Herod.

---

29. *Zechariah* 13:2.

30. These first three examples are interpolated from Malbim to *Bereishis* 27:40.

# פרשת ויצא
# PARASHAS VAYEITZEI

## Seeing Versus Knowing:
## The Rungs of Prophecy

וַיֵּצֵא יַעֲקֹב מִבְּאֵר שָׁבַע וַיֵּלֶךְ חָרָנָה: וַיִּפְגַּע בַּמָּקוֹם וַיָּלֶן שָׁם כִּי־
בָא הַשֶּׁמֶשׁ וַיִּקַּח מֵאַבְנֵי הַמָּקוֹם וַיָּשֶׂם מְרַאֲשֹׁתָיו וַיִּשְׁכַּב בַּמָּקוֹם
הַהוּא:
וַיַּחֲלֹם וְהִנֵּה סֻלָּם מֻצָּב אַרְצָה וְרֹאשׁוֹ מַגִּיעַ הַשָּׁמָיְמָה וְהִנֵּה
מַלְאֲכֵי אֱלֹקִים עֹלִים וְיֹרְדִים בּוֹ: וְהִנֵּה ה' נִצָּב עָלָיו ...
... וַיִּיקַץ יַעֲקֹב מִשְּׁנָתוֹ וַיֹּאמֶר אָכֵן יֵשׁ ה' בַּמָּקוֹם הַזֶּה וְאָנֹכִי לֹא
יָדָעְתִּי

*And Yaakov left Be'er Sheva and went toward*
*Charan. He chanced upon the place and spent the*
*night there, for the sun had set; and he took from*

*the stones of the place, and he put them at his*
*head, and he lay down in that place.*
*And he dreamed, and behold, a ladder was standing*
*earthward, with its head reaching to the heavens,*
*and, behold, angels from God were going up and*
*down upon it. And, behold, Hashem was standing*
*upon him ....*
*... And Yaakov awoke from his sleep and he said,*
*"In truth, Hashem is here in this place,*
*and I did not know."*
*(Bereishis 28:10-13,16)*

Being a prophet required such an extremely lofty level of holiness that today we can barely relate to it.

Nonetheless, even among the ancient Jewish prophets, there were many different levels of prophecy, one above the other. These levels depended upon several things, including the individual capabilities of the particular prophet, and upon his particular state of preparedness at the time of the prophecy.

In relating Yaakov's vision of the ladder, the angels climbing it, and finally of God speaking to him, the Torah here gives us a picture of a prophecy that, as exalted as it was, was relatively low level, "deficient" in some sense, especially when compared with that of Moshe Rabbeinu.

This "deficiency" expressed itself in several ways, whether in terms of the place of the prophecy, Yaakov's preparation for the prophecy, and in regard to the properties of the vision itself, as follows:

Perfection of prophecy requires that it occur in a holy place, as our Sages[1] point out that all the prophets prophesied exclusively in Eretz Yisrael, whereas this prophecy occurred after Yaakov had already *"left Be'er Sheva and went toward Charan."* For, although he had not yet left the Holy Land, yet Yaakov had already initiated the *process* of uprooting himself from it, and

---

1. *Sifri: Shoftim 32.*

this was enough to begin to dim the prophetic glow that radiates only in the Land of Israel.

Next comes the question of Yaakov's prophetic capabilities. The Sages[2] tell us that among the preconditions of prophecy are that the prophet be a person of might, wealth, and wisdom. Here the Torah depicts Yaakov as "deficient" in all three of these areas:

- **Might:** The Torah tells us that Yaakov "*chanced upon the place and spent the night there, for the sun had set.*" Afraid to travel at night, and afraid to enter any settlement where Esav might be able to track him down, Yaakov spent the night out in the wild. Apparently, Yaakov felt he lacked the physical and emotional strength needed to face his enemies.

- **Wealth:** The Torah says that Yaakov "*took from the stones of the place, and he put them at his head,*" because he had nothing else, neither cushion nor pillow, upon which to place his head. Thus, having fled his father's house with nothing more than his walking stick,[3] Yaakov lacked another prerequisite of prophecy: wealth.

- **Wisdom:** The Torah states that Yaakov "*lay down in that place*" to go to sleep, illustrating Yaakov's lack of preparedness[4] in the third prerequisite of prophecy: wisdom. For it is not enough that the prophet be a wise person, as Yaakov surely was; rather, he must be actively engaged in wisdom as a prelude to the prophecy, mentally preparing himself through deep and contemplative Torah study, not lying down and going to sleep.

---

2. *Shabbos 92a.*

3. Or because Eliphaz, the son of Esav, caught up to him and took everything he possessed, as our Sages tell us (*Rashi to Bereishis* 29:11) [Malbim].

4. No lack, *chas v'shalom*, is implied in Yaakov's essential wisdom, only in his lack of preparedness at that prophetic moment.

"*And he dreamed ....*" Now the Torah relates the four deficiencies in the prophecy itself; these are the four ways in which the prophecy of Moshe Rabbeinu differs from that of all the other prophets:

- **Dreaming Versus Waking:** The lower-level prophecy comes in a dream, as opposed to the prophecy of Moshe to whom God spoke while he was in a waking state. Thus it says here, "*and he dreamed.*"

- **Image Versus Speech:** The lower-level prophecy comes in allegorical form, in puzzling imagery; the less understandable the imagery, the lower the prophetic level. To this the Torah states, "*and behold, a ladder was standing earthward, with its head reaching to the heavens*"; a rather puzzling image, and one that until today is not clearly understood[5] (see next section for Malbim's explanation of it). By contrast, Moshe's prophecy was as clear as "a man who speaks to his friend, face-to-face."[6]

- **Directly Versus Proxy:** The prophecy that comes via the "*aspeklaria she'einah me'irah,*" the "nonradiant prism," comes via a *malach*, a heavenly emissary, as opposed to directly from God. To this it states, "*and behold, angels from God were going up and down upon it,*" these being the angels who were the conveyors of this prophecy to Yaakov.

- **Visualization Versus Pure Cognizance:** Intertwined with the lower-level prophecy are the prophet's own powers of visualization and imagination. To this it states, "*And behold, Hashem was standing upon him*"; in Yaakov's imagination, it appeared as though Hashem were standing there in that place. The prophecy of Moshe, by

---

5. Although Malbim himself does offer an explanation here in his *Torah Or* commentary, nonetheless the ladder imagery remains rather obscure (Editor).

6. *Shemos* 33:11.

contrast, went beyond the level of *seeing* to the level of *knowing*.

This last point is made in the verse in *Sefer Shemos, Parashas Va'eira.*[7] There Hashem tells Moshe: "I *appeared* to Avraham, to Yitzchak, and to Yaakov ... but with My Name, Hashem, I was not *known* to them." The *Zohar*[8] contrasts the two verbs used in this verse, "*appearing*" as opposed to "*knowing*": Hashem "*appeared* to them," a prophetic experience limited by visualization, but "was not *known* to them." Moshe's prophecy, via the "*aspeklaria meirah,*" the "radiant prism," brought him to the higher level of *knowing*, beyond that which any visualization can afford.

Thus, when Yaakov awoke he said, "*In truth, Hashem is here in this place, and I did not know.*" He meant: "Since I envisioned Hashem '*here in this place,*' an almost physical description, it must be that '*I did not know,*' i.e., I did not reach the level of prophecy characterized by 'knowing,' only that of 'seeing.' "

# Angelic Directions

T he symbolism of "Jacob's Ladder" has always been a puzzling one. It has no immediately apparent connection to the narrative, nor to the prophetic promise of Divine protection that follows it. What particular message was Yaakov Avinu meant to learn from this vision?

In answer, let us ask another question: One would expect

*The vision of "Jacob's Ladder" is a rather puzzling one, and one that until today is not clearly understood.*

7. *Shemos* 6:3.
8. *Zohar Chelek B*, 23b.

"*angels of God*" to first descend from the heavens, and only afterward — after completing the Divine mission for which they were sent to earth — to go back up. Why did Yaakov envision the opposite, angels first "*going up*" and only afterward "*going down*"?

In *Pirkei Avos,*[9] the Sages teach that each time a person performs a mitzvah, he creates a spiritual energy, an "angel." This angel then ascends to Heaven and advocates on behalf of the person who created it.

In response to this, Hashem sends other angels, heavenly emissaries, down to earth. These guardian angels protect and guide the person, and infuse his world with positive influences.

Thus, the ascending angels, by their very essence, trigger a cascade of blessing, Divine energy flowing from above to below; and in this way the person himself, through his own actions, creates the degree of Divine Providence and protection that he receives.

> *The ascending angels, by their very essence, trigger a cascade of blessing, Divine energy flowing from above to below.*

This is what Yaakov was being shown here: The angels going up the ladder were those that *he himself* had created: his "mitzvah angels," born of his righteous deeds, and his "Torah angels," born through his intensive Torah study. Ascending, these aroused other angels, angels of Providence, to descend and protect him.

According to the Midrash,[10] this ladder had four rungs. Through sanctifying his interactions with all four levels of the lower realm — *domeim* (inert matter), *tzomei'ach* (plant life), *chai* (animals), and *medabeir* ("the speaker," i.e., human beings) — Yaakov drew Divine energy down through all four hierarchical channels of the upper realms, known in Kabbalah[11] as the worlds of *Atzilus* (Emanations), *Beriyah* (Creation), *Yetzirah* (Formation), and *Asiyah* (Action).

---

9. *Pirkei Avos* 4:13.

10. Brought in *Kli Yakar Bereishis* 1:1, *Shelah,* and elsewhere.

11. *Sefer Chesed L'Avraham* 4:30.

With this explanation in mind, an obscure Midrash suddenly becomes clear. The Midrash[12] says that the *"angels from God were going up and down,"* not *"upon it"* (Hebrew having no gender-neutral pronoun), but *"upon him,"* on Yaakov himself. Yaakov, through his deeds, regulates the Divine flow from above; the angels go up and down *on him*, by him, and for him. He is the ladder.

Now, having explained the symbolism of the ladder somewhat, we may yet ask what was the purpose of sending Yaakov this message at this particular time.

The Torah's depiction of Yaakov at this point is one of a person afraid, afraid of many things: Afraid of his brother, he flees the Holy Land … *"and he went toward Charan."* Afraid of wild animals, *"he took from the stones of the place, and he put them at his head"* for protection. And, afraid to travel in the dark[13] *"for the sun had set,"* he sleeps out in the wild. The objects of his fear span all four levels of creation, from humans to animals to plants and inanimate objects.

With this vision, Yaakov is shown that, by virtue of his extreme righteousness, Hashem will offer him protection at all levels, a fitting prelude to Hashem's promise that follows: *"… And, behold, I am with you, and I will protect you wherever you go …"* (28:15).

# A Swindler's Logic

‫... וַיֹּאמֶר אֶל־לָבָן מַה־זֹּאת עָשִׂיתָ לִּי‬
‫הֲלֹא בְרָחֵל עָבַדְתִּי עִמָּךְ וְלָמָּה רִמִּיתָנִי:‬
‫וַיֹּאמֶר לָבָן לֹא־יֵעָשֶׂה כֵן בִּמְקוֹמֵנוּ לָתֵת הַצְּעִירָה‬
‫לִפְנֵי הַבְּכִירָה: מַלֵּא שְׁבֻעַ זֹאת וְנִתְּנָה לְךָ גַּם־אֶת־זֹאת‬
‫בַּעֲבֹדָה אֲשֶׁר תַּעֲבֹד עִמָּדִי עוֹד שֶׁבַע־שָׁנִים אֲחֵרוֹת:‬

---

12. *Bereishis Rabbah* 68:12.
13. Lest he injure himself on rocks, trees, thorns, etc.

*... [Yaakov] said to Lavan, "What is this you have done to me? Was it not on behalf of Rachel that I worked for you? So why have you deceived me?"*

*And Lavan said, "Such is not done in our place, to give the younger girl before the elder one. Complete the week of this one, and this one will have been given to you in consideration of the work that you will do for me for another seven years."*

*(Bereishis 29:25-27)*

L avan's answer does not really seem to address Yaakov's questions: Didn't the work of the first seven years give Yaakov the right to marry Rachel? And why was he tricked into marrying Leah?

Rather, the Torah here portrays for us the most sinister of cheats cloaking his trickery in the soundest of logic:

Lavan told Yaakov the following: "Don't think my intention in giving you Leah in this manner was to force you into marrying her against your will, or to deny you the chance to marry Rachel, as you deserve.

"On the contrary! Everything I did was in order to make good on my promise to you, to allow you to marry Rachel as soon as possible. You worked for Rachel, and you deserve her fair and square, and as soon as possible!

"However, as you may know, the custom in our place is that the younger daughter is not allowed to marry before her older sister. *'Such is not done in our place,'* and the people of the place would not allow such a thing to happen!

"So you see, I did you a favor! If you would have waited to marry Rachel until some other man came along to marry Leah, you would have needed to wait another seven years *at least*!

"You see, seven years' labor is what I require as Leah's bride-price, and I require that such labor be done *in advance* of any marriage, because I don't trust anybody.

"Except for you, that is. Therefore, as a special favor to you, I gave you Leah *on credit*. Now you are free to marry Rachel, for whom you worked, immediately after '*the week of this one,*' i.e., after Leah's seven-day marriage celebration, instead of waiting seven years for someone else to marry Leah."

"Since I trust you, I gave you Leah first, and am letting you do the work for her afterward. In other words, '*this one [Leah] will have been given to you*' now, retroactively, '*in consideration of the work that you will do for me for another seven years.*'

"I assumed that you would agree to this. You are free to dispute me, of course. You can send Leah home, if you wish, claiming that your marriage to her was a case of mistaken identity. Keep in mind, however, that if you do so, I won't be able to let you marry Rachel until Leah marries someone else first, and that could take a long, long time.

> *"You can send Leah home, if you wish, claiming that your marriage to her was a case of mistaken identity ...."*

"So, you see, I had only your best interest at heart in everything that I did!"

# Barren and Bearing[14]

וַיַּרְא ה' כִּי־שְׂנוּאָה לֵאָה וַיִּפְתַּח אֶת־רַחְמָהּ וְרָחֵל עֲקָרָה
***And God saw that Leah was hated, so He opened
her womb, while Rachel remained barren [akarah].
(Bereishis 29:31)***

Like Sarah and Rivkah before her, Rachel was barren. Leah, too, was originally barren by nature, until God intervened and "*opened her womb.*" Thus, all four Matriarchs of the Jewish people were barren, a phenomenon that requires explanation. Why should this have been so?

---

14. Parts of this essay are adapted from Malbim's Hebrew commentary to *Bereishis* 25:21; see there.

Having children is natural. Just as for plants and animals, reproduction in humans ensures the continued survival of the species.

Producing offspring who are the pinnacle of holiness, however, is "counternatural." Left to themselves, the forces of nature are unequipped to produce souls worthy to be chosen as God's treasured nation. For this, special Divine assistance is required.

This Divine energy was to be aroused through prayer, through the unremitting prayers of Avraham, Yitzchak, and Yaakov. Their prayers, joining those of the Matriarchs, would draw down into this world that holy soul, that *neshamah*, which emanates directly from God Himself.[15]

It is for this reason, then, that the Matriarchs were barren: to arouse those prayers that would turn their childbearing from a natural occurrence into a supernatural one.

> *It is for this reason, then, that the Matriarchs were barren: to arouse the prayers that would turn their childbirth from a natural occurrence into a super-natural one.*

With this in mind, the above verse takes on a new understanding: Had Yaakov loved Leah, she, like Rachel, would have remained barren, arousing Yaakov's prayers on her behalf. But, since "*God saw that Leah was hated*" — that Rachel was Yaakov's primary focus, and that Yaakov would pray only for Rachel but not for Leah[16] — therefore, God intervened and "*opened her womb*" miraculously. "*Rachel,*" on the other hand, "*remained barren,*" to arouse Yaakov's prayers on her behalf.

The Midrash[17] on this verse makes the homographic equation between Rachel's being *akarah* (barren) to her being *ikarah* (the mainstay) of Yaakov's home. Other than the fact that these two

---

15. As it were.

16. Or, if he would pray, he would not focus his primary prayer energy in her direction, but rather toward Rachel (Editor).

17. *Bereishis Rabbah* 71:2; *Yalkut Shimoni Bereishis* 29:125.

Hebrew words are spelled the same, what connection do they have to each other?

Based on our explanation of the above verse, the meaning of this Midrash becomes eminently clear: Rachel was barren exactly *because* she was the mainstay, the beloved wife, and therefore the one on whose behalf Yaakov would pray to conceive. Had he not loved her, she would not have been barren!

# An Encounter With Angels

... וַיֵּשֶׁב לָבָן לִמְקֹמוֹ: וְיַעֲקֹב הָלַךְ לְדַרְכּוֹ וַיִּפְגְּעוּ־בוֹ מַלְאֲכֵי אֱלֹקִים: וַיֹּאמֶר יַעֲקֹב כַּאֲשֶׁר רָאָם מַחֲנֵה אֱלֹקִים זֶה וַיִּקְרָא שֵׁם־ הַמָּקוֹם הַהוּא מַחֲנָיִם

*... [Lavan] left and returned to his place. Yaakov went upon his way, and angels from God encountered him. And Yaakov said when he saw them, "This is God's camp [machaneh]," and he called the name of that place "machanayim [twin-camps]." (Bereishis 32:1-3)*

Yaakov here achieves a very high level of prophecy, much higher than the vision of the "Ladder" that he saw when fleeing from his brother twenty years earlier. In this case, "angels from God encountered him" while in a waking state — "he saw them" with his flesh-and-blood eyes — in contrast to the dream-vision of the angels going up and down the ladder.

*Even though he was still far away, yet, by merely beginning the journey, Yaakov already begins to experience the prophetic glow that emanates from the Land of Israel.*

The cause of his newly elevated state was that now "*Yaakov went upon his way,*" toward the Holy Land. Even though he was still far away, yet, by merely beginning the journey, Yaakov already begins to experience the prophetic glow that emanates from the Land of Israel.

Yaakov's angelic encounter comes immediately upon his separation from the evil Lavan, who "*left and returned to his place*." This juxtaposition of events is no coincidence: It parallels the incident of Avraham and Lot in which "Hashem spoke to Avram after Lot separated from him ...."[18] In both of these instances, the Torah contrasts the spiritual slump caused by associating with evildoers to the ethereal elevation achieved by separating from them.

When Yaakov "*saw them*," i.e., when he grasped the purpose of their agency[19] — which was to help him in his encounter against the belligerent Esav — "*he said, 'This is God's camp [machaneh].'*" The Hebrew word for camp always implies an encamped brigade preparing for war. Seeing this battalion of angels, Yaakov realizes that Esav must be coming against him with a militia of his own. Thus, "he called the name of that place "*machanayim*" twin-camps, indicating that the two opposing camps would ultimately meet face-to-face on the battlefield.

---

18. *Bereishis* 13:14.

19. The Hebrew word for angel, "*malach*," implies agency.

# פרשת וישלח
# PARASHAS VAYISHLACH

---

## We Are What We Eat

עַל־כֵּן לֹא־יֹאכְלוּ בְנֵי־יִשְׂרָאֵל אֶת־גִּיד הַנָּשֶׁה אֲשֶׁר עַל־כַּף הַיָּרֵךְ
עַד הַיּוֹם הַזֶּה כִּי נָגַע בְּכַף־יֶרֶךְ יַעֲקֹב בְּגִיד הַנָּשֶׁה

*Therefore the Children of Israel are not to eat the*
***gid hanasheh** [dislocated sinew] which is upon the*
*pulp of the thigh until this very day; for he touched*
*the pulp of Yaakov's thigh in the **gid hanasheh**.*
*(Bereishis 32:33)*

W hen a person eats meat, the flesh of the animal
nourishes him, becoming part and parcel of his flesh.
If he eats meat derived from "impure," nonkosher
animals, he absorbs into his personality the traits characteristic

of those animals. It is for this reason[1] that the Torah legislated against eating those animals that it defines as "not kosher," for those creatures are typically predatory, cruel, and repulsive as well.

This is the concept behind the prohibition of eating the *gid hanasheh* — the organ associated with earthliness and the reproductive desire. That the angel succeeded in attacking Yaakov in no place other than the *gid hanasheh* indicated that even Yaakov Avinu — as holy as he was, and as far removed from physicality as he could possibly be — remained intertwined with physicality via this organ, ever so minimally, yet to the extent that it rendered him vulnerable.

So, too, regarding the *gid hanasheh* of an animal; it is inextricably bound up with the forces of earthliness and bodily desires, such that whoever eats it is permeated by these characteristics.

*So, too, regarding the gid hanasheh of an animal; it is inextricably bound up with the forces of earthliness and bodily desires, such that whoever eats it is permeated by these characteristics.*

With its prohibition against eating this part of an animal, the Torah reminds us to distance ourselves from all base desires and helps us toward our goal of becoming a nation "holy unto God."

---

1. The Malbim does not mean to imply that this is the only reason.

# Retribution and Cunning

וַיַּעֲנוּ בְנֵי־יַעֲקֹב אֶת־שְׁכֶם ... בְּמִרְמָה וַיְדַבֵּרוּ אֲשֶׁר טִמֵּא אֵת
דִּינָה אֲחֹתָם: וַיֹּאמְרוּ אֲלֵיהֶם לֹא נוּכַל לַעֲשׂוֹת הַדָּבָר הַזֶּה לָתֵת
אֶת־אֲחֹתֵנוּ לְאִישׁ אֲשֶׁר־לוֹ עָרְלָה כִּי־חֶרְפָּה הִוא לָנוּ: אַךְ־בְּזֹאת
נֵאוֹת לָכֶם אִם תִּהְיוּ כָמֹנוּ לְהִמֹּל לָכֶם כָּל־זָכָר ... וְאִם־לֹא תִשְׁמְעוּ
אֵלֵינוּ לְהִמּוֹל וְלָקַחְנוּ אֶת־בִּתֵּנוּ וְהָלָכְנוּ:
... וַיָּבֹא חֲמוֹר וּשְׁכֶם בְּנוֹ אֶל־שַׁעַר עִירָם וַיְדַבְּרוּ אֶל־אַנְשֵׁי עִירָם
לֵאמֹר: הָאֲנָשִׁים הָאֵלֶּה שְׁלֵמִים הֵם אִתָּנוּ וְיֵשְׁבוּ בָאָרֶץ וְיִסְחֲרוּ
אֹתָהּ ... אַךְ־בְּזֹאת יֵאֹתוּ לָנוּ ... בְּהִמּוֹל לָנוּ כָּל־זָכָר כַּאֲשֶׁר הֵם
נִמֹּלִים: מִקְנֵהֶם וְקִנְיָנָם וְכָל־בְּהֶמְתָּם הֲלוֹא לָנוּ הֵם אַךְ נֵאוֹתָה
לָהֶם וְיֵשְׁבוּ אִתָּנוּ

*And the Children of Yaakov answered Shechem ...
with cunning, and they spoke [to him] who defiled
Dinah, their sister. They said to them, "We are not
able to do this thing, to give our sister to a man who
has a foreskin, for it is a disgrace to us. Through
this alone will we agree to you, if you will be like us,
circumcising every male among you ....
But, if you do not listen to us to be circumcised,
we will take our daughter and leave."
... Chamor and his son Shechem came to the gate of
their city, and they spoke to the people of their city
saying, "These people are at peace with us; they will
dwell in the land and they will engage in commerce
within it .... Only through this will they agree to us
... by our circumcising every male among us as they
are circumcised. Their livestock, their possessions,
and all their animals, they are surely ours for
merely agreeing to allow them to live among us!"
(Bereishis 34:13-15,17,20-23)*

The brothers' retribution against Shechem raises many questions: How were the brothers successfully able to fool Shechem into believing that they meant him no harm? How, indeed, was an entire town of Canaanites convinced to undergo the challenging process of circumcision? The most striking question of all, perhaps, is that of the morality of slaughtering and plundering an entire city of unsuspecting people: How could such a thing be justified?

In championing the cause of their abducted sister Dinah, the Children of Yaakov employed tremendous cunning. In order to lull Shechem into a sense of security, the brothers pretended that they sought, not justice, but honor:

Their stated complaint against Shechem *completely ignored* the violent injustices committed against their sister, capital crimes under the Noachide code. Rather, *"they answered Shechem with cunning"* in that *"they spoke [to him] who **defiled** Dinah, their sister."* That is, they harshly rebuked him — as implied by the verb *"dibeir"* — but only for the sacrilegious *defilement* and dishonor brought by Dinah's union to one who was uncircumcised.

No mention was made regarding the true cause of their anger, the crimes of kidnap and rape, crimes that could be redressed by nothing short of the death penalty. The stigma of the foreskin, however, had a remedy: *"Through this alone will we agree to you, if you will be like us, circumcising every male among you."*

By saying *"through this alone,"* the brothers meant that their *sole* requirement was a "religious" one. The issue here was not one of revenge or money, and they would forgo all the generous privileges of citizenship offered, as long as this one requirement be met. Otherwise, said the brothers, *"We are not able to give our sister to a man who has a foreskin"* for any money in the world. *"But, if you do not listen to us to be circumcised, we will take our daughter and leave,"* but we will seek no revenge; Shechem violated our laws regarding circumcision, but we can forgive him because in this respect he sinned inadvertently, for how was he supposed to know the "religious" laws of our tiny, migrant clan?

With the above, the brothers gave the impression that their only gripe was against Shechem's *accidental* violation of their unique "religious" tenets regarding circumcision, and that if Shechem had been a "Son of the Covenant," they would give Dinah to him with no compunctions. They completely disregarded the violent, criminal nature of his actions, thus lulling Shechem into a false sense of security.

> **The brothers gave the impression that their only gripe was against Shechem's accidental violation of their unique "religious" tenets regarding circumcision, but that if Shechem had been a "Son of the Covenant," they would give Dinah to him with no compunctions.**

To convince the people of Shechem to circumcise, Shechem's father, Chamor, appealed to their sense of profit and greed: "*These people are at peace with us,*" said Chamor, and will therefore come to our aid against any enemy invasion. "*They will dwell in the land,*" he added, 'and develop it from its present state of barrenness," "*and they will engage in commerce,*" bringing wealth, prosperity, and economic growth to our region.

"*Only through this,*" the only condition being that we "*circumcise every male among us,*" in which case "*their livestock, their possessions, and all their animals, they are surely ours for merely agreeing to allow them to live among us.*" Since they seek no other conditions or rights of citizenship, we will thereafter be able to threaten them with expulsion whenever we chose; they will then be forced to give us their property merely for the right to dwell among us.

Three days after the citywide circumcision, when the men were in pain, Yaakov's sons attacked the unprotected, unsuspecting city, killed every male, looted all the property, took captive all the women and children, and rescued their captive sister. Where was the justice in this?

The answer is that the Shechemites had incurred the death penalty for three reasons:

- Each of the seven Noachide laws carries capital punishment for those who violate it, and one of the Noachide laws is the prohibition against theft, including "human theft," i.e., kidnapping. For his rape and abduction of Dinah, therefore, Prince Shechem was liable to death. And because the people of Shechem neither prosecuted their prince nor protested against him for his high-handed crimes, they, too, transgressed one of the seven Noachide laws, "*dinim,*" the requirement that justice be done, that the other six Noachide laws be enforced. For this, they, too, incurred the death penalty.[2]

- Shechem never had any intentions of sending Dinah home peacefully, as we see from the fact that he held her captive during his "negotiations" with Yaakov. From this it was obvious that, had Yaakov demanded Dinah's return, Shechem was prepared to go to war for her, with all the citizens of Shechem as his soldiers. This was a tacit declaration of war against Yaakov, and afforded Yaakov the legal right to kill the entire city in self-defense in order to save his captive daughter.

- The Shechemites' sole motivation for circumcising themselves was so that they could thereafter use threats of expulsion to extort money from Yaakov and sons; another type of theft, amounting to a capital offense under the Noachide code.

Thus, the brothers committed no injustice.[3]

---

2. This comment in its entirety is based on *Rambam, Hilchos Melachim* 9:14.

3. Even Yaakov Avinu who criticizes his sons' actions (see next piece) does so only from the tactical standpoint, claiming that they enflamed the region and brought danger of counterattack from the surrounding treaty-states.

As for the spoils of war, they belonged rightly to Yaakov's family as reparations for the disgrace brought to Dinah's honor.

# Diplomacy Versus Aggression

וַיֹּאמֶר יַעֲקֹב אֶל־שִׁמְעוֹן וְאֶל־לֵוִי עֲכַרְתֶּם אֹתִי לְהַבְאִישֵׁנִי
בְּישֵׁב הָאָרֶץ בַּכְּנַעֲנִי וּבַפְּרִזִּי וַאֲנִי מְתֵי מִסְפָּר וְנֶאֶסְפוּ עָלַי
וְהִכּוּנִי וְנִשְׁמַדְתִּי אֲנִי וּבֵיתִי:
וַיֹּאמְרוּ הַכְזוֹנָה יַעֲשֶׂה אֶת־אֲחוֹתֵנוּ

*And Yaakov said to Shimon and to Levi,*
*"You have sullied me, befouling me among the*
*inhabitants of the land, among the Canaanite*
*and among the Perizzite; I am few in number,*
*and they will rally against me and attack me;*
*I will be annihilated, I and my household."*
*And they said, "Shall he treat our sister*
*like a harlot!?"*
*(Bereishis 34:30-31)*

In these short verses, Yaakov and his sons "debate" the proper approach to achieving peace with the belligerent Canaanites.

Yaakov told his sons that they had just made the situation go from bad to worse. For, according to Yaakov, the surrounding peoples *already* considered him as their enemy, and this was

---

The essential justification of their actions, however, he does not question.

In *Parashas Vayechi* (*Bereishis* 49:5-6), Yaakov does criticize Shimon and Levi for an *additional* aspect of their vengeful act, the fact that it was done out of anger, thereby invalidating either of these elder sons from assuming the position of leadership newly removed from firstborn Reuven. (Since the Shechemites converted, Yaakov felt that the brothers should have shown mercy. See Malbim there and our essay "Anger and Fury.")

for two reasons: the first being that the local peoples are the *"inhabitants of the land,"* and thus regard Yaakov as an outsider; secondly, because they are *"Canaanites and Perizzites,"* therefore Yaakov's nationality and religious values are in opposition to theirs. By attacking the city of Shechem the brothers had fanned these coals of hatred into a flame, arousing the ire of those who far outnumbered Yaakov's little tribe and who were now bound by blood ties to retaliate.

*Exactly because Yaakov and his family were outsiders and few in number did the local peoples see them as easy prey, weak and helpless.*

But the brothers answered that the opposite was true, that in passivity lay the danger: Exactly *because* Yaakov and his family were outsiders and few in number did the local peoples see them as easy prey, weak and helpless; and thus did they begin committing their injustices against them, abducting their sister and *"treating her like a harlot."*

"If we remain silent now," Yaakov's sons told him, "they will continue doing to us whatever they please. We need to show that we have the power to strike back at all those who commit evil against us."

# The Name Yisrael

וַיֹּאמֶר־לוֹ אֱלֹקִים שִׁמְךָ יַעֲקֹב לֹא־יִקָּרֵא שִׁמְךָ עוֹד יַעֲקֹב
כִּי אִם־יִשְׂרָאֵל יִהְיֶה שְׁמֶךָ וַיִּקְרָא אֶת־שְׁמוֹ יִשְׂרָאֵל:
וַיֹּאמֶר לוֹ אֱלֹקִים אֲנִי קֵל שַׁקַּי פְּרֵה וּרְבֵה גּוֹי וּקְהַל
גּוֹיִם יִהְיֶה מִמֶּךָּ וּמְלָכִים מֵחֲלָצֶיךָ יֵצֵאוּ

*And God said to him, "Your name is Yaakov;*
*your name will no longer be called Yaakov,*
*but rather Yisrael will be your name";*
*and He called his name 'Yisrael.' "*
*And God said to him, "I am **Keil Shakkai**:*
*Be fruitful and multiply; a nation and a*
*congregation of peoples will come from you,*
*and kings will issue forth from your loins."*
*(Bereishis 35:10-11)*

Regarding Avraham, the verse[4] had said, "*No longer will your name [es shimcha] be called Avram.*" The extra word "*es*" (which means "with" and denotes something secondary[5]) implies that even as a secondary name, Avram will not be used.

Yaakov, however, is told, "*Your name is Yaakov*" — the appellation "Yaakov" remains, except that it no longer describes your essence. "*Your name [shimcha],*" i.e., your essence, "*will no longer be called Yaakov, but rather Yisrael will be your name.*"

The names "Yaakov" and "Yisrael" refer to the two different ways in which the Jewish people conduct themselves, and the two corresponding ways in which God guides the affairs of the Jewish people.

"Yaakov" refers to that conduct that functions according to nature, following the natural laws and being governed by those

---

4. *Bereishis* 17:5.

5. "*Es*" means *with*, as in "*es Yaakov*" (*Shemos* 1:1). It denotes something secondary, as in "*es besaro*" (*Eiruvin* 4b). Malbim notes several other distinctions as well between Yaakov's name-change and that of Avraham.

forces that govern all nations. The name "Yisrael," on the other hand, indicates a conduct above nature, wherein the Jewish people are infused with a Divinity that causes the mighty to tremble before them and princes to serve them.[6]

> *The name "Yisrael," on the other hand, indicates a conduct above nature, wherein the Jewish people are infused with a Divinity that causes the mighty to tremble before them and princes to serve them.*

Unlike "Avram," the name "Yaakov" is not eliminated, the difference being that the name "Avram" was given by idolatrous parents, while the name "Yaakov" was given by believers in the One True God.

Through recognizing the Creator and circumcising himself, Avraham "converted," so to speak, to the Hebrew faith; and "one who converts is like a newborn child."[7] Thus, Avraham completely severed any connections to his idolatrous background, such that "whoever calls him 'Avram' has transgressed a negative commandment."[8]

The name Yaakov, on the other hand, remains, and for two reasons: One is that it is a "Jewish name," given him by believers in the faith of Israel. Secondly, it represents the natural system under which the Jewish people will sometimes find themselves, because the system beyond nature will not always be in effect.

By telling Yaakov, *"I am Keil Shaddai,"* God intended that from now on He would conduct Yaakov's affairs through hidden miracles and Divine Providence, as represented by the name Yisrael.[9]

---

6. Malbim here does not spell out clearly how these names contain these ideas. However, see above verse 32:29, Rashi and Malbim there. In addition, perhaps Malbim means that *"Yisrael"* combines the word *"yisr" from the root "yisharet"* ("will serve"), and the word *"el"* meaning "mighty one," "prince."

7. *Yevamos* 22a.

8. *Berachos* 13a.

9. *Shakkai* is related to the word *shodeid*, "plunder," meaning "The God

# His Wife's Sister

וַיְהִי בְּצֵאת נַפְשָׁהּ כִּי מֵתָה וַתִּקְרָא שְׁמוֹ בֶּן־אוֹנִי וְאָבִיו קָרָא־לוֹ בִנְיָמִין

*And it was, as her soul departed — for she died — that she called his name "Ben-Oni" [the son of my strength], and his father called him "Binyamin" [the son of my right hand].*

*(Bereishis 35:18)*

Rachel's marriage to Yaakov, although it was permitted at the time, was a relationship that would subsequently become forbidden for the Jewish people: With the giving of the Torah at Mount Sinai, it became forbidden for a Jew to marry his wife's sister during his wife's lifetime.[10]

Yaakov married sisters because (1) there was no prohibition against doing so, and (2) it was God's unfathomable plan that the Holy Tribes of Israel be brought into existence in this fashion.

> **But now, since God had changed Yaakov's name to Yisrael and had blessed him to be under God's direct influence, that spark of Divinity that would illuminate the Jewish nation at the Giving of the Torah already began to glimmer.**

But now, since God had changed Yaakov's name to Yisrael and had blessed him to be under God's direct influence, that spark of Divinity that would illuminate the Jewish nation at the Giving of the Torah already began to glimmer. At this point, therefore, it would be a spiritual blemish for Yaakov to be married to two sisters, especially now that

---

Who despoils the natural system" through hidden miracles (Malbim to *Bereishis* 17a citing *Ibn Ezra* ad loc.).

10. Yaakov married Leah first, so Rachel was the forbidden one.

Binyamin had been born and the Twelve Tribes were complete. Therefore, Rachel dies at this time, and is not to be buried next to Yaakov.

# The Death of Rachel

וַיִּסְעוּ מִבֵּית אֵל וַיְהִי־עוֹד כִּבְרַת־הָאָרֶץ לָבוֹא אֶפְרָתָה
וַתֵּלֶד רָחֵל וַתְּקַשׁ בְּלִדְתָּהּ: וַיְהִי בְהַקְשֹׁתָהּ בְּלִדְתָּהּ
וַתֹּאמֶר לָהּ הַמְיַלֶּדֶת אַל־תִּירְאִי כִּי־גַם־זֶה לָךְ בֵּן:
וַיְהִי בְּצֵאת נַפְשָׁהּ כִּי מֵתָה וַתִּקְרָא שְׁמוֹ
בֶּן־אוֹנִי וְאָבִיו קָרָא־לוֹ בִנְיָמִין:
וַתָּמָת רָחֵל וַתִּקָּבֵר בְּדֶרֶךְ אֶפְרָתָה הִוא בֵּית לָחֶם: וַיַּצֵּב
יַעֲקֹב מַצֵּבָה עַל־קְבֻרָתָהּ הִוא מַצֶּבֶת קְבֻרַת־רָחֵל עַד־הַיּוֹם

And they traveled from Bethel, and there was
another stretch of land to get to Efrat
when Rachel went into labor; and she had
a difficult labor. And it was, as she was having
a difficult labor, that the midwife said to her,
"Do not fear, for this, too, is a son for you."
And it was, as her soul departed — for she died —
that she called his name "Ben-Oni"
[the son of my strength], and his father called him
"Binyamin" [the son of my right hand].
And Rachel died and was buried on the way
to Efrat — this is Bethlehem — and Yaakov
erected a monument for her grave. This is
the monument of Rachel's Tomb until today.
(Bereishis 35:16-20)

A s earlier when Rachel tells Yaakov, "Give me children, and if not, I am dead,"[11] here, too, we see Rachel's tremendous righteousness, and her great longing to have

---

11. *Bereishis* 30:1.

children. Even though she had arrived at death's door, Rachel's only concern was for the welfare of her new child. She worries that perhaps due to the unusually severe travails of her labor that the baby is somehow damaged or not viable.

Thus, "and she had a difficult labor," i.e., because she was having a difficult labor and worried about the safety of her child, therefore the midwife said to her, "Do not fear, for this, too, is a son for you," meaning a "son of life," i.e., a healthy child.[12]

"And it was, as her soul departed ...." Even with her dying breath, Rachel thought not about herself, but rather about her newborn child and giving him a name.

She called him "the son of my strength," meaning that she died by giving birth to him, and thus gave all her strength for his sake. Yaakov called him "Binyamin," which means "the son of my right hand"; with this, Yaakov changed the name but not the essential meaning, the right hand signifying a person's strength and power.

> **By burying Rachel "on the way to Efrat," and not in Efrat itself, Yaakov made sure that Rachel was buried in the portion of the Land that would later be alloted to her own descendants, to the Tribe of Binyamin.**

"Rachel died and was buried on the way to Efrat — this is Bethlehem ...." The verse here is explaining why Rachel was buried "on the way to Efrat," and not taken the short distance to be buried in Efrat itself. Because "this is Bethlehem," a portion of the Land that in the future would be alloted to the Tribe of Judah, Leah's descendants, it was therefore not ideal that Rachel be buried there. By burying Rachel "on the way to Efrat," and not in Efrat itself, Yaakov made sure that Rachel was buried in the portion of the Land that would later be alloted to her own descendants, to the Tribe of Binyamin.

---

12. Through this interpretation, Malbim addresses the verse's apparent redundancy.

*"And Yaakov erected a monument for her grave. This is the monument of Rachel's Tomb until today."*

The purpose of a monument erected for the deceased is in order to commemorate his good deeds, so that they should not be forgotten by future generations.

For Rachel, however, such a thing did not apply. As the *ikeres habayis*, the mainstay of the House of Israel, Rachel's renown and her good deeds would be remembered forever without any need for a monument. As the Sages say, "We do not make monuments [*nefashos*] for the righteous, because their words are their monuments."[13]

The monument that Yaakov erected upon Rachel's Tomb, therefore, was only a way to mark the grave's location, but not to commemorate her good deeds. To make this point, this verse says that Yaakov erected a monument *"for her grave"* but not *"for her,"* and that this was the monument *"of Rachel's Tomb,"* not the monument *"of Rachel,"* for she herself could never be forgotten.

# Reuven's Transgression

וַיְהִי בִּשְׁכֹּן יִשְׂרָאֵל בָּאָרֶץ הַהִוא וַיֵּלֶךְ רְאוּבֵן וַיִּשְׁכַּב אֶת־בִּלְהָה
פִּילֶגֶשׁ אָבִיו וַיִּשְׁמַע יִשְׂרָאֵל וַיִּהְיוּ בְנֵי־יַעֲקֹב שְׁנֵים עָשָׂר

*And it was when Yisrael dwelled in that land that*
*Reuven went and lay with Bilhah, the concubine*
*of his father; and Yisrael heard [this] —*
*and the children of Yaakov were twelve.*
*(Bereishis 35:22)*

According to the Sages,[14] no sin was actually committed by Reuven, at least not one of the magnitude attributed to him by the above verse. Rather, they explain that the

---

13. *Yerushalmi, Shekalim* 11a; brought in *Tosefos Eiruvin* 53a.
14. *Shabbos* 55b.

verse is referring to the fact that Reuven interfered in his father's sleeping arrangements, a breach of filial honor as shocking as if he had committed adultery.

The view that Reuven remained sinless is supported by the fact that, with its "very next breath," the verse goes out of its way[15] to point out that *"the children of Yaakov were twelve,"* thereby equating all twelve sons in terms of their righteousness.

The kabbalists provide an additional insight into this seeming non sequitur — *"and the children of Yaakov were twelve"* — as follows:

The very night of Reuven's sin, Yaakov was destined to have fathered two more tribes, Menasheh and Ephraim. Reuven, through desecrating his father's sleeping arrangements, negated this possibility, requiring that these two tribes later be brought into being by Yoseph instead. Thus, *"the children of Yaakov were twelve"* only, and not fourteen[16] as originally decreed; and for this reason the verse considers Reuven as having consorted with his father's concubine.[17]

This insight enables us to understand a subsequent incident in the Torah, where we find that Yaakov elevates Menasheh and Ephraim to "Tribe" status, even though they were his grandsons rather than his sons: *"And now,"* Yaakov tells Yoseph, *"your two sons, born to you in the Land of Mitzrayim before I came*

---

15. *Chazal's* view here is supported here by the *piskah b'emtza pasuk*, a paragraph break starting midverse (Malbim). I.e., the phrase *"and the children of Yaakov were twelve"* begins the following paragraph and therefore deserved to be considered a verse unto itself. But since the Torah considers it rather as the end of the previous verse, the Torah means for us to draw inferences from it.

16. Here, Malbim's explanation follows that of the kabbalists whom he cites. Later, (see e.g., *Parashas Vayechi,* "The Tree of Twelve Branches) Malbim follows the mainstream approach, which is that originally Yaakov was intended to have been the father of twelve children only.

17. Arizal in *sefer "Eitz Hadaas Tov" Parashas Vayechi; sefer "Kanfei Yonah."*

*to you to Mitzrayim, **they are mine;** Menasheh and Ephraim will be just as Reuven and Shimon are to me.*[18] Why indeed would Yaakov consider Menasheh and Ephraim to be "his," as though he himself had fathered them? According to the above explanation, the answer is clear: Yaakov considers them as his own because they were originally meant to issue from him.

When Hashem told Yaakov to *"be fruitful and multiply,"*[19] Rachel was already expecting Binyamin; yet Yaakov is promised that he would *"be fruitful"* and father even more children. At first, Yaakov assumed that Rachel would be the mother of these promised offspring; but, once Rachel died, Yaakov moved his personal effects into Bilhah's tent and took up residence there. He did this believing that Bilhah was the most fitting one to mother these future children, because, as Rachel's maidservant, the children born to her would be considered like Rachel's children.[20]

> **When Hashem told Yaakov to "be fruitful and multiply", Rachel was already expecting Binyamin; yet Yaakov is promised that he will "be fruitful" and father even more children.**

Reuven disagreed. Aware of this prophecy, he felt that the promised offspring should descend from his mother, Leah. Therefore, he "mixed up his father's sleeping arrangements" so that his father's bed be placed in Leah's tent, intending that she would be the one to mother these future children.

Although Reuven acted out of concern for his mother's honor, yet he dishonored his father and his father's concubine Bilhah, and as a result of his actions Menasheh and Ephraim did not emerge from Yaakov. For this brazenness, the verse faults him as though he had committed immorality.

---

18. *Bereishis* 48:5.
19. Ibid. 35:11.
20. See *Bereishis* 30:3.

According to the above, the verse reads as follows:

"*And it was when Yisrael dwelled in that land*" and in that fashion, with his tent next to Bilhah's, "*that Reuven went*" to confound this arrangement, "*and*" this was when "*he lay with Bilhah, the concubine*" — who lay? — "*his father*" Yaakov. That is, while Yaakov was attempting to bring about God's promise via Rachel's handmaiden, Reuven went to stop it, claiming that Bilhah was merely a concubine, and that his mother, Leah, deserved primacy because she was Yaakov's wife.

"*And Yisrael understood*" ("*vayishma*" can mean both "heard" and "understood") the ramification of Reuven's actions, that now "*the children of Yaakov were twelve*" only, and that due to Reuven's desecration, "*Yaakov's bed*" was no longer fitting to produce Menasheh and Ephraim.

With this, it is understood why Reuven forfeited his double portion in the Land of Israel, which was his rightful due as the firstborn. As the verse says in *Divrei HaYamim*:[21] "*And in his desecrating his father's bed, his firstborn status was given to the sons of Yosef ....*" This was not a punishment, per se, but rather a consequence. Because Hashem had promised Yaakov to be "*fruitful and multiply ... and the Land which I have given to Avraham and to Yitzchak, to you and to your seed shall I give it ....*"[22] Yaakov therefore understood that there would be two more children born who would each inherit a portion in the Land. Had Menasheh and Ephraim been born from Yaakov, they each would have received this portion by rights; but now that they were to be born from Yoseph and only elevated to "Tribe" status by special bequest from Yaakov, it would be unfair to give them each a portion in the Land, as this would diminish the portion due to the other brothers.[23] Reuven, therefore, as the cause of this

---

21. *I Divrei HaYamim* 5:1.

22. *Bereishis* 35:11,12.

23. With 14 brothers, the land is divided 15 ways; the firstborn gets two shares while the others get one. With only 12 brothers, the land is divided 13 ways, and each brother gets a larger share. Considering Menasheh and

situation, forfeits half of his anticipated double-portion to his brother Yoseph, so that Yoseph's two sons can each inherit one portion without diminishing the portion due to any of the other brothers.

# Seventy Souls, Seventy Princes, Seventy Nations[24]

וְאֵלֶּה תֹּלְדוֹת עֵשָׂו אֲבִי אֱדוֹם בְּהַר שֵׂעִיר

*These are the generations of Esav,*
*the father of Edom, in Mount Seir.*
*(Bereishis 36:9)*

אֵלֶּה בְנֵי־שֵׂעִיר הַחֹרִי יֹשְׁבֵי הָאָרֶץ לוֹטָן וְשׁוֹבָל וְצִבְעוֹן וַעֲנָה ...

*These are the children of Seir,*
*the Chorite, the inhabitants of the land:*
*Lotan, Shoval, Tzivon, and Anah ... etc.*
*(Bereishis 36:20)*

Seir and his family were the original inhabitants of *Eretz Seir* until *"the children of Esav ... wiped them out and dwelled in place of them."*[25] As such, they play an extremely minor role in the Torah's narrative. One might well ask, what is the point of the Torah's telling us these genealogical details — not only of the children

**What is the point of the Torah's telling us these genealogical details — not only of the children of Esav — but of the family of Seir and his twenty-six male descendants?**

---

Ephraim as "Tribes" would therefore diminish each brother's share from ⅟₁₃ to ⅟₁₅.

24. Malbim here refers the reader to his commentary to *Divrei HaYamim* (*I Chronicles*, Ch. 1), upon which this essay is based.

25. *Devarim* 2:12.

of Esav — but of the family of Seir and his twenty-six male descendants?

Rather, the Torah is teaching us how Hashem directs the affairs of human history such that there remains a balance, a "one-to-one"[26] correspondence between the Jewish people and the World Powers, as follows:

Not including the Jewish People, a scrupulous accounting of the "Descendants of Avraham" brings us to the number seventy, as follows:

Yishmael and the princes descended from him were thirteen,[27] and the children of Keturah were thirteen,[28] a total of twenty-six.

Esav and his princely descendants listed in this chapter are another sixteen, for a subtotal of forty-two.

Now, the Torah tells us that the children of Esav wiped out the children of Seir and dwelled "in place of them," suggesting that we should consider the twenty-six princes of Seir as though they were princes of Esav, bringing our total to sixty-eight.

Finally, by including Amon and Moav, who were also from the family of Avraham,[29] we arrive at a total of 70.

We learn from this that, just as there arose seventy nations in the world at large,[30] so, too, there arose seventy princes and chieftains from the seed of Avraham; and corresponding to these were the seventy souls of the children of Yaakov,[31] the roots of

---

26. "Zeh le'umas zeh, asah Elokim"—"God made this corresponding to that" (Koheles 7:14).

27. Bereishis 25:13-16.

28. Ibid. verses 1-4.

29. Amon and Moav were the sons of Avraham's nephew Lot. Perhaps, too, we can loosely consider them "Avraham's offspring" because they were conceived after Lot was rescued from Sodom, and Lot was rescued from Sodom only in Avraham's merit (ibid. 19:29).

30. As derived from a careful count of Noach's descendants listed in Chapter 10 of Bereishis.

31. Ibid. 46:27.

*Klal Yisrael,* the Jewish people, as the Arizal writes in the *Sefer Hagilgulim.*[32] Thus, we see the Divinely guided equilibrium of human history.

---

32. *Hakdamah* 38.

# פרשת וישב
# PARASHAS VAYEISHEV

---

## The Sale of Yoseph —
## Its Ultimate Purpose

וַיֵּשֶׁב יַעֲקֹב בְּאֶרֶץ מְגוּרֵי אָבִיו בְּאֶרֶץ כְּנָעַן

*And Yaakov settled in the land of his*
*father's sojourning, in the land of Canaan.*
*(Bereishis 37:1)*

At the crux of the story of the sale of Yoseph is the fact
that it was part of God's plan designed to bring the
Jewish people to Mitzrayim and to purify them there in
the "iron furnace."[1] For this reason, the Torah begins by explain-

---

1. This is a running theme throughout Malbim's commentary to the
"Yoseph Story."

ing why God didn't simply bring a famine or the like to induce Yaakov to go to Mitzrayim, as He had in the days of Avraham.

First of all, this was "the land of his father's sojourning," Yaakov's ancestral homeland. Furthermore, this was "the Land of Canaan," known for its inherent holiness and Divine Providence.

> **At the crux of the story of the sale of Yoseph is the fact that it was part of God's plan designed to bring the Jewish people to Mitzrayim and to purify them there in the "iron furnace."**

For these two reasons, "Yaakov settled," permanently, in the Holy Land, and could not be convinced to leave it under normal circumstances. Therefore, the "Cause of all causes" wove the chain of events, beginning with the sale of Yoseph, which brought Yaakov and his family down to Mitzrayim.

# The Brothers' Motives for Selling Their Brother

אֵלֶּה תֹּלְדוֹת יַעֲקֹב יוֹסֵף בֶּן־שְׁבַע־עֶשְׂרֵה שָׁנָה הָיָה רֹעֶה
אֶת־אֶחָיו בַּצֹּאן וְהוּא נַעַר אֶת־בְּנֵי בִלְהָה וְאֶת־בְּנֵי זִלְפָּה
נְשֵׁי אָבִיו וַיָּבֵא יוֹסֵף אֶת־דִּבָּתָם רָעָה אֶל־אֲבִיהֶם

*These are the chronicles of Yaakov:*
*When Yoseph was seventeen years old,*
*he was shepherding his brothers among the sheep,*
*and he was a youth with the children of Bilhah*
*and with the children of Zilpah, his father's wives;*
*and Yoseph brought their evil talk to their father.*
*(Bereishis 37:2)*

**I**f Yaakov's sons, whom the verse refers to as the "Tribes of God,"[2] agreed to sell their brother (this itself was an improvement over their original plan to kill him) it must be that they

---

2. *Tehillim* 122:4.

considered him a wicked, destructive person, one whom it was a mitzvah to rid the world of.

For it is unthinkable to conclude that due to petty jealousy over a fine woolen tunic that their father had made for Yoseph that these towering, world-class *tzaddikim* suddenly metamorphosed into a band of murderers and savage beasts.

> *For it is unthinkable to conclude that due to a petty jealousy over a fine woolen tunic that their father had made for Yoseph that these towering, world-class tzaddikim suddenly metamorphosed into a band of murderers and savage beasts.*

With the verses that follow, the Torah comes to justify the brothers in one sense, in that they acted *l'shem Shamayim*, for the sake of Heaven. This will likewise clarify why we never find that the brothers were punished for their actions; because as far as their intentions were concerned, not only were the brothers perfectly blameless, but it was as though they had performed a mitzvah.

The Torah reveals Yoseph's righteousness as well, relating how the brothers hated him without just cause, and yet he never retaliated; on the contrary, he returned their evil with goodness and kindness, providing food for them during the famine.[3]

The verse begins by telling us that even though Yoseph was merely seventeen years old, younger than his other brothers, yet *"he was shepherding his brothers among the sheep,"* leading and teaching them the art of pasturing sheep, at which he was more proficient than they. Alternatively, while the brothers were watching the flock, Yoseph was "shepherding them" regarding spiritual matters, reproving them in issues of fear of God and teaching them wise conduct.

At first, this seems like haughtiness on Yoseph's part, until the verse informs us the exact opposite, that Yoseph was an extremely humble person, so much so that *"he was a youth*

---

3. Translation based on Malbim's Hebrew commentary to *Bereishis* 49:24.

*with the children of Bilhah and with the children of Zilpah."* The word *na'ar* or "youth" connotes a servant-boy, implying that Yoseph served his brothers, even though they were the children of the handmaidens and thus of lesser status than the brothers who were the sons of Leah, and even Yoseph himself.

*"And Yoseph brought their evil talk to their father."* The other brothers, the children of Leah, considered the children of the handmaidens to be slaves by dint of their mothers. They spoke evil of them, referring to them as slaves, and the children of the handmaidens spoke evil about the children of Leah (as our Sages explain[4]). It was this "evil talk" between the two factions that Yoseph conveyed to their father, in the expectation that Yaakov would rebuke them and bring peace between them.

The classical works of Jewish ethics and character development explain that God planted within each person diametrically opposite extremes, such as pride and humility, generosity and stinginess, mercy and cruelty, etc. Each person has a natural tendency that generally pushes him toward one or the other of these extremes, except that he, by implementing his free will, has the power to bend himself toward the opposite extreme if he so desires.

Thus, we can separate people into three general categories:

First, there is the person who always goes along with his natural tendency toward a certain character trait. Even if his character trait is a good one, such as mercy or humility, this cannot be considered an accomplishment. Because this person does not consciously choose to follow this trait, but rather does so by instinct, therefore, he will also be merciful, humble, etc., even toward evildoers.[5]

Next, there is the elevated person, someone who acts according to the dictates of the intellect; he is humble, kind, and

---

4. *Yerushalmi Pe'ah* 4:1, *Bereishis Rabbah* 84:7.

5. Malbim is obviously referring to a case where it is inappropriate to have mercy on the evildoers, such as where harm will result to innocents.

generous toward righteous people, but high-handed, cruel, and begrudging toward evildoers.[6]

The evildoer, on the other hand, takes the third route, implementing both extremes, but in the opposite way: The *rasha* is self-effacing toward immoral people, lowering himself before them and donating generously in order to be accepted into their society where he believes he will find his heart's desires. Toward those who are righteous and good, he acts haughty and mean.

> **The rasha is self-effacing toward immoral people, lowering himself before them and donating generously in order to be accepted into their society where he believes he will find his heart's desires. Toward those who are righteous and good, he acts haughty and mean.**

Yoseph implemented his character traits according to the dictates of his intellect. "*He was a youth,*" humbly serving his lower-echelon brothers, the sons of the handmaidens, while, at the same time, "*his heart was haughty in the ways of Hashem,*"[7] and he was not afraid to stand up and teach wise conduct to his brothers when he saw a need for this, even though they were older than he was. Similarly, when he heard the brothers quarreling with one another, his love for them — coupled with the love of truth and peace that he had developed — drove him to relate their dispute to their father so that Yaakov would rebuke the brothers and make peace among them.

The brothers, however, judged Yoseph unfavorably, viewing all the above in the wrong light: That Yoseph admonished and instructed them issued — so they thought — from his haughtiness and his manipulative mind, while his humility toward the handmaiden's children sprang from his lowly character that

---

6. Malbim refers to cases where such high-handedness is appropriate (see previous note).

7. A reference to the righteous king Yehoshafat who boldly removed idol worship from the Land of Israel (*II Divrei HaYamim* 17:6).

attracted him to these brothers whom they held in lower esteem. Conveying their quarrel to Yaakov was, by their estimation, Yoseph's way of disgracing them in Yaakov's eyes, in order to drive a wedge between them and their father.

# The Brothers' Mistaken Calculation

וְיִשְׂרָאֵל אָהַב אֶת־יוֹסֵף מִכָּל־בָּנָיו כִּי־בֶן־זְקֻנִים הוּא לוֹ
וְעָשָׂה לוֹ כְּתֹנֶת פַּסִּים: וַיִּרְאוּ אֶחָיו כִּי־אֹתוֹ אָהַב אֲבִיהֶם
מִכָּל־אֶחָיו וַיִּשְׂנְאוּ אֹתוֹ וְלֹא יָכְלוּ דַּבְּרוֹ לְשָׁלֹם

*And Yisrael loved Yoseph more than all*
*his sons because he was his **ben zekunim***
*[son of old age], and he made for him a*
*fine woolen tunic. And his brothers saw that*
*he was the one [oso] whom their father loved*
*more than all his brothers, and they hated him*
*and could not [bear] his speaking peacefully.*
*(Bereishis 37:3-4)*

The reason for Yaakov's special love to Yoseph, as the verse states, was that Yoseph was Yaakov's "*ben zekunim*," which connotes both a son who is born when the father is old, as well as the youngest son whom the father takes to serve him in his old age.

This being the case, Yaakov "*made for him a fine woolen tunic.*" The other brothers, who were always out in the field with the flock, dressed like shepherds. Yoseph, who stayed at home and served his father, wore more distinguished clothing out of respect for his father. In the Midrash,[8] we find the same thing regarding

---

8. *Pesikta Rabbasi 23.*

Esav, who, in honor of his father Yitzchak, wore elegant clothing while serving him. Dressing nicely is one of the ways of showing endearment for the mitzvah of honoring parents, and this was Yaakov's sole intention in making this special garment for Yoseph.

The brothers, however, misunderstood Yaakov's intentions here, and they thought that "*he,*" Yoseph, in his essence, "*was the one whom their father loved more than all the brothers.*"[9] A father's fondness for one particular child *over and above* his other children is not a love of the child's essence, a love that springs from that child's inherent goodness or superiority over the other children; rather it is a natural infatuation, a love toward the child with whom he most closely identifies.[10] Yet the brothers misinterpreted Yaakov's fatherly fondness toward Yoseph as a love of Yoseph's essence, as though Yaakov saw Yoseph as essentially superior to them.

> **A father's fondness for one particular child over his other children is not a love of the child's essence, a love that springs from that child's inherent goodness or superiority over the other children; rather it is a natural infatuation.**

This, then, was the basis of their hatred toward Yoseph. Because in each preceding generation, only one of the children became the "heart and treasure" of the chosen people, while the other children were given at most a secondary position. Yishmael and the children of the *pilagshim* were passed over in favor of Yitzchak; Esav was passed over in favor of Yaakov. Both Yitzchak and Yaakov inherited the blessings of Avraham, the birthright, the Holy Land, and the ability to draw close to God, while the others were thrust aside.

---

9. Grammatically, the word "*oso*" (him) is emphasized by its unusual placement before the verb *ahav* (loved).

10. Our interpretation of the Malbim here is based on Malbim's original Hebrew commentary to *Bereishis* 29:20 (see there).

What the brothers did not comprehend was that the time had finally come for this Divinity to take root among the *entire* family of Yaakov and that *each one* of the brothers was to become the "heart and treasure" of the Jewish nation, together comprising the Tribes of Yisrael. Not realizing this, however, and seeing that Yaakov loved Yoseph above them all, they thought that Yaakov was grooming Yoseph to be the next "heart and treasure" of the Jewish people, while they themselves were slated as the next "peels and husks."

When Yaakov made Yoseph a special garment, the brothers' concerns escalated, for they saw this as further indication of their father's desire to single out Yoseph for the Divine service and to bestow upon him the advantages of the birthright. Why else, they reasoned, would Yaakov distinguish Yoseph with these "priestly garments"?

Insofar as the brothers considered Yoseph to be a haughty, manipulative person, bossing them around and maligning them to their father, and, in addition, since they regarded Yoseph's dreams as windows into his secret aspirations to rule over them, the brothers asked themselves the following question: If Yoseph truly desires the Divine birthright and the Godly endowments, how at the same time can he covet temporal power and worldly sway?

Based upon all these considerations, the brothers concluded that if Yoseph would succeed in convincing their father to push them aside in his favor, Yoseph would bring disgrace and destruction upon the House of Yaakov. Thus, they decided that this painful thornbush needed to be weeded out from the Divine vineyard for the general good, to preserve the pride and sanctity of the House of Yisrael, and not out of personal jealousy and enmity.

# Words of Peace

... וַיִּשְׂנְאוּ אֹתוֹ וְלֹא יָכְלוּ דַּבְּרוֹ לְשָׁלֹם

*... And they hated him and could
not [bear] his speaking peacefully.*

**(Bereishis 37:4)**

Usually, hatred cools when one's enemy speaks friendly,
conciliatory words. As the verse in *Mishlei* states, "A soft
answer turns aside wrath."[11]

Hatred born out of jealousy, albeit not personal in nature,
however, and certainly hatred born of the conviction that the
enemy is a predator,
lying in wait for his
chance to kill and disgrace, such hatred
grows even greater with
each kind word the
enemy utters. His flattering mouth itself is
seen as the instrument
of destruction; peace
and love are upon his lips, while in his heart lies ambush.

> **Hatred born out of jealousy,
> and certainly hatred born of the
> conviction that the enemy is a
> predator, lying in wait for his
> chance to kill and disgrace, such
> hatred grows even greater with
> each kind word the enemy utters.**

With this perspective of Yoseph, the brothers could not tolerate his friendly and peaceful manner toward them, for they
saw this as just another element of his manipulative deception,
designed to put them off their guard and to render them vulnerable to all of his machinations.

---

11. *Mishlei* 15:1.

# Yoseph's Dreams

וַיַּחֲלֹם יוֹסֵף חֲלוֹם וַיַּגֵּד לְאֶחָיו וַיּוֹסִפוּ עוֹד שְׂנֹא אֹתוֹ׃
וַיֹּאמֶר אֲלֵיהֶם שִׁמְעוּ־נָא הַחֲלוֹם הַזֶּה אֲשֶׁר חָלָמְתִּי׃
וְהִנֵּה אֲנַחְנוּ מְאַלְּמִים אֲלֻמִּים בְּתוֹךְ הַשָּׂדֶה וְהִנֵּה קָמָה אֲלֻמָּתִי
וְגַם־נִצָּבָה וְהִנֵּה תְסֻבֶּינָה אֲלֻמֹּתֵיכֶם וַתִּשְׁתַּחֲוֶיןָ לַאֲלֻמָּתִי׃
וַיֹּאמְרוּ לוֹ אֶחָיו הֲמָלֹךְ תִּמְלֹךְ עָלֵינוּ אִם־מָשׁוֹל תִּמְשֹׁל
בָּנוּ וַיּוֹסִפוּ עוֹד שְׂנֹא אֹתוֹ עַל־חֲלֹמֹתָיו וְעַל־דְּבָרָיו׃
וַיַּחֲלֹם עוֹד חֲלוֹם אַחֵר וַיְסַפֵּר אֹתוֹ לְאֶחָיו
וַיֹּאמֶר הִנֵּה חָלַמְתִּי חֲלוֹם עוֹד וְהִנֵּה הַשֶּׁמֶשׁ וְהַיָּרֵחַ
וְאַחַד עָשָׂר כּוֹכָבִים מִשְׁתַּחֲוִים לִי׃
וַיְסַפֵּר אֶל־אָבִיו וְאֶל־אֶחָיו וַיִּגְעַר־בּוֹ אָבִיו
וַיֹּאמֶר לוֹ מָה הַחֲלוֹם הַזֶּה אֲשֶׁר חָלָמְתָּ הֲבוֹא
נָבוֹא אֲנִי וְאִמְּךָ וְאַחֶיךָ לְהִשְׁתַּחֲוֹת לְךָ אָרְצָה׃
וַיְקַנְאוּ־בוֹ אֶחָיו וְאָבִיו שָׁמַר אֶת־הַדָּבָר׃

Yoseph dreamed a dream, and he told it [va'yageid]
to his brothers, and they increased their hatred
toward him. And he said to them, "Listen,
please, to this dream that I have dreamed.
Behold, we were bundling sheaves in the midst of
the field, and, behold, my sheaf rose up and also
remained standing steadfast; and, behold, your
sheaves surrounded and bowed down to my sheaf."
And his brothers said to him, "Will you really
reign [maloch] over us if you indeed rule [mashol]
over us?" And they increased their hatred for him
because of his dreams and because of his words.
And he dreamed again, a different dream,
and he related it [va'yesapeir] to his brothers,
and he said, "Behold I dreamed another dream,
and behold the sun, the moon, and eleven
stars were bowing down to me."
He related it to his father and to his brothers,
and his father berated him and said to him,

*"What is this dream that you have dreamed?!*
*Will we really come — I, your mother, and your*
*brothers — to bow down to you to the ground?!"*
*Yet his brothers were jealous of him,*
*and his father kept the matter in mind.*
*(Bereishis 37:5-11)*

**T**he Talmud says, "All dreams go according to the mouth," [12]
meaning that they come true according to the way they are
interpreted orally; therefore, if a person wants his dreams
to come true for the good, he should tell them to a beloved friend
who he knows will give his dreams a favorable interpretation.

Yoseph, in his righteousness and his pure-heartedness, thought
that his brothers loved him and that they would therefore offer a
positive interpretation to his dream, which is why he told it to them.

Furthermore, since the dream was relevant to them, Yoseph
*"told it (va'yageid)"* to his brothers. There is a difference between
the root word *"haggadah,"* "telling," used in connection with the
first dream, and *"sippur,"* "relating," used in connection with the
second dream. The difference is that *"sippur"* is a mere telling of
something, such as a story, which has no direct relevance to the
listener, whereas *"haggadah"* refers to a telling of some information that is relevant to the listener and that he needs to know.

The brothers, however, who couldn't even bear to hear Yoseph
speaking civilly (see previous essay), were now even more
enraged at this very loving approach of his. They considered him
shamelessly brazenfaced, trying to camouflage his hatred of them
behind a smoke screen of friendliness. Thus, *"they increased*
*their hatred toward him,"* because of what they saw as his new
ploy, and did not even want to listen to the dream.

Yet Yoseph persisted, saying, *"Listen, please,"* using the same
Hebrew phrase *"shimu na"* which, as the Midrash remarks, [13]
would later be employed by the prophets when rebuking the

---

12. *Berachos* 55b.
13. *Bereishis Rabbah* 84:10.

Jewish people. In this way, Yoseph intimated that the dream contained a prophetic message to them from God and that they should therefore listen to it.

The dream itself had three distinct messages, accounting for the thrice-repeated "*henei,*" "behold," a word that indicates the introduction of a new element:

- Yoseph's rise to power would come about through grain, as pictured at the dream's beginning: "*Behold, we were bundling sheaves in the midst of the field ....*"

- At first, the brothers would stand against Yoseph, but he would forcefully overpower them. Symbolizing this was the next part of the dream: "*And, behold, my sheaf rose up*" by itself, indicating that Yoseph would rise to power without the brothers' consent, "*and remained standing steadfast,*" despite the opposition of those who sought his downfall.

- Eventually, though, the brothers would willingly, of their own accord, submit to Yoseph's leadership, as the dream predicts: "*And, behold, your sheaves surrounded and bowed down to my sheaf,*" the gathering into a circle symbolizing goodwill and acceptance.

Misinterpreting the above, the brothers confronted Yoseph with what they saw as a contradiction in his dream. First he dreamed "*my sheaf rose up ...,*" indicating that he would rise by force, but then he dreamed "*behold, your sheaves surrounded ...,*" indicating the opposite, that the brothers would accept his rule willingly.

They expressed this contradiction by saying, "*Will you really reign [maloch] over us if you indeed rule [mashol] over us?*" The difference between a *melech* (king) and a *moshel* (ruler) is that the *melech* is chosen for his position, governing with the will and consent of the people, while the *moshel* is a dictator who rules by force. A *moshel*, then, cannot be called a *melech*, since the *melech* has the will of the people while the *moshel* does not. "How," the brothers asked Yoseph rhetorically, "could you possibly[14] be a *melech* over us, ruling us with our will, if you rise against us and subjugate us by force?"

A dream containing a self-contradiction could not possibly be a Divine prophecy; rather, the brothers concluded, this dream could be nothing more than the nocturnal expression of Yoseph's daytime reveries and cogitations, as the Talmud states, "a person is shown (in his dreams) only the (daytime) musings of his heart."[15] Therefore, "*they increased their hatred for him because of his dreams*," which they believed exposed his secret aspirations to rule over them.

> **A dream containing a self-contradiction could not possibly be a Divine prophecy; rather, the brothers concluded, this dream could be nothing more than the nocturnal expression of Yoseph's daytime reveries and cogitations ....**

Their hate increased also "*because of his words*"; not only did Yoseph fantasize about ruling over them, he even had the audacity to say this straight to their faces, as if he wanted them all to suddenly agree to accept him as their king!

"*And he dreamed again, a different dream ....*" Yoseph's second dream added a new element to the first dream, that after the brothers would bow down to him of their own accord when coming to Mitzrayim to purchase grain, their father Yaakov and all his household[16] would come to Mitzrayim in honor and grandeur.[17] Then, Yaakov, his wives, and all Yaakov's household would bow down to Yoseph.

---

14. With this comment, the Malbim explains the emphatic verb repetition "*hamaloch timloch,*" "*hamashol timshol.*" The added emphasis here implies that fulfillment of the dream is not merely unlikely but impossible.

15. *Berachos* 55b.

16. The moon symbolized Yaakov's household, and not Yoseph's mother Rachel, as Yaakov interprets it.

17. Just as the sun, moon, and stars are grand and exalted in the sky.

"And he related it [va'yesapeir] to his brothers ...." Seeing that he had made enemies of his brothers by telling them his first dream in a manner of "haggadah," a conveyance of information that has relevance for the listener, Yoseph now wanted to remove their enmity by telling his second dream in a manner of "sippur," "storytelling," a relating of matters that have no bearing on the listener. This dream, thought Yoseph, was so preposterous that it would discredit his first dream, causing his brothers to disregard his dreams altogether. The symbolism of the sun, moon, and stars all bowing down to Yoseph was so utterly absurd that it obviously could be nothing more than a deluded flight of fancy. As such, it proved retroactively that Yoseph's first dream had been meaningless as well. Thus, "va'yesapeir," Yoseph "told this tale" to his brothers, admitting that it, along with its precursor, was an irrelevant "tall tale" to be disregarded.

Now, had Yoseph told his brothers only, this approach would have succeeded in quelling their hatred. However, since "he related it to his father and to his brothers," it backfired, as follows:

Yaakov, on the one hand, wanted to interpret Yoseph's dream for the good; but, on the other hand, he did not want the brothers to be jealous of Yoseph. Therefore, "his father berated him," implying with his harsh words and tone that the dream was absurd, and on three counts: "Will I, your mother, and your brothers come to bow down to you to the ground?!" meaning, "Does a father bow down to his son? Could your mother, who has already died, bow down to you? And, would your brothers, who are stronger and more numerous than you, come to bow down to you?"

"Yet, his brothers were jealous of him ...." Yaakov's attempt to quell the brothers' jealousy through his words of rebuke achieved the exact opposite, for the brothers therein realized that these dreams of Yoseph's did indeed have some substance after all, and they felt that their father wanted to put Yoseph as their king by granting him the birthright and the blessings.

For his part, Yaakov *"kept the matter in mind,"* for he understood that this dream contained a prophetic message.

# The Divine Plan Versus Free Will

וַיֵּלְכוּ אֶחָיו לִרְעוֹת אֶת־צֹאן אֲבִיהֶם בִּשְׁכֶם:
וַיֹּאמֶר יִשְׂרָאֵל אֶל־יוֹסֵף הֲלוֹא אַחֶיךָ רֹעִים
בִּשְׁכֶם לְכָה וְאֶשְׁלָחֲךָ אֲלֵיהֶם וַיֹּאמֶר לוֹ הִנֵּנִי:
וַיֹּאמֶר לוֹ לֶךְ־נָא רְאֵה אֶת־שְׁלוֹם אַחֶיךָ וְאֶת־שְׁלוֹם
הַצֹּאן וַהֲשִׁבֵנִי דָּבָר וַיִּשְׁלָחֵהוּ מֵעֵמֶק חֶבְרוֹן וַיָּבֹא שְׁכֶמָה

*And his brothers went to pasture their father's*
*sheep in Shechem. And Yisrael said to Yoseph,*
*"Aren't your brothers pasturing in Shechem?*
*Come, and I will send you to them,"*
*and Yoseph said, "Behold, I am ready."*
*And he said to him, "Go, now, and see the*
*well-being of your brothers and the well-being*
*of the flock and bring me back word";*
*and he sent him from the deep [valley]*
*of Chevron, and he came to Shechem.*
*(Bereishis 37:12-14)*

The Torah now relates how the germ of hatred sprouted bitter fruit; that in order to distance themselves from Yoseph, his machinations and his *lashon hara*, the brothers went all the way to Shechem to pasture their father's flock, far from their father's house, trusting that their father would not send Yoseph to such a dangerous place. Furthermore, even if Yoseph did come and the brothers would kill him, Yaakov would assume that people of the surrounding cities had killed him out of hatred and revenge for his sons' massacre of the people of Shechem.

Yaakov, however, sent Yoseph to Shechem specifically *because* of the danger. Yaakov said to Yoseph: *"Aren't your brothers pasturing in Shechem?* Since it is a dangerous place for them to be, we need to find out how they are doing."

*"Go, now, and see ... and bring me back word ...."* Yaakov appointed Yoseph as a *"shaliach mitzvah,"* an agent to perform a commandment, thus ensuring that no harm would befall him, as our Sages say, "Mitzvah agents go unharmed."[18]

Still, the difficulty arises as to how Yaakov could possibly send Yoseph, his favorite son, on his own to enemy territory, to a place where he feared even for the fate of his stronger, more numerous sons and their servants who were prepared against attackers!

The answer lies in a statement of our Sages, who interpret the verse, *"and he sent him from the deep [valley] of Chevron,"* as "Yaakov sent Yoseph because of the deep counsel of Avraham, who is buried in Chevron."

What the Sages mean to convey by this is the following:

Although it is true that God's general plan will ultimately be done despite human intervention, humans have the free will as to what specific part they will play in this plan. This, for example, explains why the Egyptians were punished for their role in subjugating the Jews, even though such subjugation was Divinely decreed in advance at the *Bris Bein Habesarim*.[19]

Based on this principle, one might therefore assume that the same could be said about the sale of Yoseph; that even if God's plan was for Yoseph to become viceroy of Mitzrayim and for Yaakov and his family to ultimately migrate there, this could have come about through any number of scenarios, and not necessarily through the brothers selling Yoseph as a slave. (Indeed, this approach is the one taken by the author of the *"Akeidah,"* who writes that while the overall outcome was God's plan, yet all the interim steps in the story of Yoseph were products of human free will.[20])

---

18. *Pesachim* 8a.
19. *Bereishis* 15:13.
20. *Sefer Akeidas Yitzchak: Sha'ar* 28.

The above statement of our Sages, however, indicates that the sale of Yoseph was something of an exception to this. While the brothers were not Divinely *forced* into selling Yoseph, as such would have constituted an interference with their free will, but, because they were acting with good intentions (see above[21]), God should have intervened to save them from this sin.

By way of example, we see that God saved Avimelech from sinning with Sarah, saying that because *"with simplicity of heart you did this ..."* therefore *"I held you back from sinning against Me, and I did not allow you to touch her...."*[22] How much more so should God have intervened here on behalf of the righteous brothers from the holy family of Yisrael.

> **While the sale of Yoseph was done with free choice, the events leading up to it were Divinely orchestrated: Yaakov's making a special garment for Yoseph; Yoseph's relating his dreams ...; even the hatred itself that drove the brothers to sell Yoseph was planted in their hearts by God, as the Midrash says.**

In addition, while the sale of Yoseph was done with free choice, the events leading up to it were Divinely orchestrated: Yaakov's making a special garment for Yoseph; Yoseph's relating his dreams ...; even the hatred itself that drove the brothers to sell Yoseph was planted in their hearts by God, as the Midrash says.[23]

So, too, Yaakov's sending his beloved Yoseph on this dangerous mission defies natural explanation; it can only be understood as the Hand of God fulfilling the "deep counsel of the righteous Avraham who is buried in Chevron," promised by God that his offspring would be enslaved and oppressed in a foreign land.

---

21. "The Brothers' Mistaken Calculation" (*Bereishis* 37:3-4).

22. *Bereishis* 20:6.

23. *Yalkut Shimoni: Bereishis* 37:141.

# The Sale of Yoseph: The Plot, the Deed, and the Cover-up

וַיִּשְׁמַע רְאוּבֵן וַיַּצִּלֵהוּ מִיָּדָם וַיֹּאמֶר לֹא נַכֶּנּוּ נָפֶשׁ: וַיֹּאמֶר אֲלֵהֶם
רְאוּבֵן אַל־תִּשְׁפְּכוּ־דָם הַשְׁלִיכוּ אֹתוֹ אֶל־הַבּוֹר הַזֶּה אֲשֶׁר בַּמִּדְבָּר
וְיָד אַל־תִּשְׁלְחוּ־בוֹ לְמַעַן הַצִּיל אֹתוֹ מִיָּדָם לַהֲשִׁיבוֹ אֶל־אָבִיו:
... וַיִּקָּחֻהוּ וַיַּשְׁלִכוּ אֹתוֹ הַבֹּרָה וְהַבּוֹר רֵק אֵין בּוֹ מָיִם: וַיֵּשְׁבוּ
לֶאֱכָל־לֶחֶם וַיִּשְׂאוּ עֵינֵיהֶם וַיִּרְאוּ וְהִנֵּה אֹרְחַת יִשְׁמְעֵאלִים
בָּאָה מִגִּלְעָד וּגְמַלֵּיהֶם נֹשְׂאִים נְכֹאת וּצְרִי וָלֹט הוֹלְכִים לְהוֹרִיד
מִצְרָיְמָה:
וַיֹּאמֶר יְהוּדָה אֶל־אֶחָיו מַה־בֶּצַע כִּי נַהֲרֹג אֶת־אָחִינוּ וְכִסִּינוּ
אֶת־דָּמוֹ: לְכוּ וְנִמְכְּרֶנּוּ לַיִּשְׁמְעֵאלִים וְיָדֵנוּ אַל־תְּהִי־בוֹ כִּי־אָחִינוּ
בְשָׂרֵנוּ הוּא וַיִּשְׁמְעוּ אֶחָיו:
וַיַּעַבְרוּ אֲנָשִׁים מִדְיָנִים סֹחֲרִים וַיִּמְשְׁכוּ וַיַּעֲלוּ אֶת־יוֹסֵף מִן־הַבּוֹר
וַיִּמְכְּרוּ אֶת־יוֹסֵף לַיִּשְׁמְעֵאלִים בְּעֶשְׂרִים כָּסֶף וַיָּבִיאוּ אֶת־יוֹסֵף
מִצְרָיְמָה:
וַיָּשָׁב רְאוּבֵן אֶל־הַבּוֹר וְהִנֵּה אֵין־יוֹסֵף בַּבּוֹר וַיִּקְרַע אֶת־בְּגָדָיו:
וַיָּשָׁב אֶל־אֶחָיו וַיֹּאמַר הַיֶּלֶד אֵינֶנּוּ וַאֲנִי אָנָה אֲנִי־בָא:
וַיִּקְחוּ אֶת־כְּתֹנֶת יוֹסֵף וַיִּשְׁחֲטוּ שְׂעִיר עִזִּים וַיִּטְבְּלוּ אֶת־הַכֻּתֹּנֶת
בַּדָּם: וַיְשַׁלְּחוּ אֶת־כְּתֹנֶת הַפַּסִּים וַיָּבִיאוּ אֶל־אֲבִיהֶם וַיֹּאמְרוּ זֹאת
מָצָאנוּ הַכֶּר־נָא הַכְּתֹנֶת בִּנְךָ הִוא אִם־לֹא:
וַיַּכִּירָהּ וַיֹּאמֶר כְּתֹנֶת בְּנִי חַיָּה רָעָה אֲכָלָתְהוּ טָרֹף טֹרַף
יוֹסֵף: וַיִּקְרַע יַעֲקֹב שִׂמְלֹתָיו וַיָּשֶׂם שַׂק בְּמָתְנָיו וַיִּתְאַבֵּל עַל־בְּנוֹ
יָמִים רַבִּים: וַיָּקֻמוּ כָל־בָּנָיו וְכָל־בְּנֹתָיו לְנַחֲמוֹ וַיְמָאֵן לְהִתְנַחֵם
וַיֹּאמֶר כִּי־אֵרֵד אֶל־בְּנִי אָבֵל שְׁאֹלָה וַיֵּבְךְּ אֹתוֹ אָבִיו:

*And Reuven heard and he rescued him from their
hand, and he said, "Let us not kill him." And
Reuven said to them, "Do not spill blood; cast him
into this pit in the desert, but do not lay a hand
upon him"; [he said this] in order to save him from
their hand, to return him to his father.
... And they took him and cast him into the pit; the*

*pit was empty, there was no water in it.*
*Then, they sat down to eat bread, and they lifted*
*their eyes and looked, and behold, there was a cara-*
*van of Ishmaelites coming from Gilead,*
*their camels bearing spices, balsam,*
*and lotus, bringing them down to Mitzrayim.*
*And Yehudah said to his brothers, "What profit is*
*there if we kill our brother and cover his blood? Let*
*us go and sell him to the Ishmaelites, and our hand*
*will not be in it, for he is our brother, our flesh,"*
*and his brothers agreed.*
*Then there passed by Midianite merchant people;*
*they drew Yoseph up and out of the pit,*
*and they sold Yoseph to the Ishmaelites for twenty*
*silver pieces, and they brought Yoseph to Mitzrayim.*
*Reuven returned to the pit and, behold, Yoseph was*
*not in the pit; so he ripped his clothing; he returned*
*to his brothers and he said, "The boy is not there,*
*and I, where should I go?"*
*They took Yoseph's tunic, slaughtered a kid-goat,*
*and immersed the tunic in the blood. Then they*
*sent the fine woolen tunic and they brought it to*
*their father, and they said, "We found this; identify,*
*please, whether this is your son's tunic or not."*
*He recognized it, and he said, "My son's tunic!*
*A wild beast ate him! Yoseph was surely torn apart!"*
*Yaakov ripped his garments, put sackcloth upon his*
*loins, and he mourned for his son for many days.*
*All his sons and all his daughters arose to comfort*
*him, but he refused to be comforted, and he said,*
*"I will descend to the grave mourning for my son,"*
*and his father wept for him.*
*(Bereishis 37:21-35)*

hen the verse says that Reuven *"rescued him,"* it means that he first urged the brothers to leave Yoseph alone altogether. They ignored this request, so Reuven tried another tack, *"and he said, 'Let us not kill him* but rather let us punish him some other way.' "* When the brothers refused this as well, *"Reuven said to them, 'Do not spill blood'"* directly, but rather kill him indirectly by throwing him into this pit which, since it is *"in the desert,"* no one will pass by to save him. To this the brothers agreed; they threw Yoseph into a pit, not to drown, for *"there was no water in it,"* but to die there, being unable to climb out.

*"And they sat down to eat bread,"* a clear indication that they had no guilt feelings about their decision; the brothers were wholeheartedly convinced that Yoseph was the aggressor who had left them no choice but to do what they did.

> *"And they sat down to eat bread," a clear indication that they had no guilt feelings about their decision ....*

One who murders does so for one of four reasons; either for monetary gain, out of vengeance and hatred, to inspire fear in others, or in self-defense.

The first three of these reasons, Yehudah told his brothers, were not applicable to their situation:

- In regard to monetary gain, Yehudah said, *"What profit is there ...?"*
- *"... If we kill our brother"*; because he is our brother, family loyalty requires that we forgive him for any past wrongs and not take revenge.
- As far as making an example out of Yoseph to inspire fear in others, Yehudah said, *"... and cover his blood"*; no one is going to know that we did this.

Since our primary goal, said Yehudah, is to distance him from our father's house so that he will not rise to subjugate us, this can be achieved by selling him as a slave.[24] Therefore, *"Let us go and sell him to the Ishmaelites ...."*

---

24. Malbim cites Abarbanel as the source of this comment.

Some of the commentaries explain that the brothers did not actually sell Yoseph at all, but that the traveling merchants themselves were the ones who took Yoseph out of the pit, and the verses seem to support this view. According to this view, Yehudah told his brothers, "*Let us go*" away from the pit, and when the Ishmaelites pass by and see Yoseph thrown into the pit, they will assume him to be a man condemned to death, and they will therefore take him as a slave (as was the practice of the day). In this way, Yoseph will become a slave without our intervention. Therefore, "*Let us go*," away, "*and sell him*" — meaning "give him over," or "indirectly cause him to be sold"[25] — "*to the Ishmaelites; and our hand will not be in it*," we will not be directly involved in this sale. "*His brothers agreed*" to his plan, and they left the place.

In the meantime however, "*there passed by Midianite merchant people*" who got to the pit before the Ishmaelites, "*and they drew Yoseph up and out of the pit*," and subsequently "*they sold Yoseph to the Ishmaelites*" who brought him to Mitzrayim.

The reason that Hashem brought the Midianites to the pit first was so that Reuven would not succeed in his plan to save Yoseph. Originally, Reuven was together with his brothers when they deserted Yoseph, calculating that he could return to the pit in time to save Yoseph before the Ishmaelites got there. What Reuven didn't realize was that there were Midianites approaching the pit from the opposite direction who were closer to it than the Ishmaelites were.[26]

---

25. This comment requires that "I am Yoseph whom you sold to Mitzrayim" (*Bereishis* 45:4) be interpreted "whom you caused to be sold," as Malbim points out. Malbim cites Rabbeinu Bachaya and Maharaf that many simple active verbs are to be understood as causative.

26. For certainly the brothers had already distanced themselves from the pit far enough so as not to hear Yoseph's cries for help. By way of illustration, if the brothers were west of the pit and saw Ishmaelites approaching from farther west, and then they withdrew to the north, they would not necessarily have seen the Midianites approaching from the east, even though the Midianites were closer to the pit (Malbim).

Therefore, when Reuven returns to his brother and tells them that *"the boy is not there,"* he is not telling them something obvious; rather, he means to inform them that Yoseph was *already* missing from the pit by the time the Ishmaelites arrived there. *"Where should I go,"* Reuven asks rhetorically, "to look for Yoseph, which is something my father will surely require of me?"[27]

Yaakov's reaction was disbelief on three counts: First of all, how could it be that *"a wild beast ate him"*? Even if it were decreed upon Yoseph for some sin that he should die by wild animals, surely he should have been spared the additional disgrace of having his remains devoured by the beasts. We see this point in the episode of the prophet sent to Beth-el[28] who was killed by a lion as punishment for his disobedience to God, yet the lion did not eat him.

> **Even if it were decreed upon Yoseph for some sin that he should die by wild animals, surely he should have been spared the additional disgrace of having his remains devoured by the beasts.**

Secondly, a wild beast will not attack a human being unless the human being "appears to the beast like an animal"[29] (i.e., his control over his inborn animalistic tendencies is not total, and this animalistic nature is sensed by the animal). How, then, could it be that *"Yoseph was torn apart,"* Yoseph, the paradigm of righteousness and self-control?

Thirdly, he said, *"This is my son's [outer] tunic,"* and if indeed *"a wild beast ate him,"* then there should be some remnants of his undergarments as well.

---

27. As the verse stated, the brothers had seen that the Ishmaelites were headed toward Mitzrayim. But since now they do not know who took Yoseph out of the pit, Reuven therefore has no idea where to start looking for him.

28. *I Kings* 13:24-29.

29. *Shabbos* 151b.

Based on all these questions, Yaakov concluded that "*Yoseph was surely torn apart*" by humans who exercise free will, and not by any animal. Therefore, he did not want to be consoled.

Not only did Yaakov rip his garments, he also "*put sackcloth upon his loins*" as a form of repentance, in accordance with the concept found in the response of the Mahariv[30] that if one sends an agent on a dangerous mission and that agent is killed, the sender needs to accept a regimen of repentance upon himself.

"*I will descend to the grave mourning for my son ....*" Yaakov was in possession of an oral tradition that the Tribes of Yisrael needed to be no less than twelve, and that otherwise the House of Yisrael would not be built upon a firm foundation. Thus, Yaakov said that he would mourn his whole life for this incident, as it meant much more than just the loss of a child, but rather indicated a fundamental flaw in Yaakov's own service of God, and for this he would be punished.

# The End Before the Beginning

וַיְהִי בָּעֵת הַהִוא וַיֵּרֶד יְהוּדָה מֵאֵת אֶחָיו
וַיֵּט עַד־אִישׁ עֲדֻלָּמִי וּשְׁמוֹ חִירָה ...

*And it was at that time that Yehudah went down from his brothers until he came to an Adulamite man whose name was Chirah ....*
*(Bereishis 38:1)*

The Torah interrupts the story of Yoseph to relate the details of Yehudah's union with Tamar and the birth of their offspring. Why?

The sale of Yoseph by his brothers was the cause of much more than just the Egyptian exile; rather, it was the seed of all future exiles and foreign dominations under which the Jewish

---

30. Cited by *Magen Avraham, Orach Chaim* 603.

people would suffer throughout history until the coming of the *Mashiach*.

Thus, "*it was at that time*" specifically, immediately after the sale of Yoseph, that God began planting the Messianic seed. Even before the first exile had begun, Hashem was already "busy" preparing the light of redemption, the *Mashiach*, who would bring the end and culmination of all future exiles.

> **Even before the first exile had begun, Hashem was already "busy" preparing the light of redemption, the Mashiach, who would bring the end and culmination of all future exiles.**

So, "*at that time,*" while Yoseph (and, symbolically, "*Mashiach ben Yoseph*"[31]) descended to Egypt to ultimately rule there, the Messianic scion, the seed of David that was to emerge through the Tribe of Yehudah, was already taking embryonic form.

As the Sages say in the Midrash on this verse, "Before having any birth pangs, she will have already given birth …." (*Yeshayahu* 66:7), "Before the first oppressor was born, the final redeemer was born."[32]

---

31. *Chazal* teach that there are two redeemers: one descended from Yoseph and one descended from David HaMelech, from the Tribe of Yehudah (*Sukkah* 52b).

32. *Bereishis Rabbah* 85a.

# Yoseph in the House of Potiphar

וְיוֹסֵף הוּרַד מִצְרָיְמָה וַיִּקְנֵהוּ פּוֹטִיפַר סְרִיס פַּרְעֹה שַׂר הַטַּבָּחִים אִישׁ מִצְרִי מִיַּד הַיִּשְׁמְעֵאלִים אֲשֶׁר הוֹרִדֻהוּ שָׁמָּה: וַיְהִי ה׳ אֶת־יוֹסֵף וַיְהִי אִישׁ מַצְלִיחַ וַיְהִי בְּבֵית אֲדֹנָיו הַמִּצְרִי: וַיַּרְא אֲדֹנָיו כִּי ה׳ אִתּוֹ וְכֹל אֲשֶׁר־הוּא עֹשֶׂה ה׳ מַצְלִיחַ בְּיָדוֹ: וַיִּמְצָא יוֹסֵף חֵן בְּעֵינָיו וַיְשָׁרֶת אֹתוֹ וַיַּפְקִדֵהוּ עַל־בֵּיתוֹ וְכָל־יֶשׁ־לוֹ נָתַן בְּיָדוֹ: וַיְהִי מֵאָז הִפְקִיד אֹתוֹ בְּבֵיתוֹ וְעַל כָּל־אֲשֶׁר יֶשׁ־לוֹ וַיְבָרֶךְ ה׳ אֶת־בֵּית הַמִּצְרִי בִּגְלַל יוֹסֵף וַיְהִי בִּרְכַּת ה׳ בְּכָל־אֲשֶׁר יֶשׁ־לוֹ בַּבַּיִת וּבַשָּׂדֶה: וַיַּעֲזֹב כָּל־אֲשֶׁר־לוֹ בְּיַד־יוֹסֵף וְלֹא־יָדַע אִתּוֹ מְאוּמָה כִּי אִם־הַלֶּחֶם אֲשֶׁר־הוּא אוֹכֵל וַיְהִי יוֹסֵף יְפֵה־תֹאַר וִיפֵה מַרְאֶה

*Yoseph had been brought down to Mitzrayim, and Potiphar, Pharaoh's minister, the Chief Executioner, an Egyptian man, bought him from the hand of the Ishmaelites who had brought him down there.*

*And Hashem was with Yoseph; he was a successful man, and he was in the house of his master, the Egyptian. His master saw that Hashem was with him and that everything he did Hashem made prosper in his hand.*

*Yoseph found favor in his eyes and he served him; he appointed him over his household, and everything that he had, he put into his hand.*

*And it was from the time that he appointed him upon his household and upon all that he had that Hashem blessed the house of the Egyptian because of Yoseph, and Hashem's blessing was upon all that he had, in the house and in the field. He forsook all that he had in Yoseph's hand, and he did not know anything that was with him,*

*except for the bread he ate; and Yoseph*
*was beautiful of form and good looking.*
*(Bereishis 39:1-6)*

The Torah now returns to the narrative of Yoseph's descent to Mitzrayim, and we immediately see the Divine Providence whereby Yoseph was acquired by none other than a minister of the Pharaoh himself, the great and wealthy Potiphar.

Yoseph's endeavors were blessed with two types of success: natural and Providential, which came despite two opposing factors; a) his being a slave b) to an immoral master:

As the Torah tells us, Yoseph "*was a successful man*" in the natural sense, combining his talents and decision-making abilities with a healthy dose of good luck.

In addition, "*Hashem was with Yoseph*," blessing him with Providential levels of success beyond the natural. Thus, even "*his master saw that Hashem was with him*," because "*everything he did*," even in those situations where poor decisions had been made, nevertheless, "*Hashem made prosper in his hand*," granting uncanny reversals from bad to good to any project as long as it was in Yoseph's hands.

These two types of success, natural and beyond, came despite two forces working against them:

Potentially impeding the rise of Yoseph's "lucky star" was the fact that "*he was in the house of his master*." Success bestowed through the natural system graces only free people, but not slaves whose success is that of their masters.

**Opposing Yoseph's Providential success was, as the Torah points out, the fact that his master was in every sense "the Egyptian," Egypt being the Torah's paradigm of base morality and debauched practices. As such, Potiphar's home repelled God's presence more than it invited it.**

Opposing Yoseph's Providential success was, as the Torah

points out, the fact that his master was in every sense *"the Egyptian,"*[33] Egypt being the Torah's paradigm of base morality and debauched practices.[34] As such, Potiphar's home repelled God's presence more than it invited it.

Yoseph's elevation in Potiphar's household came in stages. First, *"he served him,"* becoming Potiphar's personal servant, being freed from hard slave labor to a position of light "service." Next, *"he appointed him over his household,"* a post that entails two separate tasks, overseeing both a) income and b) expenses. Usually, these two responsibilities are given to two different people to protect the owner against embezzlement. Yet, Potiphar trusted Yoseph, and so *"he appointed him over his household,"* referring to the expenses, *"and everything that he had,"* even his income and his treasure houses, *"he put into his hand."*

*"From the time that he appointed him upon his household and upon all that he had ...."* With Yoseph now in charge of everything, *"Hashem blessed the house of the Egyptian."* Even though it was an Egyptian house and therefore unfitting for Divine blessing, nevertheless, Hashem blessed it *"because of Yoseph"*; since Yoseph was in charge, he was considered in a sense the surrogate owner, such that *"Hashem's blessing was upon all that he had,"* even upon that which he acquired before Yoseph arrived, *"in the house,"* the expenses, *"and in the field,"* the income.

At first, Pharaoh kept tabs on Yoseph, but eventually *"he forsook all that he had in Yoseph's hand,"* trusting Yoseph totally. The sole item not entrusted to Yoseph was *"the bread Potiphar ate,"* since the Egyptian religion forbade Egyptians to eat bread together with Hebrews.

The Torah now remarks that *"Yoseph was beautiful of form and good looking"* as a prelude to the upcoming episode of Potiphar's wife.

---

33. Otherwise, the phrase *"the Egyptian"* is redundant, as the verse above already stated that Potiphar was an Egyptian.

34. *Va'eira* 18:3.

# Potiphar's Wife

וַיְהִי אַחַר הַדְּבָרִים הָאֵלֶּה וַתִּשָּׂא אֵשֶׁת־אֲדֹנָיו אֶת־עֵינֶיהָ אֶל־יוֹסֵף
וַתֹּאמֶר שִׁכְבָה עִמִּי:
וַיְמָאֵן וַיֹּאמֶר אֶל־אֵשֶׁת אֲדֹנָיו הֵן אֲדֹנִי לֹא־יָדַע אִתִּי מַה־בַּבָּיִת
וְכֹל אֲשֶׁר־יֶשׁ־לוֹ נָתַן בְּיָדִי: אֵינֶנּוּ גָדוֹל בַּבַּיִת הַזֶּה מִמֶּנִּי וְלֹא־חָשַׂךְ
מִמֶּנִּי מְאוּמָה כִּי אִם־אוֹתָךְ בַּאֲשֶׁר אַתְּ־אִשְׁתּוֹ וְאֵיךְ אֶעֱשֶׂה הָרָעָה
הַגְּדֹלָה הַזֹּאת וְחָטָאתִי לֵאלֹקִים:
... וַתִּתְפְּשֵׂהוּ בְּבִגְדוֹ לֵאמֹר שִׁכְבָה עִמִּי וַיַּעֲזֹב
בִּגְדוֹ בְּיָדָהּ וַיָּנָס וַיֵּצֵא הַחוּצָה:
וַיְהִי כִּרְאוֹתָהּ כִּי־עָזַב בִּגְדוֹ בְּיָדָהּ וַיָּנָס הַחוּצָה: וַתִּקְרָא לְאַנְשֵׁי
בֵיתָהּ וַתֹּאמֶר לָהֶם לֵאמֹר רְאוּ הֵבִיא לָנוּ אִישׁ עִבְרִי לְצַחֶק בָּנוּ
בָּא אֵלַי לִשְׁכַּב עִמִּי וָאֶקְרָא בְּקוֹל גָּדוֹל ...
וַתְּדַבֵּר אֵלָיו ... בָּא אֵלַי הָעֶבֶד הָעִבְרִי אֲשֶׁר־הֵבֵאתָ לָּנוּ לְצַחֶק
בִּי: וַיְהִי כַּהֲרִימִי קוֹלִי וָאֶקְרָא וַיַּעֲזֹב בִּגְדוֹ אֶצְלִי וַיָּנָס הַחוּצָה:
וַיְהִי כִשְׁמֹעַ אֲדֹנָיו אֶת־דִּבְרֵי אִשְׁתּוֹ ... וַיִּחַר אַפּוֹ: וַיִּקַּח אֲדֹנֵי יוֹסֵף
אֹתוֹ וַיִּתְּנֵהוּ אֶל־בֵּית הַסֹּהַר מְקוֹם אֲשֶׁר־אֲסוּרֵי [אֲסִירֵי] הַמֶּלֶךְ
אֲסוּרִים וַיְהִי־שָׁם בְּבֵית הַסֹּהַר: וַיְהִי ה' אֶת־יוֹסֵף וַיֵּט אֵלָיו חָסֶד
וַיִּתֵּן חִנּוֹ בְּעֵינֵי שַׂר בֵּית־הַסֹּהַר

*And it was after these things that the wife of his*
*master lifted her eyes toward Yoseph,*
*and she said, "Lie with me."*
*But he refused, and he said to his master's wife,*
*"Look, my master doesn't keep track of me*
*regarding what is in the house, and everything*
*that he owns he has put into my hand.*
*No one in this household is greater than I am,*
*and he has not withheld from me anything,*
*except for you, because you are his wife. How, then,*
*can I do this great evil, and sin against God?"*
*... She grabbed him by his garment, saying,*
*"Lie with me," but he left his garment in her hand,*
*and he fled and went outside.*

*And it was, when she saw that he left his garment in her hand and that he fled outside, that she called to the people of her house and said to them, "See! He brought us a Hebrew man to sport with us; he came to me to lie with me, but I called out in a loud voice ...."*
*And she said to [Potiphar] ... "The Hebrew slave whom you brought to us came to me, to sport with me; and when I raised my voice and called out, he left his garment by me and he ran outside."*
*And it was when his master heard his wife's words ... his anger flared. And Yoseph's master took him and put him in the prison, in the place where the king's prisoners were locked up, and he was there in the prison. And Hashem was with Yoseph and granted him kindness, and gave him grace in the eyes of the prison warden ....*
*(Bereishis 39:7-21)*

Initially, Potiphar's wife would never have even considered committing adultery with a lowly slave. "*It was after these things,*" however, only after seeing Yoseph advanced to a high position in his master's house, that "*the wife of his master lifted her eyes toward Yoseph ....*"

"*But he refused ....*" According to the sense of the Hebrew verb used here,[35] Yoseph refused her advances only externally. Yet, in his heart, he desired to acquiesce, except that he controlled his urges.

Yoseph asked:

How could I be so ungrateful to my master, who has given me both trust and honor? He trusted me to the extent that "*he doesn't keep track of me regarding what is in the house,*" i.e., the expenses, "*and everything that he owns he has put into*

---

35. "*Yema'ein,*" he refused, as opposed to "*lo avah,*" he did not desire (Malbim).

*my hand,"* i.e., the income. He has honored me to the extent that *"no one in this household is greater than I am."* Such an act would be especially treacherous, because the one and only thing he has not given me is specifically *"you, because you are his wife."*

*"How, then, can I do this great evil"* against my master, and, in addition, Yoseph asks, How could I *"sin against God?"*

*"And it was, when she saw that he left his garment in her hand and that he fled and went outside ...."* Potiphar's wife chose to accuse Yoseph now[36] because she was afraid that people would ask Yoseph why he was walking around without his clothing and that everyone would therefore find out what had actually happened.

> **Potiphar's wife chose to accuse Yoseph now because she was afraid that people would ask Yoseph why he was walking around without his clothing and that everyone would therefore find out what had actually happened.**

Therefore, *"she called to the people of her house,"* her maidservants,[37] and said to them, *"He brought us a Hebrew man to sport with us,"* using the plural to imply that Yoseph surely must have committed indecencies with them as well, since he was unashamed to approach even the lady of the house. In this way, she hoped to incite them all against Yoseph.

She was careful to say, *"he left his garment by me,"* as opposed to "in my hand" as was the truth, claiming instead that Yoseph of his own accord had doffed the garment and left it nearby.

*"And it was when his master heard ...,"* meaning that Potiphar heard and understood the truth of the matter. By saying that *"the slave came to me,"* she implied that, in addition to tak-

---

36. Not because she was angry with Yoseph for refusing.

37. The verse above stated that *"no man"* was in the house, allowing for the presence of women.

ing off his clothing, Yoseph had actually committed the intended act. From this, Potiphar realized that she was lying, knowing that the slave[38] would never be so brazen to do either of these things.

Thus, the verse says that *"his anger flared,"* but it does not say at whom. It obviously could not have been against Yoseph, for otherwise Potiphar would have killed him. Rather, Potiphar was angry about the whole situation because he understood exactly what had happened, but he could no longer allow Yoseph to remain in his house under the circumstances.

Therefore, *"Yoseph's master,"* because he cared for Yoseph as a master cares for his slave, *"took him,"* he himself took Yoseph compassionately, not having him arrested by the police, *"and he put him in the prison."* Because Potiphar was the Chief Executioner, the prison was under his jurisdiction and he needed servants there as well. Therefore, he had the authority to place servants there to do his bidding without their being guilty of anything.

Because the prison had a wing where the commoners were housed, therefore the verse tells us that Yoseph was placed not with them but rather in *"the place where the king's prisoners were locked up,"* with the ministers and high-ranking officials.

*"... And he was there in the prison"*; in contrast to the other prisoners, Yoseph *was there in the prison* but was not *locked up*; rather, he was free to roam the prison in order to carry out his duties.

Even in jail *"Hashem granted him kindness,"* such that others regarded Yoseph as innocent, *"and gave him grace in the eyes of the prison warden"* — who normally tends to be a cruel person — to the extent that the warden delegated all his authority to Yoseph.

---

38. It is not clear whether Malbim means specifically Yoseph or any slave.

# The Butler and the Baker

וַיְהִי אַחַר הַדְּבָרִים הָאֵלֶּה חָטְאוּ מַשְׁקֵה מֶלֶךְ־מִצְרַיִם וְהָאֹפֶה
לַאֲדֹנֵיהֶם לְמֶלֶךְ מִצְרָיִם: וַיִּקְצֹף פַּרְעֹה עַל שְׁנֵי סָרִיסָיו עַל שַׂר
הַמַּשְׁקִים וְעַל שַׂר הָאוֹפִים: וַיִּתֵּן אֹתָם בְּמִשְׁמַר בֵּית שַׂר הַטַּבָּחִים
אֶל־בֵּית הַסֹּהַר מְקוֹם אֲשֶׁר יוֹסֵף אָסוּר שָׁם: וַיִּפְקֹד שַׂר הַטַּבָּחִים
אֶת־יוֹסֵף אִתָּם וַיְשָׁרֶת אֹתָם וַיִּהְיוּ יָמִים בְּמִשְׁמָר:
וַיַּחַלְמוּ חֲלוֹם שְׁנֵיהֶם ... וַיָּבֹא אֲלֵיהֶם יוֹסֵף בַּבֹּקֶר וַיַּרְא אֹתָם
וְהִנָּם זֹעֲפִים: וַיִּשְׁאַל אֶת־סְרִיסֵי פַרְעֹה ... מַדּוּעַ פְּנֵיכֶם רָעִים הַיּוֹם

*And it was after these things that the butler to
the king of Mitzrayim and the baker sinned against
their masters (sic), against the king of Mitzrayim.
And Pharaoh was enraged against his
two ministers, against the Chief Butler and
against the Chief Baker; and he put them under
guard in the house of the Chief Executioner in the
prison, in the place where Yoseph was incarcerated.
The Chief Executioner appointed Yoseph
to be with them, and he served them,
and they were [many] days under guard.
And they dreamed a dream, both of them ... and
Yoseph came to them in the morning,
looked at them, and saw that they were upset;
so he asked Pharaoh's ministers ...
"Why do your faces look troubled today?"*
(Bereishis 40:1-7)

The Torah does not say why the baker and butler were jailed, but our Sages provide the missing information: The butler's crime was that a fly was found in Pharaoh's wine glass, while the baker's crime was that a pebble was found baked inside Pharaoh's bread.

A little thinking about this reveals that the baker's sin against the king was an act of gross negligence; for, even a baker to a lesser minister would be considered negligent if dirt or pebbles were found in the bread.

The butler, on the other hand, had committed a relatively minor offense, since a fly landing in a cup is quite a common occurrence and almost impossible to prevent.

Yet, even the butler's sin was gross, since he was no ordinary butler, but rather the butler of the king, toward whom even a small transgression is considered large. This is why in reference to his sin the verse calls him *"the butler to the king of Mitzrayim"*; but, had he been a butler to anyone else, his act would not have been considered a transgression. The same verse calls his friend *"the baker,"* without reference to his being "the king's baker," because his act was an intrinsic sin, even had he been the baker to someone of lesser stature than the king.

Paying close attention to the exact wording of the verses reveals that sometimes the text refers to the "butler" and "baker," whereas other times the terms used are "Chief Butler" and "Chief Baker."

This lends support to the commentaries who explain that in the days of Pharaoh — as is still true today in the royal courts — the king would appoint from among the high ministers of his inner circle a "Chief Butler" whose great privilege it would be to place the cup in Pharaoh's hand. Another high minister would be awarded the prestigious title "Chief Baker," and he had the great honor of serving the breads and baked goods on the table that stood before the king.

As high-ranking officials, these men did not busy themselves with the actual baking of the bread or preparing of the wine; rather, they had trusty servants, expert chefs and master wine-makers, whom they relied upon to carry out these tasks flawlessly and without fail. Any blunder or negligence that evidenced itself in the king's bread or wine would lead to the punishment of not only the worker but the minister in charge as well, since he accepted upon himself responsibility for the actions of his under-lings whom he appointed to carry out his duties.

According to this, when the verse states that "*the butler to the king of Mitzrayim and the baker sinned*," this refers to the workers appointed by the ministers, and not to the ministers themselves.

It also implies, as mentioned above, that that butler's transgression was less severe than the baker's, because his error was a only a sin in light of his being "*the butler to the king of Mitzrayim*," but had he been a butler to anyone lesser, such a thing would not have been a crime.

The verse explains that they sinned "*against their masters*," plural; i.e., the baker sinned against his master the Chief Baker, while the butler sinned against his master the Chief Butler. At the root of it all, their sin was against "*the king of Mitzrayim.*"

"*And Pharaoh was enraged.*" Scrutinizing the matter more closely, we find that even though the sin of the baker was much worse than the sin of the butler, this was only insofar as the workers themselves were concerned. However, in regard to the ministers, the Chief Butler's sin was far worse than that of the Chief Baker. After all, the Chief Baker did not bake the bread; his servant did. How, then, was he to know that there were pebbles baked inside? He himself, therefore, did nothing

> **The Chief Butler's sin was far worse than that of the Chief Baker. After all, the Chief Baker did not bake the bread; his servant did. How was he to know that there were pebbles baked inside?**

wrong, except that he bears responsibility for the actions of his underling, the baker, whose fault it was.

The Chief Butler, on the other hand, he himself sinned, for he should have looked to see if the wine in the cup was free of fetid flies. Why didn't he inspect the cup before handing it to the king?

Thus, were Pharaoh to become angry with the underlings, he would first and foremost be angry with the baker; only afterward and secondarily would he be angry with the butler. However, because the king became angry not with the workers but "*with his two ministers,"* therefore, his foremost anger was against 'the Chief Butler" because not only did his worker err, but he himself erred by not checking the cup. Only secondarily was Pharaoh angry with the Chief Baker, who himself did nothing wrong, but rather took responsibility for the sin of his worker.

Now, one might ask, what is the point is of this whole story, with all these subtle nuances about who sinned more and who less? The answer is that the Torah here is teaching a very important lesson, showing us just how extraordinary was the special Providence that Hashem provided Yoseph in catapulting him to power:

The first stage was Pharaoh's anger that brought the ministers to the jail where Yoseph was found. However, had Yoseph interpreted their dreams in a way that was analagous to the severity of their crimes, with the Chief Butler hanged from the tree and the Chief Baker reinstated, then Yoseph would not have risen to power. Because, if that had been the case, they would have said that Yoseph's "interpretation" was merely an educated guess, a logical calculation that each man would get what he deserved according to the severity of his crime.

When they saw, however, that Yoseph interpreted their dreams *contrary* to logic and *contrary* to what simple justice would dictate and that his interpretation was accurate, from this they realized that Yoseph was a person infused with the Divine spirit. Thus, these verses are fundamental in understanding the first stage of Divine Providence in Yoseph's rise to become the viceroy of Mitzrayim.

Providence evidenced itself as well by having both ministers put in the section of the prison *"of the Chief Executioner,"* and not in some other wing, and that the executioner put them in the prison *"in the place where Yoseph was ...."*

Further Providence was seen in this that *"the Chief Executioner appointed Yoseph to be with them, and he served them"* bringing them into daily contact with Yoseph, and that *"they were [many] days under guard,"* meaning one full year, which enabled Yoseph to become very familiar with them. Otherwise, Yoseph would not have had the audacity to ask them why their *"faces looked troubled"*; he would not have asked such a thing unless he had earned their trust as a faithful servant over *"many days."*

## The Two Dreams

וַיַּחַלְמוּ חֲלוֹם שְׁנֵיהֶם אִישׁ חֲלֹמוֹ בְּלַיְלָה אֶחָד אִישׁ
כְּפִתְרוֹן חֲלֹמוֹ הַמַּשְׁקֶה וְהָאֹפֶה אֲשֶׁר לְמֶלֶךְ מִצְרַיִם אֲשֶׁר
אֲסוּרִים בְּבֵית הַסֹּהַר ... וַיְסַפֵּר שַׂר־הַמַּשְׁקִים אֶת־חֲלֹמוֹ
לְיוֹסֵף וַיֹּאמֶר לוֹ בַּחֲלוֹמִי וְהִנֵּה־גֶפֶן לְפָנָי: וּבַגֶּפֶן שְׁלֹשָׁה
שָׂרִיגִם וְהוּא כְפֹרַחַת עָלְתָה נִצָּהּ הִבְשִׁילוּ אַשְׁכְּלֹתֶיהָ עֲנָבִים:
וְכוֹס פַּרְעֹה בְּיָדִי וָאֶקַּח אֶת־הָעֲנָבִים וָאֶשְׂחַט אֹתָם
אֶל־כּוֹס פַּרְעֹה וָאֶתֵּן אֶת־הַכּוֹס עַל־כַּף פַּרְעֹה:
וַיֹּאמֶר לוֹ יוֹסֵף זֶה פִּתְרֹנוֹ שְׁלֹשֶׁת הַשָּׂרִגִים שְׁלֹשֶׁת יָמִים הֵם:
בְּעוֹד שְׁלֹשֶׁת יָמִים יִשָּׂא פַרְעֹה אֶת־רֹאשֶׁךָ וַהֲשִׁיבְךָ עַל־כַּנֶּךָ וְנָתַתָּ
כוֹס־פַּרְעֹה בְּיָדוֹ ... כִּי אִם־זְכַרְתַּנִי אִתְּךָ ... וְהִזְכַּרְתַּנִי אֶל־פַּרְעֹה
וְהוֹצֵאתַנִי מִן־הַבַּיִת הַזֶּה:
... וַיַּרְא שַׂר־הָאֹפִים כִּי טוֹב פָּתָר וַיֹּאמֶר אֶל־יוֹסֵף אַף־אֲנִי בַּחֲלוֹמִי
וְהִנֵּה שְׁלֹשָׁה סַלֵּי חֹרִי עַל־רֹאשִׁי: וּבַסַּל הָעֶלְיוֹן מִכֹּל מַאֲכַל
פַּרְעֹה מַעֲשֵׂה אֹפֶה וְהָעוֹף אֹכֵל אֹתָם מִן־הַסַּל מֵעַל רֹאשִׁי:
וַיַּעַן יוֹסֵף וַיֹּאמֶר זֶה פִּתְרֹנוֹ שְׁלֹשֶׁת הַסַּלִּים שְׁלֹשֶׁת יָמִים הֵם:
בְּעוֹד שְׁלֹשֶׁת יָמִים יִשָּׂא פַרְעֹה אֶת־רֹאשְׁךָ מֵעָלֶיךָ וְתָלָה אוֹתְךָ
עַל־עֵץ וְאָכַל הָעוֹף אֶת־בְּשָׂרְךָ מֵעָלֶיךָ:
וַיְהִי בַּיּוֹם הַשְּׁלִישִׁי יוֹם הֻלֶּדֶת אֶת־פַּרְעֹה ... וַיָּשֶׁב אֶת־שַׂר
הַמַּשְׁקִים עַל־מַשְׁקֵהוּ וַיִּתֵּן הַכּוֹס עַל־כַּף פַּרְעֹה: וְאֵת שַׂר הָאֹפִים
תָּלָה כַּאֲשֶׁר פָּתַר לָהֶם יוֹסֵף:

*And they dreamed a dream, both of them,*
*each one's dream on the same night,*
*each man according to the interpretation of his*
*dream, the butler and the baker of the king of*
*Mitzrayim, who were locked up in the prison ....*
*And the Chief Butler told his dream to Yoseph, and*

*he said to him, "In my dream, behold, there was a grapevine before me. Upon the grapevine were three branches, and as it was budding, its flowers blossomed, and its clusters ripened with grapes; and Pharaoh's cup was in my hand, and I took the grapes and I squeezed them into Pharaoh's cup, and I put the cup into Pharaoh's palm."*

*Yoseph said to him, "This is its interpretation: The three branches are three days. In three more days, Pharaoh will lift up your head and restore you to your position, and you will put Pharaoh's cup into his hand .... Only, if you will remember me ... and mention me to Pharaoh ... and take me out of this jailhouse ...."*

*... The Chief Baker saw that he had interpreted well, so he said to Yoseph, "I, too, was in my dream, and behold, there were three wicker baskets upon my head. And in the uppermost basket were all types of Pharaoh's food, baked goods, and the birds were eating them from the basket from upon my head."*

*Yoseph answered and said, "This is its interpretation: The three baskets are three days. In three days, Pharaoh will lift up your head from upon you and hang you on a tree, and the birds will eat your flesh from upon you."*

*And it was on the third day, Pharaoh's birthday .... He restored the Chief Butler to his butlership, and he put the cup into Pharaoh's hand. And the Chief Baker he hanged, as Yoseph interpreted for them.*

*(Bereishis 40:5-22)*

As explained above, the judgment warranted by the ministers, the Chief Butler and the Chief Baker, was the exact opposite of that deserved by their servants, the butler and the baker. Indeed, we can safely assume that, during their year in jail, their cases had been reviewed and decided by the judges of the land, and that the Chief Butler had already been sentenced to death and the Chief Baker restored to his post, in accordance with the severity of their actions (see previous essay.)

Thus, the verse states that each ministers dreamed "*according to the interpretation of his dream, the butler and the baker ...*" meaning that the interpretation of each man's dream applied aptly not to himself but to his servant, the butler and the baker who were also there in the prison. That is, the Chief Butler's good dream was fitting for his servant the butler, while the Chief Baker's bad dream was fitting for his servant, the baker. Astonishingly, Pharaoh reversed the judgment of his ministers, judging each one not for his own action but for the actions of his servant.

The Chief Butler's dream begins with a barren, empty vine, symbolic of the fact that he had already been condemned to death. Suddenly, however, over the next three days, symbolized by the three vines, his judgment would change for the good, and he would be restored to his old position in every sense.

Yoseph interpreted the three symbols of flowering, blossoming, and ripening grapes as the three levels of the Chief Butler's redemption: a) "*Pharaoh will lift up your head,*" meaning he will pardon you from the death penalty, b) "*and restore you to your position*" of wealth, for till now you were judged as a "rebel" whose property is forfeit to the crown,[39] c) "*and you will put Pharaoh's cup into his hand*" as though you had never done anything wrong.

"However," Yoseph told him, "*only if you will remember me ... and mention me to Pharaoh ... and take me out of this pit*" will God's purpose be served in staging such a dramatic, life-and-death turn of events on your behalf. The sole reason that this miracle will happen to you, Yoseph told the Chief Butler, is as a vehicle for me to gain my freedom.

The Chief Baker's dream begins just the opposite; instead of

---

39. *Rambam, Hilchos Gezeilah* 5:13.

the symbol of the empty vine, his dream starts with a basket full of delicious bread ready to be served upon the king's table. This symbolized that the Chief Baker had been acquitted of his crimes and was slated for reinstatement to his post. Instead of the king, however, a bird from heaven eats the bread, meaning that over the next three days, symbolized by the three baskets, his judgment would change from good to bad.

> *Instead of the symbol of the empty vine, the Chief Baker's dream starts with a basket full of delicious bread ready to be served upon the king's table. This symbolized that he had been acquitted of his crimes and was slated for reinstatement to his post.*

Three days later, Pharaoh reinstated the Chief Butler and hanged the Chief Baker. This dramatic turn of events was *"as Yoseph interpreted for them,"* coming about *because of* Yoseph's interpretation. Hashem made things happen the way that Yoseph said they would in order to raise Yoseph to power.

# פרשת מקץ
# PARASHAS MIKEITZ

---

# The Dreams of a King

וַיְהִי מִקֵּץ שְׁנָתַיִם יָמִים וּפַרְעֹה חֹלֵם
*It was at the end of two full years,*
*and Pharaoh was dreaming ....*
*(Bereishis 41:1)*

I n the grammar of *Lashon Hakodesh* (Biblical Hebrew), the
subject normally follows the verb. If the verb follows the
subject, it signifies a specific emphasis on the subject. Here,
where the verb "*was dreaming*" follows the subject "*Pharaoh,*"
this implies an emphasis on Pharaoh dreaming to the exclusion
of the dreams of others.

By this, the verse means to point out that the dreams of the ministers did not help Yoseph at all; only the dreams of Pharaoh himself helped Yoseph.[1]

Another explanation is offered by the Midrash[2] on this verse, which asks the following: "Weren't the rest of the people in the world also dreaming?" Again, this question springs from the word order that emphasizes "Pharaoh," implying that Pharaoh and only Pharaoh was dreaming. The Midrash answers: "Rather, the dream of the king is the dream of the whole world."

The Midrash means to explain why the king's conjurers failed in their attempts to explain Pharaoh's dream. Their failure lay in perceiving and interpreting his dreams in relation to issues that pertained to Pharaoh personally, as though these were the dreams of a private individual.

*This was not a private person dreaming; rather, it was Pharaoh who was dreaming, and thus his dream was a message for the entire kingdom.*

Their mistake was in not realizing that the dreams of a king emanate from his aspect as a universal person, a person who represents the entire collective of society. This was not a private person dreaming; rather, it was *Pharaoh* who was dreaming, and thus his dream was a message for the entire kingdom.

# Pharaoh's "Second" Dream

וְהִנֵּה מִן־הַיְאֹר עֹלֹת שֶׁבַע פָּרוֹת יְפוֹת מַרְאֶה וּבְרִיאֹת בָּשָׂר וַתִּרְעֶינָה בָּאָחוּ: וְהִנֵּה שֶׁבַע פָּרוֹת אֲחֵרוֹת עֹלוֹת אַחֲרֵיהֶן מִן־ הַיְאֹר רָעוֹת מַרְאֶה וְדַקּוֹת בָּשָׂר וַתַּעֲמֹדְנָה אֵצֶל הַפָּרוֹת עַל־שְׂפַת

---

1. The point being to teach that Yoseph's trust in the Chief Butler was misplaced, as Malbim points out in his commentary (40:23).

2. *Bereishis Rabbah* 89:4.

הַיְאֹר: וַתֹּאכַלְנָה הַפָּרוֹת רָעוֹת הַמַּרְאֶה וְדַקֹּת הַבָּשָׂר אֵת שֶׁבַע
הַפָּרוֹת יְפֹת הַמַּרְאֶה וְהַבְּרִיאֹת וַיִּיקַץ פַּרְעֹה:
וַיִּישָׁן וַיַּחֲלֹם שֵׁנִית וְהִנֵּה שֶׁבַע שִׁבֳּלִים עֹלוֹת בְּקָנֶה אֶחָד בְּרִיאוֹת
וְטֹבוֹת: וְהִנֵּה שֶׁבַע שִׁבֳּלִים דַּקּוֹת וּשְׁדוּפֹת קָדִים צֹמְחוֹת אַחֲרֵיהֶן:
וַתִּבְלַעְנָה הַשִּׁבֳּלִים הַדַּקּוֹת אֵת שֶׁבַע הַשִּׁבֳּלִים הַבְּרִיאוֹת
וְהַמְּלֵאוֹת וַיִּיקַץ פַּרְעֹה וְהִנֵּה חֲלוֹם:
וַיְהִי בַבֹּקֶר וַתִּפָּעֶם רוּחוֹ וַיִּשְׁלַח וַיִּקְרָא אֶת־כָּל־חַרְטֻמֵּי
מִצְרַיִם וְאֶת־כָּל־חֲכָמֶיהָ וַיְסַפֵּר פַּרְעֹה לָהֶם אֶת־חֲלֹמוֹ
וְאֵין־פּוֹתֵר אוֹתָם לְפַרְעֹה

*And, behold, from the Nile rose seven good-looking,*
*healthy-fleshed cows, and they grazed in the marsh.*
*And, behold, seven other cows rose from the Nile*
*after them, bad looking and thin fleshed, and they*
*stood next to the cows on the bank of the Nile.*
*And the bad-looking, thin-fleshed cows ate the seven*
*healthy, good-looking cows; and Pharaoh woke up.*
*And he slept and dreamt a second time:*
*And, behold, seven healthy and good ears of grain*
*arose upon one stalk. And behold, seven ears,*
*thin and smitten by an eastern wind,*
*sprouted after them. And the thin ears of grain*
*swallowed the seven healthy and full ears, and*
*Pharaoh woke up, and behold, it was a dream.*
*And it was in the morning that his heart pounded,*
*so he sent and called for all the necromancers of*
*Mitzrayim and for all its wise men, and Pharaoh*
*related to them his dream, yet there was no one*
*to interpret them to Pharaoh.*
*(Bereishis 41:2-8)*

The Egyptians believed in the Nile River, attributing Divine power to it because of its life-giving ability to irrigate the land. They worshipped the cow as well for its power to pro-duce crops from the earth through plowing. Hashem therefore chose these two symbols of agricultural prosperity to show Pharaoh in his dream.

"*Seven other cows rose from the Nile after them,*" immediately after them, meaning that no time would lapse between the good years and the famine years. The bad cows rose "*from the Nile,*" because the famine would occur due to a drying of the Nile.

"*They stood next to the cows,*" because at the beginning of the famine there was still bread in Mitzrayim, and thus the famine and the bounty existed side by side.[3]

"*And he slept and dreamt a second time, and behold, seven healthy and good ears of grain arose upon one stalk ....*" The second dream is more easily understood than the first dream, and is actually the interpretation of it; the cows represent plowing and planting while the stalks represent the purpose of this activity, i.e., harvesting a crop.

> **The second dream is more easily understood than the first dream, and is actually the interpretation of it; the cows represent plowing and planting, while the stalks represent the purpose of this activity, i.e., harvesting a crop.**

Five things about Pharaoh's dream marked it as a true portent of the future:

a) It was a repeated dream. b) It was a dream interpreted within a dream, the stalks being the interpretation of the cows. This indicates a true dream, as our Sages teach.[4]

c) "*And Pharaoh woke up, and behold, it was a dream.*" The word "*hinei*" (behold) indicates a new element. Until Pharaoh woke up, it was not a dream; that is, the dream seemed as real to Pharaoh as though he were seeing everything in a waking state.

---

3. Meaning that, although the people of Mitzrayim still had bread, yet **a)** the famine had begun in other lands, or **b)** the famine conditions were evident in Mitzrayim itself.

4. *Berachos* 55b.

d) *"And it was in the morning,"* the dream occurred toward morning, another indication of its prophetic nature, as our Sages tell us.[5] e) And, finally, *"his heart pounded"* because he was very moved by the dream, a further indication of the veracity of a dream.[6]

Pharaoh called for the *"necromancers,"* those schooled in magic and in the world's physical make-up, and for the *"wise men,"* the astronomers and astrologers. Ultimately, he rejected all of their attempted interpretations, and for two reasons:

For one, *"Pharaoh related to them his **dream**,"* singular, for in truth the two dreams were really one. The advisers, however, incorrectly believed it to be two dreams, and thus, *"there was no one who could interpret **them**,"* plural.

Secondly, no one could interpret them *"to Pharaoh,"* the king. This was no ordinary dream, but rather a "Pharaohic" one, a royal dream whose interpretation must be relevant to matters of state. The advisers, on the other hand, offered interpretations of a personal, private nature, such as "You will have seven daughters …," as our Sages explain.[7]

---

5. Ibid.

6. According to *Sefer Hachalomos* [Malbim].

7. *Bereishis Rabbah* 89:6.

# Yoseph's Interpretation

וַיֹּאמֶר יוֹסֵף אֶל־פַּרְעֹה חֲלוֹם פַּרְעֹה אֶחָד הוּא אֵת אֲשֶׁר הָאֱלֹקִים
עֹשֶׂה הִגִּיד לְפַרְעֹה: שֶׁבַע פָּרֹת הַטֹּבֹת שֶׁבַע שָׁנִים הֵנָּה וְשֶׁבַע
הַשִּׁבֳּלִים הַטֹּבֹת שֶׁבַע שָׁנִים הֵנָּה חֲלוֹם אֶחָד הוּא: וְשֶׁבַע הַפָּרוֹת
הָרַקּוֹת וְהָרָעֹת הָעֹלֹת אַחֲרֵיהֶן שֶׁבַע שָׁנִים הֵנָּה וְשֶׁבַע הַשִּׁבֳּלִים
הָרֵקוֹת שְׁדֻפוֹת הַקָּדִים יִהְיוּ שֶׁבַע שְׁנֵי רָעָב: הוּא הַדָּבָר אֲשֶׁר
דִּבַּרְתִּי אֶל־פַּרְעֹה אֲשֶׁר הָאֱלֹקִים עֹשֶׂה הֶרְאָה אֶת־פַּרְעֹה:
הִנֵּה שֶׁבַע שָׁנִים בָּאוֹת שָׂבָע גָּדוֹל בְּכָל־אֶרֶץ מִצְרָיִם: וְקָמוּ שֶׁבַע
שְׁנֵי רָעָב אַחֲרֵיהֶן וְנִשְׁכַּח כָּל־הַשָּׂבָע בְּאֶרֶץ מִצְרָיִם וְכִלָּה הָרָעָב
אֶת־הָאָרֶץ: וְלֹא־יִוָּדַע הַשָּׂבָע בָּאָרֶץ מִפְּנֵי הָרָעָב הַהוּא אַחֲרֵי־כֵן
כִּי־כָבֵד הוּא מְאֹד: וְעַל הִשָּׁנוֹת הַחֲלוֹם אֶל־פַּרְעֹה פַּעֲמָיִם כִּי־נָכוֹן
הַדָּבָר מֵעִם הָאֱלֹקִים וּמְמַהֵר הָאֱלֹקִים לַעֲשֹׂתוֹ:
וְעַתָּה יֵרֶא פַרְעֹה אִישׁ נָבוֹן וְחָכָם וִישִׁיתֵהוּ עַל־אֶרֶץ מִצְרָיִם

*And Yoseph said to Pharaoh, "Pharaoh's dream is
one; that which God is doing, He told to Pharaoh.
The seven good cows are seven years, and the seven
good ears of grain are seven years; it is one dream.
And the seven thin, bad cows rising after them are
seven years, as are the seven empty, wind-smitten
ears of grain, they will be seven years of famine.
This is the matter that I have said to Pharaoh, that
which God is doing, He showed Pharaoh."*

*"Behold, seven years are coming of great abundance
in the whole land of Mitzrayim; but seven years of
famine will arise after them, and all the abundance
will be forgotten in the land of Mitzrayim, and the
famine will destroy the land. The abundance will
not be known in the land due to the famine that
follows it, for it will be extremely severe."*

*And regarding the dream's being repeated to
Pharaoh twice, this is because the matter is prepared before God, and God is hastening to do it.*

*So, now, let Pharaoh find a wise and discerning man
and appoint him over the land of Mitzrayim ....
(Bereishis 41:25-33)*

Yoseph's perception of Pharaoh's dreams differed from
that of the advisers in three ways, two of which were
alluded to above:
Firstly, Yoseph recognized that *"Pharaoh's dream is one,"*
unlike the advisers who saw them as two separate dreams with
two separate interpretations.

Secondly, whereas the advisers saw the dreams in terms
of Pharaoh's private affairs, Yoseph said, *"that which God is
doing"* in terms of general, worldwide "acts of God," *"He told
to **Pharaoh**,"* Pharaoh, the king and ruler of nations.

Thirdly, the advisers interpreted the dreams symbolically, as
though they were riddles or
analogies, but ignored their plain
meaning. Yoseph, on the other
hand, read the dream in its most
simple sense: "Good grain, bad
grain." Thus, he said, *"God
told Pharaoh,"* telling plainly
without any hinting or analogy.

Everything God does is first
decreed in potential in the heavenly realms, revealed only to the
angelic beings. Sometimes such
a decree does not apply until the distant future. Later, when the
time comes for the decree to go into effect on earth, the prophets sense it with their prophetic "eye."

*The advisers interpreted
the dreams symbolically, as
though they were riddles
or analogies, but ignored
their plain meaning.
Yoseph, on the other
hand, read the dream in its
most simple sense: "Good
grain, bad grain."*

This explains why Pharaoh's dream was repeated *in two different forms*, first with cows and then with grain: The first was
to show that the decree had been issued in the Heavenly realm,
and *"that which God is doing, He **told** Pharaoh,"* telling and
informing him of a hidden, heavenly decree via the symbol of

cows that represent agricultural productivity in *potential*.

With the second dream, *"that which God is doing, He showed Pharaoh,"* showing him palpably through images of grain that the famine was ready to actualize *immediately*.

According to Yoseph, Pharaoh's dream presaged *"great abundance in the whole land of Mitzrayim."* Unlike the famine that would be worldwide, the abundance would grace the land of Mitzrayim alone. Yoseph saw this by virtue of the fact that Pharaoh saw *"the good cows rising from the Nile,"* whereas regarding the bad cows Pharaoh did not mention that they "rose from the Nile."[8] God caused Pharaoh to relate his dream in this way, Yoseph told Pharaoh, to indicate that the famine would be universal, not limited to the Nile, whereas the abundance would be Nile based.

Thus, *"all the abundance will be forgotten in the land of Mitzrayim"* alone, where there was once abundance to be forgotten; *"and the famine will destroy the land"* in general, referring to the rest of the world, but where the abundance will not be "forgotten," because even initially there was never abundance there.

Even during the years of plenty, Yoseph adds, *"the abundance will not be known in the land"* of Mitzrayim itself, and this will be *"due to the famine,"* in anticipation of which all spare grain will be placed in storage and not enjoyed.

The actual repetition of the dream indicated three things:[9]

- Although sometimes a Heavenly decree is issued conditionally and can be averted if the people repent, this decree was unconditional and would definitely come about. This dream was repeated to show that *"the matter is prepared before God"* without any hope of its being rescinded.

8. Although in his dream the cows did indeed rise from the Nile, yet when recounting his dream Pharaoh omits this detail (*Bereishis* 41:19).

9. Above Malbim explained why the repeated dream came in two different *forms*: cows and grains. Here he explains the purpose of the *repetition* itself.

- Secondly, the repetition showed that *"God is hastening to do it"* immediately.

- Finally, the dream's repetition was meant to rouse Pharaoh to the urgency of appointing *"a wise and understanding man"* to store up provisions in preparation for the famine.

This last reason explains why only in regard to the cows did Pharaoh say, *"it was not known that they came inside them,"* whereas he did not make this point regarding the grain. The dream itself is predicting that Pharaoh — alerted to the total devastation *in potential* foretold by the dream of the cows — would store the grain. These preparations would result in the fulfillment of the second dream, wherein the thin grain *does* become fuller from swallowing the fat grain, indicating that the plenty would *in actuality* serve to sustain the land in famine.

With this last point, we can answer another question: Who asked Yoseph to advise the king on how to deal with the famine?[10] Yoseph was called upon to interpret the dream, not to give advice.

Based on the above, however, we can see that Pharaoh's preparations for the famine were alluded to in the dream, and therefore formed an intrinsic part of its interpretation.

---

10. Oddly, Malbim asks this question not here, but rather in his introduction to his next comment, in which he does not seem to answer it. We took Malbim's question from there and combined it with his comment here.

# Autocracy or Rule by Committee?

וְעַתָּה יֵרֶא פַרְעֹה אִישׁ נָבוֹן וְחָכָם וִישִׁיתֵהוּ עַל־אֶרֶץ
מִצְרָיִם: יַעֲשֶׂה פַרְעֹה וְיַפְקֵד פְּקִדִים עַל־הָאָרֶץ וְחִמֵּשׁ אֶת־
אֶרֶץ מִצְרַיִם בְּשֶׁבַע שְׁנֵי הַשָּׂבָע: וְיִקְבְּצוּ אֶת־כָּל־אֹכֶל הַשָּׁנִים
הַטֹּבוֹת הַבָּאֹת הָאֵלֶּה וְיִצְבְּרוּ־בָר תַּחַת יַד־פַרְעֹה אֹכֶל בֶּעָרִים
וְשָׁמָרוּ: וְהָיָה הָאֹכֶל לְפִקָּדוֹן לָאָרֶץ לְשֶׁבַע שְׁנֵי הָרָעָב אֲשֶׁר
תִּהְיֶיןָ בְּאֶרֶץ מִצְרָיִם וְלֹא־תִכָּרֵת הָאָרֶץ בָּרָעָב

*"So, now, let Pharaoh find a wise and discerning
man and appoint him over the land of Mitzrayim.
Let Pharaoh do this, and he will appoint officers
over the land and he will enact a twenty percent tax
upon the land of Mitzrayim in the seven years of
abundance. And they will gather all the
food of these good years that are coming,
and they will hoard grain under Pharaoh's hand,
food in the cities, and they will guard it. The food
will be a surety for the land for the seven years of
famine that will be in the land of Mitzrayim,
and the land will not be cut off in hunger."*

*(Bereishis 41:33-36)*

Political scientists argue as to whether delegation of responsibilities is a good way to run a country.

Some say that the best policy is to have many appointees, with each one responsible for a specific task; for example, one person in charge of collecting taxes, while another is treasurer, and yet a third oversees spending, etc. For if one person were empowered with all these responsibilities, he would be unable to oversee all the requisite details and various activities to make sure that they are all done in the optimum way.

Others argue that, no, it is better for all the administration to be under the control of one person, because otherwise *"many ministers cause the land to rebel,"*[11] with each minister pursuing a different goal, each with different interests, and there is no definitive leadership.

*It is better for all the administration to be under the control of one person, because otherwise "many ministers cause the land to rebel," with each minister pursuing a different goal, each with different interests, and there is no definitive leadership.*

We see in Yoseph's advice to Pharaoh that each of the above views has its place. Matters in general must all be under the authority of one person who makes sure that everything advances more or less toward one overall goal. To this, Yoseph said, *"Now, let Pharaoh find a wise and discerning man and appoint him over the land of Mitzrayim"*; the country's main leadership should be under the authority of one person.

That accomplished, *"let Pharaoh do this"* as well, empowering that wise man such that *"he will appoint officers over the land,"* assigning specialized tasks to however many underlings are necessary to ensure that the job is done right.

Now Yoseph specifies more particularly what are to be the various roles of the general overseer and of his officers. The general overseer will enact a tax whereby twenty percent of all the grain produced will go the king's storehouses. Such a heavy tax requires great wisdom and good oratory skills to convince the entire populace to accept it.[12]

---

11. *Mishlei* 28:2; see Malbim there. Our translation here is justified by the context.

12. By today's standards, this tax rate does not seem exorbitant. Yet, it may have **a)** been *in addition to* other taxes they were already paying; **b)** not have allowed for deduction of expenses; and **c)** applied to the poor as well; these and other factors, such as contemporary farming conditions, may have made this a difficult tax [Editor].

The lesser officers appointed in each city will "*gather all the food*," not only grain. "*They will hoard grain under Pharaoh's hand*"; the grain from the twenty percent tax will be hoarded in huge amounts and guarded in the capital city's treasure-houses. In addition, they will also store "*food in the cities, and guard it.*" The other food, grain, and produce that the lesser officers gather will be stored in each city's storehouses where it must be carefully guarded against theft, unlike the grain in the capital city that is safe in the royal treasure vaults.

The food in the cities "*will be a surety for the land for the seven years of famine,*" to provide for the needs of the people within the city. By contrast, the grain in the capital city will not be a surety for the land, but rather will be sold to the surrounding nations during the famine, bringing great wealth to the royal coffers.

# The Good Within the Bad

וַיִּקְרָא יוֹסֵף אֶת־שֵׁם הַבְּכוֹר מְנַשֶּׁה כִּי־נַשַּׁנִי אֱלֹקִים
אֶת־כָּל־עֲמָלִי וְאֵת כָּל־בֵּית אָבִי: וְאֵת שֵׁם הַשֵּׁנִי קָרָא
אֶפְרָיִם כִּי־הִפְרַנִי אֱלֹקִים בְּאֶרֶץ עָנְיִי

**And Yoseph called the name of the firstborn
Menasheh — "Because Hashem caused me to forget
all my travails and all my father's household."
And the name of the second one he called
Ephraim — "Because Hashem has made me
prosper me in the land of my affliction."
(Bereishis 41:51-52)**

One of the character traits of the righteous is that they remember the bad times even when all is going well.

This is why we are commanded to eat matzah and bitter herbs the first night of Passover, to enable us in times of freedom to remember the bitter exile; because it is the exile that brings the redemption, the bad that brings the good.

Thus, we see here that Yoseph, in his righteousness, gave his children symbolic names to help him during his triumph to remember his travails:

He called his firstborn "*Menasheh*," from the Hebrew root meaning "to forget," in *lament* at having forgotten all his troubles and all his father's household.

> *One of the character traits of the righteous is that they remember the bad times even when all is going well.*

The second son he called "*Ephraim*," related to the root word for "fruitfulness" and "prosperity," and he said, "*Hashem has made me prosper* only *in the land of my affliction*," recognizing that all his prosperity and success was born out of affliction and pain.

# The Brothers Accused/ Yoseph's Motives

וַיָּבֹאוּ בְּנֵי יִשְׂרָאֵל לִשְׁבֹּר בְּתוֹךְ הַבָּאִים כִּי־הָיָה הָרָעָב בְּאֶרֶץ
כְּנָעַן: וְיוֹסֵף הוּא הַשַּׁלִּיט עַל־הָאָרֶץ הוּא הַמַּשְׁבִּיר לְכָל־עַם
הָאָרֶץ וַיָּבֹאוּ אֲחֵי יוֹסֵף וַיִּשְׁתַּחֲווּ־לוֹ אַפַּיִם אָרְצָה:
וַיַּרְא יוֹסֵף אֶת־אֶחָיו וַיַּכִּרֵם וַיִּתְנַכֵּר אֲלֵיהֶם וַיְדַבֵּר אִתָּם קָשׁוֹת
וַיֹּאמֶר אֲלֵהֶם מֵאַיִן בָּאתֶם וַיֹּאמְרוּ מֵאֶרֶץ כְּנַעַן לִשְׁבָּר־אֹכֶל:
וַיִּזְכֹּר יוֹסֵף אֵת הַחֲלֹמוֹת אֲשֶׁר חָלַם לָהֶם וַיֹּאמֶר אֲלֵהֶם ...
מְרַגְּלִים אַתֶּם

*And the Children of Yisrael came to buy food among those who came, for the famine was in the Land of Canaan. Yoseph was the ruler over the land, he was the one who sold food to all the people of the land, and Yoseph's brothers came and bowed down to him, face to the ground.*

*Yoseph saw his brothers and he recognized them;*
*yet he pretended to be a stranger to them; he spoke*
*to them harshly, and said to them, "Where are you*
*coming from!" And they said, "From the Land of*
*Canaan to buy food."*
*... Yoseph remembered the dreams that he dreamed*
*about them, and he said to them, "You are spies ...."*
*(Bereishis 42:5-9)*

E ven though *"Yoseph was the ruler over the land,"* nevertheless, he was also *"the one who sold food to all the people of the land,"* and therefore, *"Yoseph's brothers came"* before him to buy food. Because he was the ruler, they *"bowed down to him, face to the ground,"* thus fulfilling, at least partially, his first dream, for they bowed down to his *"sheaf of grain."*

Regardless of Yoseph's motives (discussed below) for accusing the brothers of being spies, finding some plausible pretext for doing so was a challenge: First of all, they were not from a belligerent, warlike tribe, but rather they were *"Children of Yisrael,"* reputed to be people of peace. It was clear that they *"came to buy food,"* because they were *"among those who came"* for the same purpose. These others were not a few individuals but rather great multitudes who thronged to Mitzrayim *"because the famine was in the Land of Canaan."*

> **Wordiness in the presence of a powerful, venerated prince of the land reveals that the speaker has a "guilty conscience," a secret motive that he is attempting to conceal.**

Yoseph found his pretext when he asked his brothers in an accusing tone, *"Where are you from!"* They should have answered simply, *"from the Land of Canaan".* By adding the words *"to buy food,"* they volunteered an answer to a question that had not been asked. Yoseph used this as his excuse to accuse them of being

spies, because wordiness in the presence of a powerful, vener-
ated prince of the land reveals that the speaker has a "guilty
conscience," a secret motive that he is attempting to conceal.[13]

The question arises as to why Yoseph would put his brothers
through all this tribulation. Is this the same righteous, forgiving
Yoseph who later says (*Bereishis* 45:8), "*It wasn't you who sent
me here, but, rather, it was God ...*"?

The above verse gives us part of the answer: "*Yoseph remembered the dreams that he dreamed about them, and he said to
them, "You are spies ...."* As explained previously,[14] Yoseph's
dreams indicated events occurring in three distinct stages: a) His
sheaf rising indicated that first Yoseph would rise to a position
of power above them against their will, which already occurred;
b) next they would bow to him willingly, as indicated by their
sheaves *surrounding* and bowing to his sheaf; this had not yet
been fulfilled because Binyamin was not with them; and, finally,
c) their father and his household would all bow down to Yoseph,
as shown by the dream of the sun, moon, and stars. Accusing
them of being spies was the initial stage of Yoseph's plan to bring
about the fulfillment of the second and third stages of his dreams.

Yoseph had additional reasons for his method:

For one, Yoseph wanted to put his brothers to the test: When
Binyamin was enslaved for his "theft," would the brothers voluntarily sacrifice themselves for his sake? If so, that would indicate
that they harbored no jealousy or grudge against the children of
Rachel.

Furthermore, Yoseph wanted to aggrieve his brothers so that
they would receive their punishment[15] measure for measure.
Just as they suspected him of being a "spy" and a talebearer, he
accused them of being spies. Just as it was Shimon, according to
our Sages,[16] who flung Yoseph into the pit with the agreement

---

13. Malbim credits *Mahari Bei Rav* for this insight.

14. See above, "Yoseph's Dreams" to *Bereishis* 37:5-11.

15. In this world, to purge them from sin in the next.

16. *Bereishis Rabbah* 91:6.

of all the brothers, so too Yoseph put them all in jail for three days, and afterward he imprisoned only Shimon. Just as they sold him for twenty silver pieces, so too he subjected them to the fear and anxiety caused by finding their money returned in their sacks; and, just as they sold him as a slave, he caused them to say, "*Behold, we are [your] slaves*" (*Bereishis* 44:16), and for Yehudah to accept upon himself to remain as a slave in place of Binyamin.

# The Purpose of
# Mitzrayim's Prosperity

וַיֹּאמֶר שָׁלוֹם לָכֶם אַל־תִּירָאוּ אֱלֹקֵיכֶם וֵאלֹקֵי אֲבִיכֶם
נָתַן לָכֶם מַטְמוֹן בְּאַמְתְּחֹתֵיכֶם כַּסְפְּכֶם בָּא אֵלָי

*And he said, "Peace unto you, do not fear; your God*
*and the God of your fathers has given you a cache*
*in your sack; your money came to me ...."*
**(Bereishis 43:23)**

Simply speaking, the man overseeing Yoseph's house was reassuring the brothers that he indeed had received their money, and that they were under no suspicion of theft; the money they found in their sacks was a gift to them from Hashem.

Based on a Midrash,[17] however, we can read another intention in his words.

Hashem's purpose in bringing abundance and then famine in the land of Mitzrayim was in order to fulfill His promise to Avraham that "*afterward, they will go out with vast wealth.*"[18] Because Mitzrayim at that time was not a wealthy country,

---

17. *Bereishis Rabbah* 92:4.

18. *Bereishis* 15:14.

Hashem arranged matters such that all the nations would bring their gold and silver there to purchase grain during the famine so that the Jews could take it all with them at the time of the Exodus.

The above concept is what the overseer of Yoseph's house was hinting to the brothers: "Your money came to me," meaning, all the money that has come to me from all the nations is actually your money that you are going to take out when you leave Mitzrayim. Why, then, should you give me more?"

*Because Mitzrayim at that time was not a wealthy country, Hashem arranged matters such that all the nations would bring their gold and silver there to purchase grain during the famine so that the Jews could take it all with them at the time of the Exodus.*

# פרשת ויגש
# PARASHAS VAYIGASH

## The Two Paths to Acquittal

וַיִּגַּשׁ אֵלָיו יְהוּדָה וַיֹּאמֶר בִּי אֲדֹנִי יְדַבֶּר־נָא עַבְדְּךָ דָבָר בְּאָזְנֵי
אֲדֹנִי וְאַל־יִחַר אַפְּךָ בְּעַבְדֶּךָ כִּי כָמוֹךָ כְּפַרְעֹה

*Yehudah approached him and said, "Please, my
lord, let your servant please speak a word into my
lord's ears, and do not be angry with your servant,
because you are just like Pharaoh."*
*(Bereishis 44:18)*

One who has been convicted in court has two options
open to him: Either he can try to prove his innocence
via all legal channels, or he can throw himself on the
mercy of the court.

There are two differences between these options: a) One who

tries to prove his innocence through the legal system needs to speak at length in presenting all his proofs and arguments, whereas the one requesting clemency needs only to admit his guilt and to ask for mercy; b) going through the legal channels can be accomplished via the judges, whereas clemency must be granted by the king himself, for only the king has the power to commute a sentence once it has been issued.

Yehudah saw no chance to prove Binyamin's innocence, and so he took the second approach, the request for mercy. In doing so, he needed to approach Yoseph himself, because Yoseph had the kingly powers to grant clemency. Therefore, the verse states, *"Yehudah approached him"* directly, for until now the legal give-and-take had been presented in front of all the courtiers and judges who stood at hand.

*"Please, my lord,"* he asked plaintively, *"let your servant please speak a word,"* one brief word to beg for clemency, as opposed to the long, protracted arguments and proofs of the legal system; *"into my lord's ears,"* and not into the ears of the judges who have no authority to overlook or forgive; *"and do not be angry with your servant,"* as though I am asking you to pervert justice, *"because you are just like Pharaoh"* and have the royal power to pardon.

> *"And do not be angry with your servant," as though I am asking you to pervert justice, "because you are just like Pharaoh" and have the royal power to pardon.*

# Yaakov's Descent to Mitzrayim

וַיֹּאמֶר יִשְׂרָאֵל רַב עוֹד־יוֹסֵף בְּנִי חָי אֵלְכָה וְאֶרְאֶנּוּ בְּטֶרֶם אָמוּת:
וַיִּסַּע יִשְׂרָאֵל וְכָל־אֲשֶׁר־לוֹ וַיָּבֹא בְּאֵרָה שָּׁבַע וַיִּזְבַּח זְבָחִים לֵאלֹקֵי
אָבִיו יִצְחָק: וַיֹּאמֶר אֱלֹקִים לְיִשְׂרָאֵל בְּמַרְאֹת הַלַּיְלָה וַיֹּאמֶר יַעֲקֹב
יַעֲקֹב וַיֹּאמֶר הִנֵּנִי:
וַיֹּאמֶר אָנֹכִי הָקֵל אֱלֹקֵי אָבִיךָ אַל־תִּירָא מֵרְדָה מִצְרַיְמָה
כִּי־לְגוֹי גָּדוֹל אֲשִׂימְךָ שָׁם: אָנֹכִי אֵרֵד עִמְּךָ מִצְרַיְמָה
וְאָנֹכִי אַעַלְךָ גַם־עָלֹה וְיוֹסֵף יָשִׁית יָדוֹ עַל־עֵינֶיךָ:
וַיָּקָם יַעֲקֹב מִבְּאֵר שָׁבַע וַיִּשְׂאוּ בְנֵי־יִשְׂרָאֵל אֶת־יַעֲקֹב אֲבִיהֶם
וְאֶת־טַפָּם וְאֶת־נְשֵׁיהֶם בָּעֲגָלוֹת אֲשֶׁר־שָׁלַח פַּרְעֹה לָשֵׂאת אֹתוֹ

*Yisrael said, "It is much that Yoseph my son is still*
*alive; I will go and see him before I die."*
*Yisrael traveled — with all that was his — and he*
*came to Be'er Sheva, and he slaughtered offerings*
*to the God of his father, Yitzchak. And God spoke*
*to Yisrael in night visions, and he said, "Yaakov,*
*Yaakov." And he said, "Here I am."*
*And He said, "I am the God, God of your father;*
*do not be afraid to descend to Mitzrayim,*
*for I will make you a large nation there.*
*I will descend with you to Mitzrayim,*
*and, I will take you out, also ascending;*
*and Yoseph will put his hand upon your eyes."*
*Then Yaakov arose from Be'er Sheva,*
*and the Children of Yisrael carried their father*
*Yaakov, their young children, and their wives,*
*upon the wagons that Pharaoh sent to carry him.*
*(Bereishis 45:28-46:5)*

The brothers described Yoseph's majesty and power in
Mitzrayim for Yaakov, but Yaakov had no use for any
of these details. "*It is much,*" he said, "*that Yoseph my*
*son is still alive,*" meaning: It is enough for me that he is alive

and that he remained "*my son*," i.e., righteous. Had he turned wicked, he would not be considered "*my son*," nor would he be considered "*alive*" in the human aspect, but only in the animal aspect.

Yaakov says, "*I will go and see him before I die*," because Yaakov did not originally intend to go to Mitzrayim to settle there, but rather to see Yoseph one last time and then return to the Land of Canaan.

This explains why the verse says that "*Yisrael traveled ... to Be'er Sheva*" but does not mention that he used the wagons that Pharaoh sent to carry him. Yaakov understood that these wagons were sent to enable him to relocate to Mitzrayim, and not merely to visit as he intended; he therefore considered it tantamount to theft to make use of them for an unauthorized purpose.

> **Yaakov did not originally intend to go to Mitzrayim to settle there, but rather to see Yoseph one last time and then return to the Land of Canaan.**

"*Yisrael traveled to Be'er Sheva*" because that is where his father had built an altar and brought offerings, "*and he slaughtered offerings to the God of his father, Yitzchak.*" Although we know that Yaakov's father was Yitzchak, the name Yitzchak is mentioned here as the paradigm of one who did not leave the Land of Israel during famine, having been commanded by God not to do so. Yaakov was thus attempting to identify himself with this aspect of "*Yitzchak,*" for Yaakov intended only to visit his son and then to return to the Holy Land.

However, God told Yaakov otherwise, commanding him to go to Mitzrayim until God would bring him out.

Yaakov was afraid to go to Mitzrayim on six counts, and God reassured Yaakov regarding all of them:

- Yaakov feared that his children would assimilate into Egyptian culture, to which God said, "*Do not be afraid to descend to Mitzrayim, for I will make you a large nation there,*" meaning that even there the Jewish people would not (totally) assimilate but rather would be identifiable as a distinct nation.

- Moreover, they would be a *"large nation,"* allaying Yaakov's fears that their numbers would dwindle.
- To his concern that the Divine Presence would not alight upon him there, God says, *"I will descend with you to Mitzrayim."*
- Yaakov feared that he would be buried in Mitzrayim, to which God says, *"and I will take you out."*
- *"Also ascending"* would be Yaakov's children, allaying his fears that they would remain in Mitzrayim forever.
- *"And Yoseph will put his hand upon your eyes"*; Yaakov was afraid that Yoseph might yet die in his lifetime, to which God promises that Yoseph would remain alive to close Yaakov's eyelids after Yaakov passed away.

*"Then Yaakov arose"* with his newfound intention of settling in Mitzrayim. Therefore, it was only now that *"the Children of Yisrael carried their father Yaakov, their young children, and their wives **upon the wagons** that Pharaoh sent to carry him."* Until now, Yaakov had not allowed anyone to make use of these wagons that had been sent for this express purpose.

# פרשת ויחי
# PARASHAS VAYECHI

## Really Living

וַיְחִי יַעֲקֹב בְּאֶרֶץ מִצְרַיִם שְׁבַע עֶשְׂרֵה שָׁנָה וַיְהִי יְמֵי־יַעֲקֹב שְׁנֵי
חַיָּיו שֶׁבַע שָׁנִים וְאַרְבָּעִים וּמְאַת שָׁנָה

*And Yaakov lived in the land of Mitzrayim for seven-*
*teen years; and Yaakov's days, the years of his life,*
*were one hundred and forty-seven years.*
*(Bereishis 47:28)*

The end of a person's life is seen as the measure of his entire
life; one who lived all his days in pain, but who eventually
ended up happy and successful, will forget all his travails
and consider himself as having lived an entire life of peace and
happiness.

This is what the verse is telling us here: For the last seventeen years of his life, Yaakov *"lived,"* he thrived and flourished, *"in the land of Mitzrayim"* in success, happiness, and blissful reunification with his beloved son Yoseph. Therefore, it was as if *"Yaakov's days,"* i.e., his entire life, were all *"years of his life,"* i.e., years of, happiness, success, and satisfaction.

This is the meaning of the Midrash:[1] "Yaakov was in a state of happiness all those years that he was in Mitzrayim; thus that verse considers it as though he were happy his entire life."

In another vein: As mentioned above,[2] the true definition of life, the life of a human being as opposed to that of an animal, can only be considered to be those days during which the person served his Creator. In this regard, Yaakov lacked the twenty-two years of his mourning over the loss of Yoseph. During this time the Divine inspiration did not rest upon him, as our Sages[3] tell us. But now, by serving Hashem in joy during these last seventeen years of his life, Yaakov achieved the spiritual perfection that rectified even those years of anguish.

> **But now, by serving Hashem in joy during these last seventeen years of his life, Yaakov achieved the spiritual perfection that rectified even those years of anguish.**

---

1. *Tanna d'Vei Eliyahu Rabbah,* 5.

2. Malbim to *Bereishis* 47:9 and 25:7.

3. *Midrash Tanchuma, Vayeishev* 2 (see also *Pesachim* 114a, that the Divine Presence does not dwell amid sadness).

# The Oath of a Son;
# The Oath of a King

וַיִּקְרְבוּ יְמֵי־יִשְׂרָאֵל לָמוּת וַיִּקְרָא לִבְנוֹ לְיוֹסֵף וַיֹּאמֶר לוֹ אִם־נָא
מָצָאתִי חֵן בְּעֵינֶיךָ שִׂים־נָא יָדְךָ תַּחַת יְרֵכִי וְעָשִׂיתָ עִמָּדִי חֶסֶד
וֶאֱמֶת אַל־נָא תִקְבְּרֵנִי בְּמִצְרָיִם: וְשָׁכַבְתִּי עִם־אֲבֹתַי וּנְשָׂאתַנִי
מִמִּצְרַיִם וּקְבַרְתַּנִי בִּקְבֻרָתָם
וַיֹּאמַר אָנֹכִי אֶעֱשֶׂה כִדְבָרֶךָ:
וַיֹּאמֶר הִשָּׁבְעָה לִי

*And the days drew near for Israel to die, and he*
*called for his son, for Yoseph, and he said to him,*
*"If, please, I have found favor in your eyes, place,*
*now, your hand under my thigh, and perform for me*
*kindness and truth: Do not bury me in Mitzrayim.*
*For I will lie down with my fathers, and you shall*
*carry me up out of Mitzrayim and bury me in their*
*burial place."*
*And [Yoseph] said, "I will do as you have said."*
*But [Yaakov] said, "Swear to me"....*
*(Bereishis 47:29-31)*

ubtle clues in the Torah text show us that Yaakov here is
relating to Yoseph on two levels, both as an obedient son
and as the kingdom's ruler.

Thus, Yaakov calls *"for his son,"* commanding him as a father
would a son; yet he calls *"for Yoseph"* as well, mindful of the
fact his son is "Yoseph the viceroy" who can choose to or refuse
to honor any request, and as such Yaakov entreats him in a sup-
plicating manner.

In keeping with Yoseph's role as ruler, Yaakov asks beseech-
ingly, *"If, please, I have found favor in your eyes ...."* Yet, as a
father commanding a son, Yaakov makes Yoseph take an oath,
asking him to *"place, now, your hand under my thigh"* and
swear by the sign of the covenant to fulfill his request.

"And perform for me kindness and truth ...." As a ruler, acquiescing to Yaakov's request would be an act of "kindness" on Yoseph's part; as a son, it would be an act of "truth"[4] as well, an obligatory fulfillment of the requirement for a child to honor his parents.

Or, in another vein, taking the oath would be a "kindness"; but once the oath was accepted, fulfilling it would be an act of "truth."

As for his request, Yaakov asks: "Do not bury me in Mitzrayim," even temporarily, and he gives three reasons: First, a) Yaakov seeks the spiritual goal to "lie down with [his] fathers" in the Land of Israel, the home of holiness and the Land where Yaakov's ancestors are buried. Second, b) For the sake of his body, he requests that he be carried "up out of Mitzrayim," a place of impurity. Finally, c) Yaakov stipulates burial not merely in the Holy Land, but specifically "in their burial place," in the special family plot of Me'aras HaMachpelah.

Yet, Yoseph tries to avoid the oath by saying: "I will do as you have said," without any need of an oath. Being forced to swear, Yoseph reasoned, would diminish the value of the mitzvah, making it seem as though the act was performed *not* out of Yoseph's desire to show respect for his father but rather as a compulsory obligation imposed on Yoseph from without; it would be fulfilled only to satisfy the oath, in which case the good deed would not truly be accredited to Yoseph himself.[5]

> **Being forced to swear would diminish the value of the mitzvah, making it seem as though the act was performed not out of Yoseph's desire to respect his father but rather as an obligation imposed from without.**

---

4. "Emes," "truth," can refer to fulfilling one's obligations (*Rashi* to *Bereishis* 32:11).

5. Malbim is explaining the redundant "anochi," "I," in Yoseph's statement "I will do as you have said." With a first-person verb in past or future tense, anochi is redundant because it is implicit in the verb e'esah itself.

In response to Yoseph's objection, Yaakov conceded that he would not be the one to administer the oath to Yoseph, but rather that Yoseph would take the oath of his own volition. Therefore, Yaakov uses the expression *"hi'shavah li"* — *"swear to me"* — implying a voluntary oath, as opposed to *"ashbi'acha"* —*"I will administer an oath to you"* — the expression used by Avraham when charging his servant Eliezar to swear.[6]

In this way Yaakov communicated to Yoseph that the mitzvah would clearly be attributed to Yoseph's goodwill, because the oath itself will have been taken voluntarily, under no duress.

# Jewish Versus Egyptian Garb

וַיַּרְא יִשְׂרָאֵל אֶת־בְּנֵי יוֹסֵף וַיֹּאמֶר מִי־אֵלֶּה:
וַיֹּאמֶר יוֹסֵף אֶל־אָבִיו בָּנַי הֵם אֲשֶׁר־נָתַן־לִי אֱלֹקִים בָּזֶה

*And Yisrael saw Yoseph's sons, and he said, "Who are these!" And Yoseph said to his father, "They are my sons, whom God has given me here ...."*
*(Bereishis 48:8-9)*

The style of garments worn by the Hebrews was markedly different from that of the Egyptians.

Yoseph and his sons, however, being affiliated as they were with the Egyptian ruling class, wore the vestments of Egyptian royalty. We find the same phenomenon regarding the princely Rabban Gamliel, the leader of the Jewish nation during the period of Roman ascendancy; his household assumed a non-Jewish manner of deportment out of respect for the Roman royalty.[7]

Seeing his grandchildren dressed thus, Yaakov was shocked,

---

6. *Bereishis* 24:3.
7. *Bava Kamma* 83a.

and exclaimed, "Who are these!" meaning, "What kind of Israelites are these, who walk about in non-Jewish clothing?"

Yoseph reassured him that "They are my sons," righteous and God-fearing people worthy to be called "sons of Yoseph," and they only dress like Egyptians

*What kind of Israelites are these, who walk about in non-Jewish clothing?*

because "God has given them to me here," here in this place and in this situation, a situation of royalty that necessitates this mode of attire.

# The Upper Hand

וַיִּשְׁלַח יִשְׂרָאֵל אֶת־יְמִינוֹ וַיָּשֶׁת עַל־רֹאשׁ אֶפְרַיִם וְהוּא הַצָּעִיר וְאֶת־שְׂמֹאלוֹ עַל־רֹאשׁ מְנַשֶּׁה שִׂכֵּל אֶת־יָדָיו כִּי מְנַשֶּׁה הַבְּכוֹר: ... וַיֹּאמֶר יוֹסֵף אֶל־אָבִיו לֹא־כֵן אָבִי כִּי־זֶה הַבְּכֹר שִׂים יְמִינְךָ עַל־ רֹאשׁוֹ: וַיְמָאֵן אָבִיו וַיֹּאמֶר יָדַעְתִּי בְנִי יָדַעְתִּי גַּם־הוּא יִהְיֶה־לְּעָם וְגַם־ הוּא יִגְדָּל וְאוּלָם אָחִיו הַקָּטֹן יִגְדַּל מִמֶּנּוּ וְזַרְעוֹ יִהְיֶה מְלֹא־הַגּוֹיִם: וַיְבָרְכֵם בַּיּוֹם הַהוּא ... וַיָּשֶׂם אֶת־אֶפְרַיִם לִפְנֵי מְנַשֶּׁה

*And Yisrael sent forth his right hand and placed it upon the head of Ephraim, although he was the younger one, and his left hand upon Menasheh's head; he purposely guided his hands, because Menasheh was the firstborn.*
*... Yoseph said to his father, "It is not so, Father, for this one is the firstborn; place your right hand upon his head."*
*But his father refused and said, "I know, my son, I know; he too will be a nation and he too will become great, however, his younger brother* **will become great from himself** *[mimenu], and his seed will be the fullness of the nations.*

*Thus he blessed them on that day ...*
*and he put Ephraim before Menasheh.*
*(Bereishis 48:14-20)*

When crossing his arms to bless his grandchildren, Yaakov positioned his left arm above his right. This positioning seems to be at odds with the proper method of giving a blessing, a method that our Sages derive from the Torah's description of the Priestly Blessings:

When we read *aloud* from the Torah about Aharon blessing the Jewish people, we say: *"And Aharon lifted his hands (yadav) toward the people, and he blessed them...."*[8] In the actual Torah text, however, the word for "hands" is written *"yado,"* "his hand," singular, indicating that Aharon raised one hand only. Through this apparent contradiction, explains the *Zohar,*[9] the Torah is hinting that the one hand, the right hand, should be lifted higher than the left hand when giving a blessing.

Now, since Yaakov crossed his arms one over the other when blessing his grandchildren, he should have put first his left hand upon Menasheh's head and only afterward his right hand on Ephraim's head, thus positioning his right arm above his left. Yaakov, however, did just the opposite: First he *"sent forth his right hand and placed it upon the head of Ephraim,"* and only then did he put *"his left hand upon Menasheh's head,"* thus positioning his left arm above his right.

Why did Yaakov do this?

The verse itself answers this question when it says that Yaakov *"purposely guided his hands"* in this fashion, left above right, *"because Menasheh was the firstborn"* and therefore deserved the "upper hand."

Although Yaakov had his reasons for blessing the younger Ephraim with his right hand and the older Menasheh with his left

---

8. *Va'eira* 9:22.

9. *Zohar Chelek B,* 67a.

(see below), yet Menasheh remained the firstborn nonetheless. To make this point, Menasheh was blessed with the higher hand, indicating that Yaakov was not siphoning Divine energy away from Menasheh and diverting it toward Ephraim, but rather that Ephraim's blessings flowed from a wholly independent pipeline.

> **Yaakov was not "siphoning" Divine energy away from Menasheh and diverting it toward Ephraim; rather, Ephraim's blessings flowed from a wholly independent pipeline.**

Yet, Yoseph objected, saying: *"It is not so, Father, for this one is the firstborn; place your right hand upon his head."*

Yaakov responded by explaining to Yoseph two differences between Menasheh and Ephraim, one difference regarding quality, and one difference regarding time:

Ephraim's greatness, Yaakov explained, would express itself in greatness of quality, while Menasheh's greatness would express itself in greatness of quantity, as follows:

Sometimes we find a lone individual who outweighs an entire nation in his outstanding holiness and elevated character. Rabbi Akiva teaches this in the Midrash[10] by saying that there was one woman in Mitzrayim who gave birth to 600,000 children, referring to Yocheved, mother of Moshe Rabbeinu, who himself was as meritorious as all the 600,000 souls of the Jewish people who departed from Mitzrayim.

This type of greatness, the greatness of spirit that is above nature, would be typified by Ephraim, and in particular through his illustrious offspring Yehoshua. Yehoshua's entry and conquest of the Land of Israel would be replete with miraculous events in which Hashem would reveal His powerful "Right Hand." To signify this, Yaakov blesses Ephraim with his right hand.

In contrast, Menasheh's greatness would express itself in a natural way, through his vast *quantity* of future offspring. Such a blessing springs from the realm of "Nature" symbolized as the

---

10. *Shir Hashirim Rabbah* 1:65.

workings of Hashem's "Left Hand,"[11] and thus Menasheh is blessed with the left hand.

The second difference between Menasheh and Ephraim was in regard to the *time* of the fulfillment of their respective blessings. Ephraim's blessing of spirit would actualize itself immediately, because the hidden spiritual potential was already present in Ephraim's soul, while Menasheh's blessing of physical increase would not find expression until he would actually propagate into a large nation.

To express these two differences, Yaakov told Yoseph, *"I know my son, I know; he too will be a nation,"* meaning that Menasheh's greatness would first be expressed in the future when he would grow into a large nation; *"however, his younger brother will become great from himself [mimenu],"*[12] through his own spiritual growth, and not through numerical increase. Furthermore, *"his seed will be the fullness of the nations"*; one of his seed, Yehoshua, will be as great in merit as many nations combined.

Therefore, Yaakov *"blessed them* **on that day** *... and he put Ephraim before Menasheh."* Yaakov blessed Ephraim first because Ephraim's blessing was already present *"on that day"* in Ephraim's spiritual potential. Menasheh's blessing, on the other hand, was one of population increase, and therefore had no concrete expression *on that day.*

---

11. See next essay, "Shepherds and Kings."

12. *"Mimenu"* means "than him" or "from him." Most translations render *"yigdal mimenu"* as "he will become greater *than him.*" Malbim, however, renders it "will become great *from him,*" from himself.

# Shepherds and Kings

וַיְבָרֶךְ אֶת־יוֹסֵף וַיֹּאמַר הָאֱלֹקִים אֲשֶׁר הִתְהַלְּכוּ אֲבֹתַי לְפָנָיו
אַבְרָהָם וְיִצְחָק הָאֱלֹקִים הָרֹעֶה אֹתִי מֵעוֹדִי עַד־הַיּוֹם הַזֶּה:
הַמַּלְאָךְ הַגֹּאֵל אֹתִי מִכָּל־רָע יְבָרֵךְ אֶת־הַנְּעָרִים וְיִקָּרֵא בָהֶם
שְׁמִי וְשֵׁם אֲבֹתַי אַבְרָהָם וְיִצְחָק וְיִדְגּוּ לָרֹב בְּקֶרֶב הָאָרֶץ

*And he blessed Yoseph, and he said, "The God
before Whom my fathers walked, Avraham and
Yitzchak, the God Who shepherds me from the
beginning of my existence until today. The angel
who redeems me from all evil, may he bless these
youths, and may they be called by my name and by
the name of my fathers, Avraham and Yitzchak, and
may they increase like fish in the midst of the land."
(Bereishis 48:15-16)*

The Midrash[13] on this verse cites what appears to be a dispute between Rabbi Yochanan and Reish Lakish, but which can actually be seen as two sides of the same coin. The Midrash says:

*"The God before Whom my fathers walked ...."* Rabbi Yochanan says this is analogous to a shepherd who stands and gazes at his flocks before him; Reish Lakish says this is analogous to a king walking while his elder statesmen go before him. According to Rabbi Yochanan we need His honor; according to Reish Lakish, He needs our honor."

The explanation of this is as follows:

God runs the world using two distinct and different modes of operation. One is the natural, default mode; this is the fixed and constant system of nature that takes no notice of the good or evil of human actions. Under this system, God is the "initiator"of all actions.

God's second mode of running the world is the Providential

---

13. *Bereishis Rabbah* 30:10.

mode, the miraculous system that takes into account the good deeds and the moral level of the generation. Under this "merit system" God cannot[14] shower goodness and kindness without there first being an "arousal from below" (*issarusah de'le'tatta*), the prior "help" of the righteous people and their good deeds. Under this system, man initiates, God responds.

Yaakov, in his humility, considered his fathers to have been guided by this second, Providential system, while he saw himself as under the influence of the first, natural system.

Therefore, Yaakov says, "*the God before Whom my fathers walked*"; they went first, "*before*" God, priming the heavenly pipelines with their good deeds. God responded by showering them with Divine blessings.

As for himself, however, Yaakov says, "*the God Who shepherds me*," Who leads me as a shepherd leads his flock, protecting them and feeding them according to schedule, without regard to their behavior. By his own estimation, the blessings Yaakov received were undeserved, initiated by God.

Seeing himself as under the influence of God's "nature mode" of protection, Yaakov continues and says, "*the angel who redeems me from all evil.*" Because this mode is devoid of those kinds of open miracles associated with the "Providential mode," Yaakov therefore describes himself as being guided not by Hashem Himself but rather by a Divine emissary, an "angel."

In this light, we can say that the statements of Rabbi Yochanan and Reish Lakish cited above are not at odds; rather, each one refers to a *different phrase* within this verse: Rabbi Yochanan is explaining the phrase "*the God Who shepherds me,*" while Reish Lakish is explaining the phrase "*the God before Whom my fathers walked,*" as follows:

In Rabbi Yochanan's analogy, Hashem is the One Who honors his undeserving humans by providing for them, much as the shepherd provides for his undeserving sheep.

In Reish Lakish's analogy, it is the elders who bring honor to

---

14. Obviously, this limitation is imposed by God Himself.

the king by parading *before him*; so, too, do the righteous people honor Hashem through their virtuous acts. By going "before Hashem," i.e., by opening the pipeline of blessings that Hashem then showers upon them, the tzaddikim cause Hashem's goodness and love of righteousness to become known throughout the world.

> **By going "before Hashem," i.e., by opening the pipeline of blessings that Hashem then showers upon them, the tzaddikim cause Hashem's goodness and love of righteousness to become known throughout the world.**

Continuing along the "dual modal" theme, Yaakov prays that Hashem should "*bless these youths*" and prosper them under *both* modes of Divine control: In respect to the "nature mode" under which Yaakov himself prospered, Yaakov says, "*let them be called by my name*"; and in respect to the supernatural mode under which his fathers prospered, he says, "*and by the name of my fathers, Avraham and Yitzchak.*"

This duality finds further symbolic expression in Yaakov's blessing the boys with *both* hands. Ephraim is blessed with Yaakov's right hand, signifying the miraculous mode whereby Hashem's "strong hand" is revealed; Menasheh is blessed with Yaakov's left hand, signifying the natural mode wherein Hashem allows His control of the world to be harder to perceive.

Yaakov then prays that both of these blessings and both of these modes will enable his grandchildren to prosper so that they "*increase like fish in the midst of the land.*"

# Togetherness and Unity

וַיִּקְרָא יַעֲקֹב אֶל־בָּנָיו וַיֹּאמֶר הֵאָסְפוּ וְאַגִּידָה לָכֶם אֵת אֲשֶׁר־
יִקְרָא אֶתְכֶם בְּאַחֲרִית הַיָּמִים: הִקָּבְצוּ וְשִׁמְעוּ בְּנֵי יַעֲקֹב וְשִׁמְעוּ
אֶל־יִשְׂרָאֵל אֲבִיכֶם

*And Yaakov called to his sons, and he said: "Gather together [hei'asfu], and I will relate to you what will happen to you at the end of days; assemble [hi'kavtzu], and listen, O children of Yaakov; listen to Yisrael, your father."*
*(Bereishis 49:1-2)*

**K**ibbutz and *asifah* are not synonymous. *Kibbutz* (the root of *hi'kavtzu*) is the specific term for gathering together that which is dispersed, while *asifah* (the root of *hei'asfu*) is a later stage, and it means "bringing into a *designated place*."[15]

If these words are to be used together, "*kibbutz*" must come first, followed by "*asifah*." First the disparate parts are brought together from their various locations, and only afterward are they brought into a specific place.

Yet here, Yaakov first tells his sons "*hei'asfu*," and afterwards "*hi'kavtzu*."

Our Sages[16] saw this as a hint that Yaakov's original intentions were to tell his sons about a time long in the future, to reveal to them the time of the Final Redemption. To this end, Yaakov commanded his sons to band together as a unified "*asifah*" — a level of spiritual unity which follows, and is higher than, physical "*kibbutz*" — and to thereby prepare themselves for *Geulah*, the Final Redemption.

---

15. As in "*ve'asafto el toch beisecha*," "you shall gather it into your house," said in reference to a lost object (*Devarim* 22:2). Thus we see that it refers just as well to a single object as to several, and thus does not mean to gather dispersed objects.

16. *Bereishis Rabbah* 99:5.

This alludes to the statement of our Sages[17] that the *Beis HaMikdash* was destroyed due to the sin of baseless hatred, from which it follows that its rebuilding must depend on the Jewish people uniting into one nation. "If you reach such a state," Yaakov promised them, "then *I will relate to you what will happen to you at the end of days.*"[18]

**To this end, Yaakov commanded his sons to band together as a unified "asifah" — a level of spiritual unity which follows, and is higher than, physical "kibbutz" — and to thereby prepare themselves for Geulah, the Final Redemption.**

However, when Yaakov sensed that the Divine Presence had departed from him, he understood this as an indication that the Jewish people would eventually be torn with *machlokes* and internal strife, thus making it impossible for him now to reveal the time of the Final Redemption. Therefore, Yaakov changed course, telling his sons instead, "*hi'kavtzu,*" to simply assemble "*and listen to your father*" speak of other matters.

---

17. *Yoma* 9b.

18. Yaakov's promise to relate events that would occur "at the end of days" could conceivably be understood to mean some time in the future (see *Haamek Davar* here) without necessarily referring to the Final Redemption. Indeed, Yaakov proceeds to reveal prophetic information about future events, such as Korach's and Zimri's rebellions (*Bereishis* 49:6), the Davidic Dynasty (49:10), the preeminent Torah erudition of the Tribe of Yissachar (49:15), the victories of Shaul, Mordechai and Esther (49:27), etc. With Malbim's explanation here, it becomes clear how the Sages saw this verse as a reference to the literal "End of Days" as opposed to just some future date.

# The Ten "Lost" Tribes
## and the "Jews"

הֵאָסְפוּ וְאַגִּידָה לָכֶם אֵת אֲשֶׁר־יִקְרָא אֶתְכֶם בְּאַחֲרִית הַיָּמִים: הִקָּבְצוּ וְשִׁמְעוּ בְּנֵי יַעֲקֹב וְשִׁמְעוּ אֶל־יִשְׂרָאֵל אֲבִיכֶם

...*"Gather together [hei'asfu], and I will relate to you what will happen to you at the end of days; assemble [hi'kavtzu], and listen, O children of Yaakov; listen to Yisrael, your father."*
*(Bereishis 49:1-2)*

In a slightly different vein (see previous piece), the Midrash[19] explains that both *kibbutz* and *asifah* refer to the Final Redemption. According to the Midrash, Yaakov prophesied as follows: "*Hei'asfu* — let the Ten Lost Tribes be gathered in; *Hi'kavtzu*, let the Tribes of Judah and Benjamin be gathered in."

This Midrash bases itself on the verse: "*And He will gather (asifah) the lost of Israel, and the dispersed of Judea shall He assemble (kibbutz) from the four corners of the earth.*"[20]

The Ten Tribes are the *lost of Israel (nidchei Yisrael)*, "lost" in the sense that their whereabouts are unknown;[21] yet, they are not dispersed all over the globe as are the rest of the Jewish people. Therefore, they do not require "*kibbutz*," assembly, rather only "*asifah*," being brought in to the designated place, i.e., to the Land of Israel (see previous essay).

The "Jews,"[22] on the other hand, i.e., the Tribes of Judah

---

19. *Bereishis Rabbah* 98:2.

20. *Yeshayahu* 11:12.

21. Unknown to the world at large, even if they themselves have maintained their identity [Editor].

22. "*Yehudim*" ("Jews") originally referred only to those Israelites from the land of *Yehudah* (Judea), as opposed to the Ten Tribes who were from the Northern Kingdom of Israel.

and Benjamin, are the *dispersed [nefutzos] of Yehudah.* Their whereabouts are known, so they are not "lost"; yet they are dispersed to the *"four corners of the earth,"* such that they require *kibbutz,* to be gathered together.

With this Midrash in mind, we can explain Yaakov's double-invocative: *"... Hear, O children of Yaakov, and listen to Yisrael, your father."*

The words "Yaakov" and "Yisrael" parallel the words "*hei'asfu*" and "*hi'kavtzu*," and refer to the Ten Tribes and to the Tribes of Yehudah/Benjamin, respectively. Whenever the two are referred to in relation to each other, the former are called "Yaakov," whereas the latter, because of their preeminence over the Ten Tribes, are referred to by the more elevated title "Yisrael."[23]

# Reuven's Power

רְאוּבֵן בְּכֹרִי אַתָּה כֹּחִי וְרֵאשִׁית אוֹנִי יֶתֶר שְׂאֵת וְיֶתֶר עָז: פַּחַז
כַּמַּיִם אַל־תּוֹתַר כִּי עָלִיתָ מִשְׁכְּבֵי אָבִיךָ

*"Reuven, you are my firstborn; my energy [koach] and the first of my strength [ohn], advantaged in majesty and advantaged in might. Rash like water, you shall not have these advantages, because you went up upon your father's bed ...."*
*(Bereishis 49:3-4)*

Reuven had two natural advantages over his brothers: For one, he was the firstborn. This alone, even were he not formed from the "first drop," was enough to put Reuven above his brothers in regard to sovereignty, honor, and in regard to receiving a double inheritance in the Land of Israel.

---

23. Malbim writes that this is a general principle throughout *Nevi'im* and *Kesuvim.*

In addition to this, Yaakov called Reuven *"my energy and the first of my strength,"* meaning that Reuven was conceived from the very first drop of reproductive potential that Yaakov ever emitted in his lifetime. Because of this, Reuven was destined to be physically very powerful.

The difference between *koach*, energy, and *ohn*, strength, is that *koach* refers to inner power without its necessarily being outwardly revealed.[24] Yaakov meant to say that his *"koach,"* his inner, hidden potential, was revealed outwardly for the first time in Reuven, "the first of his *revealed* strength."

But because of Reuven's impetuosity, Reuven lost these advantages.

As explained previously (*Parashas Vayishlach*), Yaakov was destined to have two more children, if not for the sin for which Yaakov rebukes Reuven here. Thus, the tribes numbered only twelve, and not thirteen as originally destined. Because wherever Ephraim and Menasheh are counted as two separate tribes, there the Tribe of Levi is not counted, as in the dividing the inheritance of the Land of Israel among the tribes.

In the future, however, Levi will have a portion of the Land, at which time there will be thirteen tribes, thirteen being the *gematriya*[25] of the word *"echad"* ("one"), when the world will arrive at a higher level of recognition of God's Unity.

> **In the future, Levi will have a portion of the Land, at which time there will be thirteen tribes, thirteen being the gematriya of the word "echad" ("one") ....**

---

24. "As I wrote in my commentary to *Yeshayahu* 40:29 on the verse 'He gives *koach* to the weary'" (Malbim).

25. *Gematriya* is the numerical system whereby each Hebrew letter maps into a number; thus, *Alef* = 1, *Chet* = 8, *Daled* = 4; total = 13.

# Anger and Fury

שִׁמְעוֹן וְלֵוִי אַחִים כְּלֵי חָמָס מְכֵרֹתֵיהֶם: בְּסֹדָם אַל־תָּבֹא נַפְשִׁי
בִּקְהָלָם אַל־תֵּחַד כְּבֹדִי כִּי בְאַפָּם הָרְגוּ אִישׁ וּבִרְצֹנָם עִקְּרוּ־
שׁוֹר: אָרוּר אַפָּם כִּי עָז וְעֶבְרָתָם כִּי קָשָׁתָה אֲחַלְּקֵם בְּיַעֲקֹב
וַאֲפִיצֵם בְּיִשְׂרָאֵל

*"Shimon and Levi are brothers, violent machinations*
*are in their abode [klei chamas m'cheiroseihem[26]].*
*In their secret counsel, let my soul not come, in*
*their gathering let my honor not unite; for in their*
*anger [af] they killed people, and with their will they*
*uprooted an ox. Cursed is their anger for it is bra-*
*zen, and their fury for it is cruel; I shall divide them*
*among Yaakov, and I shall distribute them among*
*Yisrael."*
*(Bereishis 49:5-7)*

Having pronounced Reuven unfit for leadership, the most
likely candidates for this position were Shimon and Levi,
next in line by order of birth. However, Yaakov declares
that they, too, are unfit, for they were "brothers" in regard to the
attribute of vengeance and anger, a trait too destructive for one
who wields power over others.

Yaakov had no foreknowledge of their plans to kill out the
people of Shechem, although to outsiders it appeared as though
he did. To clarify this, Yaakov declares that his *"soul did not
come into their secret counsel."* Neither did he know about the
matter, nor did they seek his counsel regarding it.

---

26. *Klei* (usually translated as "vessels") refers to machinations and
plots, as in "*vayisnaklu*," "and they plotted" against Yoseph to kill him.
*M'cheiroseihem* refers to permanent dwelling places, and thus the verse
means that violent designs have found a permanent dwelling place in their
heartsc in light of what they did to the city of Shechem and to their brother
Yoseph.

Another inaccuracy that Yaakov wanted to rectify was the brothers' claim that they acted on behalf of Yaakov's honor. To counter this, Yaakov proclaims, *"In their gathering let my honor not unite,"* meaning that their gathering in war against Shechem did not bring him honor.

Yaakov goes on to curse — not anger and fury in general, for these traits are sometimes needed to punish evildoers — but rather he curses *"their* anger and *their* fury," which was "brazen and cruel" beyond the proper measure.

There is a difference between *af* (anger) and *evrah* (fury): *Af* refers to anger directed against the injuring party alone, whereas *evrah* is when this anger spills over against others who are not deserving of it. Against Dinah's abductor, Shechem ben Chamor, the brothers directed their *af,* while their *evrah* spilled over upon the inhabitants of Shechem. Both of these, said Yaakov, were out of line, because all the victims had circumcised themselves and converted to the faith of Israel.

Yet, because the traits of *af* and *evrah* are sometimes necessary, Yaakov therefore prayed that these traits be *"divided* among Yaakov," such that each tribe would receive only one-twelfth, i.e., a small fraction, of these qualities. Yaakov prays that these traits be "distributed amongst *Yisrael,"* i.e., the leaders (who are called "Yisrael" in relationship to the general populace who are called "Yaakov"), since they are the ones who require these traits in order to mete out justice and to punish evildoers.

> *The difference between af (anger) and evrah (fury) is that af refers to anger directed against the injuring party alone, whereas evrah is when this anger spills over against others who are not deserving of it.*

# The Majesty of Yehudah

יְהוּדָה אַתָּה יוֹדוּךָ אַחֶיךָ יָדְךָ בְּעֹרֶף אֹיְבֶיךָ יִשְׁתַּחֲווּ לְךָ בְּנֵי אָבִיךָ:

גּוּר אַרְיֵה יְהוּדָה מִטֶּרֶף בְּנִי עָלִיתָ כָּרַע רָבַץ כְּאַרְיֵה וּכְלָבִיא מִי יְקִימֶנּוּ:

לֹא־יָסוּר שֵׁבֶט מִיהוּדָה וּמְחֹקֵק מִבֵּין רַגְלָיו עַד כִּי־יָבֹא שִׁילֹה וְלוֹ יִקְּהַת עַמִּים:

אֹסְרִי לַגֶּפֶן עִירֹה [עִירוֹ] וְלַשֹּׂרֵקָה בְּנִי אֲתֹנוֹ כִּבֵּס בַּיַּיִן לְבֻשׁוֹ וּבְדַם־עֲנָבִים סוּתֹה [סוּתוֹ]:

חַכְלִילִי עֵינַיִם מִיָּיִן וּלְבֶן־שִׁנַּיִם מֵחָלָב:

*"You, Yehudah, are the one upon whom your*
*brothers shall confer majesty (yoducha);*
*your hand is upon the nape of your enemies' neck;*
*the children of your father will prostrate*
*themselves before you.*
*"Yehudah is a cub, a lion — from the ripping,*
*my son, you extricated yourself; he crouches,*
*lies down like a lion, and like a mother-lion,*
*who would dare to rouse him?*
*"The staff shall never be removed from Yehudah,*
*nor the legislative-chisel from between his legs,*
*until his placenta arrives, the one to whom*
*the nations will gather.*
*"He ties his donkey to the grapevine,*
*and to the prized vine his young donkey;*
*he washed his garment in wine, and his clothing*
*in the blood of grapes; eyes colored red from wine,*
*and white toothed from milk."*
*(Bereishis 49:8-12)*

After invalidating his three oldest sons, Yaakov turns to Yehudah, his fourth son, and proclaims him the one fit for monarchy and to father the Davidic dynasty. "*Yoducha*" means to confer "*hod,*" kingly majesty.[27]

As the verse[28] implies, the two requirements of royalty are that "*our king shall judge us ... and he shall fight our wars.*" Here in Yaakov's blessings to Yehudah, both of these functions are expressed: First Yaakov blesses Yehudah with military success by saying, "*Your hand is upon the nape of your enemies' neck.*" For success as the nation's judge — which depends upon the acceptance that he and his rulings engender among the populace — Yaakov says, "*The children of your father will prostrate themselves before you,*" in reverence.

Yehudah is then praised as having both the strength of an adult lion, yet the swiftness and agility of the young lion cub. Lest this comparison be misunderstood to mean that Yehudah uses his strengths to "devour" his fellow man like a ferocious lion, Yaakov hastens to add that "*from the ripping*" of Yoseph, "*you, my son, extricated yourself*" by advising the brothers not to kill him. Rather, says Yaakov, I compare you to a lion in that, just as no one in his right mind dares rouse a reposing lion, so too will your enemies sense your strength and fear to attack you.

Therefore, continues Yaakov, rulers and lawmakers will perpetually arise from Yehudah's offspring; and even in exile when the Jews have no king, yet leaders and exilarchs will emerge from the House of David. This preeminence would successively issue forth "*from between his legs,*" i.e., from his seed, until the arrival of "*shiloh,*" from the word "*shilyah,*" meaning placenta; i.e., until the "birth" of the *Mashiach,* the one to whom and against whom nations will gather in the final war of Gog and Magog.

As would the Prophet Zecharyah after him, Yaakov en-visions the *Mashiach* riding not upon a horse, the symbol of preparedness for battle, but rather upon a donkey.

---

27. As in the verse "*ammim yehoducha*" (*Tehillm* 45:18) (Malbim).

28. *I Shmuel* 8:20.

Riding only upon this nonbelligerent beast, the *Mashiach* will nevertheless cut down, crush, and stain his clothing with the blood of all those nations that rise against him, just as one cuts grapes from the vine, crushes them into wine, and becomes stained with the wine color.

> **Riding only upon this nonbelligerent beast, the Mashiach will nevertheless cut down, crush, and stain his clothing with the blood of all those nations that rise against him, just as one cuts grapes from the vine, crushes them into wine, and becomes stained with the wine color.**

The swiftness of *Mashiach's* victory is compared to one who no sooner ties his donkey to the grapevine than his clothes are already awash with wine.[29]

"*Eyes colored [chachlili einayim] from wine, and white toothed from milk.*" *Chachlili* is related to the word for eye makeup, "*kachol*," as in the verse "*kachalt einayich* — you put makeup on your eyes.*"[30] After drinking wine which makes the blood boil and colors the eyes red, drinking milk has the opposite, calming, effect. Wine symbolizes the ravages of war that cause one to "see red"; but in the end peace will reign, as symbolized by milk and its calming effects. The "teeth," the destructive power, of the messianic lion, will no longer be bloodstained, but rather whitened with the milk of peace.

---

29. With this comment, Malbim address the verse's change in tense from present to past: "He *ties* his donkey to the grapevine .... He *washed* his garment in wine ...."

30. *Yechezkel* 23:40.

# Zevulun's Seafaring Nature

זְבוּלֻן לְחוֹף יַמִּים יִשְׁכֹּן וְהוּא לְחוֹף אֲנִיֹּת וְיַרְכָתוֹ עַל־צִידֹן

*"Zevulun, at the shore of seas shall he dwell,*
*and he to the shipping shore,*
*with his thigh upon Tzidon."*
*(Bereishis 49:13)*

**P**ortions in the Land of Israel were parceled out to each tribe by means of a lottery. Here Yaakov prophesies that Zevulun's inheritance in the Land would fall out next to the shore, "*at the shore of seas shall he dwell,*" and would not be fit for farming. Yet, Zevulun will be happy with this, because "*he to the shipping shore*"; "*he*," i.e., a Zevulunite, *by nature*[31] is attracted to the mercantile, seafaring way of life, with its long, overseas journeys.

> *A Zevulunite by nature is attracted to the mercantile, seafaring way of life, with its long, overseas journeys.*

We see this expressed in the Talmud,[32] which states that if someone praises commerce and life near the ocean, he must be a descendant from the tribe of Zevulun.

Because of this tendency, Zevulun was destined to build shipping ports by the ocean shores, and his commercial exploits would take him as far as the land of the Tzidonites, the founders of maritime commerce in the ancient world.

---

31. The word "he" in the Hebrew text is redundant because it is implied by the verb. Thus Malbim explains that it refers to the Zevulunite, not by *circumstance*, but by *essence*.

32. *Pesachim* 4a.

# The Partnership of
# Yissachar and Zevulun

יִשָּׂשכָר חֲמֹר גָּרֶם רֹבֵץ בֵּין הַמִּשְׁפְּתָיִם: וַיַּרְא מְנֻחָה כִּי טוֹב
וְאֶת־הָאָרֶץ כִּי נָעֵמָה וַיֵּט שִׁכְמוֹ לִסְבֹּל וַיְהִי לְמַס־עֹבֵד

*"Yissachar is a big-boned donkey who reclines
between the borders; and he saw that rest was good,
and that the land was pleasant; so he lowered his
shoulder to bear, and he became as a serf."*
*(Bereishis 49:14-15)*

In contrast to the seafaring nature of his brother Zevulun (see above), Yissachar loved the serenity that comes with dwelling in one's own land. Therefore, Yaakov compares Yissachar to a big-boned donkey whose nature is not to travel far, but rather to *"recline between the borders."* So too, by analogy, would Yissachar remain at home within his own border, a border he shared with the neighboring Zevulun.

Zevulun the seafarer would export the high-quality produce from Yissachar's fields, and they would share the profits between them. As our Sages tell us, in the World to Come, the spiritual profits of this arrangement they share as well, as Yissachar was thus able to delve into the study of Torah, a pursuit that requires tranquility.

Thus the verse says that Yissachar *"saw that rest was good"* for the study of Torah and for the pursuit of wisdom, *"and that the land was pleas-ant,"* i.e., that this could best be achieved by remaining in the land and farming it, rather than

> **Thus the verse says that Yissachar "saw that rest was good" for the study of Torah and for the pursuit of wisdom, "and that the land was pleasant," i.e., that this could best be achieved by remaining in the land and farming it, rather than by traveling on business.**

by traveling on business. Therefore *"he lowered his shoulder to bear"* the working of the land as does a serf, and thus supported himself in peace and quiet.

According to our Sages,[33] this verse refers to Yissachar's bearing the yoke of Torah study, and the "serfdom" that comes with being a Torah leader and teaching Torah to the rest of the Jewish people.

# Dan and Gad

דָּן יָדִין עַמּוֹ כְּאַחַד שִׁבְטֵי יִשְׂרָאֵל: יְהִי־דָן נָחָשׁ עֲלֵי־דֶרֶךְ שְׁפִיפֹן עֲלֵי־אֹרַח הַנֹּשֵׁךְ עִקְּבֵי־סוּס וַיִּפֹּל רֹכְבוֹ אָחוֹר: לִישׁוּעָתְךָ קִוִּיתִי ה': גָּד גְּדוּד יְגוּדֶנּוּ וְהוּא יָגֻד עָקֵב

*"Dan will execute judgment for the sake of his nation just like any one of the tribes of Israel. Dan will be a snake upon the road, a viper on the path, that bites a horse's heels and causes its rider to fall backward. For your salvation, Hashem, I have hoped. "Gad will dispatch a battalion, and he will dispatch a surrounding battalion."*
*(Bereishis 49:16-19)*

Dan was the "gatherer of all the camps,"[34] meaning the tribe who traveled at the rear of the Israelite encampment (whereas the children of Gad traveled at the head of the camps). Thus positioned, it was Dan's task to guard against enemy attacks from the rear, and therefore the verse says that Dan would fight the enemy and *"execute judgment"* upon them *"for the sake of his nation"*; Dan would do this *"just like any one of the tribes of Israel"* would, even though Dan traveled last.

---

33. *Midrash Rabbah* 98:12; *Tanchuma, Vayechi* 11.

34. *Bamidbar* 10:25.

Soldiers who attack a camp on the march from behind generally come on horseback, because they are swift and therefore the first to arrive at the scene of battle. Thus Yaakov describes the tribe of Dan as being cunning like the snake, adept at fighting against mounted infantry even while they themselves go on foot, like the snake that slithers upon the ground.

> *... Thus Yaakov describes the tribe of Dan as being cunning like the snake, adept at fighting against mounted infantry even while they themselves go on foot, like the snake that slithers upon the ground.*

Since Dan's blessing is nonetheless characterized by an enemy pursuing and attacking from behind, a situation that indicates a state of weakness on the part of the victim, therefore Yaakov prays, *"for your salvation, Hashem, I have hoped."*

His brother Gad, on the other hand, will enjoy preemptive military prowess, dispatching battalions at the fore of the camp.

His battalions will be of two types: *"Gad will dispatch a battalion"* that attacks the enemy head-on, and *"he will dispatch a surrounding battalion"* to encircle the enemy[35] and ambush them from behind.

---

35. From the word *akov* meaning "to surround," as in *Yehoshua* 8:13 (Malbim).

# Yoseph — The "Prince of God"

בֶּן פֹּרָת יוֹסֵף בֵּן פֹּרָת עֲלֵי־עָיִן בָּנוֹת צָעֲדָה עֲלֵי־שׁוּר: וַיְמָרֲרֻהוּ
וָרֹבּוּ וַיִּשְׂטְמֻהוּ בַּעֲלֵי חִצִּים: וַתֵּשֶׁב בְּאֵיתָן קַשְׁתּוֹ וַיָּפֹזּוּ זְרֹעֵי יָדָיו
מִידֵי אֲבִיר יַעֲקֹב מִשָּׁם רֹעֶה אֶבֶן יִשְׂרָאֵל:
מֵאֵל אָבִיךָ וְיַעְזְרֶךָּ וְאֵת שַׁקַי וִיבָרְכֶךָּ בִּרְכֹת שָׁמַיִם מֵעָל בִּרְכֹת
תְּהוֹם רֹבֶצֶת תָּחַת בִּרְכֹת שָׁדַיִם וָרָחַם: בִּרְכֹת אָבִיךָ גָּבְרוּ עַל־
בִּרְכֹת הוֹרַי עַד־תַּאֲוַת גִּבְעֹת עוֹלָם תִּהְיֶין ָ לְרֹאשׁ יוֹסֵף וּלְקָדְקֹד
נְזִיר אֶחָיו

*"A fruit-bearing vine [**bein porat**] is Yoseph,
a fruit-bearing vine upon a spring, branches
advanced upon the wall. They embittered him and
shot, and they hated him, the masters of arrows; yet
he rested his bow with strength, and his arms were
cast with fine gold; from the Strong One of Yaakov,
from there he shepherds the stone of Yisrael.
"From the God of your father, may He help you,
and with Shakkai, and He will bless you,
the blessings of heaven above, blessings of the deep
waters that crouch below, the blessings of breast
and womb. The blessings of your father,
which overpowered the blessings of my parents,
until the borders of the world's hills, may they be
upon the head of Yoseph, and upon the crown
of the head of the prince of his brothers.
(Bereishis 49:22-26)*

**Y**oseph here is thrice compared to a fruit-bearing "bein"
— the word "bein" in this context meaning "vine" or
"branch."[36]
First, Yoseph is compared to a vine, healthy and fruitful;

---

36. As we find in the verse in *Tehillim* (80:16): "... *ve'al bein ematztah lach* — and upon the branch that You have nurtured" (Malbim).

secondly, to a vine planted by a spring, perpetually verdant and lush because it is next to its source of nourishment; and, finally, to a vine that climbs on a wall, becoming extremely abundant and covering the entire wall.

Thus, "*a fruit-bearing vine is Yoseph,*" a good and beautiful person by his very nature. Moreover, he is "*a fruit-bearing vine upon a spring,*" symbolizing the wellsprings of Torah and Fear of Heaven. Yoseph's innate goodness never stagnates; it continues to thrive and mature because he constantly feeds it from the source of deep waters, the Torah. Finally, Yoseph's "*branches advanced upon the wall*" — Hashem raised him to an exalted position of power and status as the viceroy of the world's superpower, Mitzrayim.

Yet the "*master of arrows,*" referring to those who spoke *lashon hara* (derogatory speech), embittered his life by shooting him with their hateful, barbed accusations. This is a reference to Potiphar's wife and her cohorts who defamed Yoseph. It is a reference to Yoseph's brothers as well.

Despite these arrowlike attacks against him, Yoseph overpowered the natural urge to respond in kind; that is, "*he rested his bow with strength,*" not using it against his enemies. On the contrary: "*His arms were cast with fine gold*"; his arms, those instruments of archery with which one might expect him to draw the bowstrings of revenge measure for measure, were instead filled with gold, silver, and rich presents that he cast upon those who sought to wrong him.

All of the above occurred to Yoseph through Divine Providence; it was all "*from the Strong One of Yaakov.*" The reference here to God is interwoven with a reference to Yaakov, because Yaakov was the epicenter of Godliness in the world, and it was in Yaakov's merit that Yoseph enjoyed such uncanny success and protection. The purpose of all this was that *"from there he shepherds the stone of Yisrael"*; from the combination of all these events, Yoseph was put in position to shepherd and provide for the Jewish people in Mitzrayim.

*"The blessings of heaven above"* refers to rain, as well as to good *mazal*, the heavenly, celestial influences that devolve through the stellar plane. *"The blessings of the deep waters that crouch below"* is a blessing that, even during times of drought, the water table will rise from below the earth and nurture Yoseph's land. And, as a blessing that there be no infertility nor inability to suckle young, Yoseph is given the *"blessings of breast and womb,"* a blessing meant to apply both to humans and to livestock as well.

Yaakov was promised by Hashem a boundless inheritance, that he would *"break out westward, eastward, northward, and southward,"*[37] while Avraham and Yitzchak were promised specific parts of the Land only. Thus, Yaakov tells Yoseph that *"the blessings of your father,"* Yaakov, *"overpowered the blessings of my parents,"* Avraham and Yitzchak, such that my blessing extends *"until the borders of the world's hills"* at the land's farthest extreme.

These blessings will come to *"the head of Yoseph"* the *"tzaddik,"* his very name symbolizing the righteousness that makes him worthy of these blessings. These blessings, too, will come to the *"crown of his head"* (the word *"kadkod"* denoting that which is even higher than the head itself), because he is crowned over and above his brothers as a *"Prince of God."*

---

37. *Bereishis* 28:14.

# The Tree of
# Twelve Branches

כָּל־אֵלֶּה שִׁבְטֵי יִשְׂרָאֵל שְׁנֵים עָשָׂר וְזֹאת אֲשֶׁר־דִּבֶּר לָהֶם אֲבִיהֶם
וַיְבָרֶךְ אוֹתָם אִישׁ אֲשֶׁר כְּבִרְכָתוֹ בֵּרַךְ אֹתָם: וַיְצַו אוֹתָם וַיֹּאמֶר
אֲלֵהֶם אֲנִי נֶאֱסָף אֶל־עַמִּי

*All these were the twelve Tribes of Israel [Shivtei
Yisrael]; and this is that which their father spoke to
them, and he blessed them, each man according to
his blessing did he bless them. And he commanded
them and said, I am being gathered up unto my
people ...."
(Bereishis 49:28-9)*

T he number twelve in regard to the Tribes of Yaakov is not
accidental. Rather it is an essential microcosmic parallel to
the inherency of the number twelve in the world at large,
where we find that there are twelve "boundaries,"[38] twelve constellations, and the twelve permutations of the Tetragrammaton[39]
through which each of the Tribes draws its blessings and spiritual
nourishment.

The number twelve remains a constant. Although the Tribe
of Yoseph splits into the two separate Tribes of Ephraim and
Menasheh, this is only where Levi is not counted. Wherever Levi
*is* counted as a separate tribe, then Menasheh and Ephraim are
not counted separately, but are considered rather as the single
Tribe of "Yoseph," as we find regarding the names engraved

---

38. Malbim refers perhaps to the twelve-line segments that define a
three-dimensional object such as a cube, thus showing the preeminence
of the number 12 in the physical, three-dimensional world. But Recanati
(*Parashas Naso*) uses similar terminology to refer to the twelve "pipelines"
through which Hashem infuses the world with wisdom.

39. The four letters of God's ineffable Name, *yud*, then *hei*, then *vav*, then
*hei*, have twelve possible ways of being rearranged.

upon the precious stones of the clothing of the Kohen Gadol[40] and at Mount Gerizim.[41]

Until this point in history, Godliness had resided with one lone individual in each generation; that individual served as the dwelling place for the Divine and as the root-conduit of all positive spiritual nourishment that flowed from Heaven to earth.

Now, however, the time had come for this root to diverge into twelve branches, twelve tribes, the Hebrew word for tribes (*shevatim*) and branches (*anafim*) being synonymous. Together with Yaakov, the sum total would be thirteen, which has the numerical value (*gematriya*) of the Hebrew word *echad*, "one."[42] This number points to the essential oneness of the Twelve Tribes and to their unified belief in the One God, paralleling Yaakov, the "root" of these twelve branches.

The properties found in any individual branch of a tree will be found in the entire tree. Thus, even though each tribe received from Yaakov its own distinct blessing, because of this inextricable unity, each tribe partakes of the blessings of all the other tribes. To make this point, the verse says "*all these [i.e., each one of these] were the twelve Tribes of Israel*," meaning that each brother alone shares an inseparable bind with all the other brothers, such that each individual is like all twelve together. "*And this is that which their father spoke to them*," this itself, this perception of their unity, is what Yaakov revealed to them.

> *The properties found in any individual branch of a tree will be found in the entire tree. Thus, even though each tribe received from Yaakov its own distinct blessing, because of this inextricable unity, each tribe partakes of the blessings of all the other tribes.*

Resulting from this unity was that "*each man according to*

---

40. *Shemos* 28:9-11, and *Rashi* ad loc.

41. *Devarim* 27:12.

42. See above, end of "Reuven's Power" to *Bereishis* 49:3-4.

*his blessing did he bless them,*" each man's individual blessing was in reality a blessing to "*them,*" to all of them. In the words of the Midrash:[43] "Because Yaakov conferred upon Yehudah the strength of a lion, upon Yoseph the strength of an ox, etc., you might think that one was greater than the other. Therefore, (to counter this misperception), he grouped them all together into one general blessing ...."

At this point Yaakov informs his sons, "*I am being gathered up unto my people ....*" Until now, all the blessings were pooled into one resource, Yaakov Avinu himself. There was no need to separate them into twelve different channels. Now, however, with Yaakov's impending passing, the root-conduit of blessing would be "gathered up" to the Next World, and therefore Yaakov conferred these blessing upon his twelve sons, uniting the twelve conduits of blessing into one.

## Yaakov's Words of Farewell

וַיְצַו אוֹתָם וַיֹּאמֶר אֲלֵהֶם אֲנִי נֶאֱסָף אֶל־עַמִּי קִבְרוּ אֹתִי אֶל־
אֲבֹתָי אֶל־הַמְּעָרָה אֲשֶׁר בִּשְׂדֵה עֶפְרוֹן הַחִתִּי: בַּמְּעָרָה אֲשֶׁר
בִּשְׂדֵה הַמַּכְפֵּלָה אֲשֶׁר־עַל־פְּנֵי מַמְרֵא בְּאֶרֶץ כְּנָעַן אֲשֶׁר קָנָה
אַבְרָהָם אֶת־הַשָּׂדֶה מֵאֵת עֶפְרֹן הַחִתִּי לַאֲחֻזַּת־קָבֶר: שָׁמָּה קָבְרוּ
אֶת־אַבְרָהָם וְאֵת שָׂרָה אִשְׁתּוֹ שָׁמָּה קָבְרוּ אֶת־יִצְחָק וְאֵת רִבְקָה
אִשְׁתּוֹ וְשָׁמָּה קָבַרְתִּי אֶת־לֵאָה: מִקְנֵה הַשָּׂדֶה וְהַמְּעָרָה אֲשֶׁר־בּוֹ
מֵאֵת בְּנֵי־חֵת

*And he commanded them, and he said to them:*
*"I am being gathered unto my people; bury me*
*with my fathers in the cave that is in the field of*
*Ephron the Hittite; in the cave that is in the field of*
*Machpelah upon the face of Mamrei, in the Land of*
*Canaan; the field that Avraham bought from Ephron*
*the Hittite as a permanent burial holding. There*

---

43. *Midrash Tanchuma Vayechi* 16.

*they buried Avraham and Sarah his wife; there they buried Yitzchak and Rivkah his wife; and there I buried Leah. The acquisition of the field and the cave within it was from the Hittites."*
*(Bereishis 49:29-32)*

Yaakov's *"commanding them"* refers to his last will, general deathbed instructions regarding how his sons were to conduct themselves after his passing. Later, in regard to Yaakov's burial, we find this verse referred to when the Torah states, *"and his sons performed for him all that he had commanded them,"*[44] without telling us the specific details of this command.

Next, Yaakov specifically instructs them regarding his burial. He begins, *"I am being gathered unto my people"*; referring to his soul that would now be "gathered inside" the partition wherein reside the souls of the righteous who are utterly connected to life. Until now, his soul had been prevented from entering there due to its being bound up with physicality. Therefore, Yaakov requests, *"bury me with my fathers,"* so that his body, too, would be together with his ancestors, and thus prepared to received its reward at the time of the Revivification of the Dead.

**With so many decades having elapsed, however, since Avraham had bought the field, it was conceivable that Ephron's name and original ownership of the field had been forgotten, and that Yaakov's sons might therefore not be able to discern its location.**

Having said this, Yaakov proceeds to demarcate the burial place in detail, each particular adding an important element. First he makes mention of the site's original owner, saying, *"in the cave that is in the field of Ephron the Hittite."*

With so many decades having elapsed, however, since

---

44. *Bereishis* 50:12.

Avraham had bought the field, it was conceivable that Ephron's name and original ownership of the field had been forgotten, and that Yaakov's sons might therefore not be able to discern its location. Therefore, Yaakov specifies the site's physical boundaries: "*In the cave that is in the field of Machpelah*" was the location; the city and locale were "*upon the face of Mamrei*"; and, finally, "*in the Land of Canaan,*" the country.

Lest it be said that Avraham bought only the cave as a temporary burial place, but not the field — for indeed it was against Hittite statute and custom to sell a permanent burial property to a foreigner — therefore, Yaakov says "*the field that Avraham bought from Ephron the Hittite*"; Avraham bought not only the cave but the entire field as well, and in order that he have full rights to it, he bought it "*as a permanent burial holding.*"

A further indication that this cave was purchased as a permanent burial holding, and not merely as a place to bury one person temporarily, is that "*there they buried Avraham and Sarah.*" In order that the descendants of Yishmael, son of Avraham, not dispute Yaakov's claims to the grave, Yaakov added, "*there they buried Yitzchak and Rivkah his wife.*" To address any claims that Esav and his children might have to the grave, Yaakov adds, "*and there I buried Leah.*"

There remained two legal claims that could potentially be brought to counter Yaakov's right to the burial site. One was the possible Hittite claim that Ephron had sold the cave illegally, transgressing the Hittite bylaws forbidding the sale of a permanent burial site to a foreigner. Secondly, there was the possibility that Ephron's family might contest the sale based on the law[45] that when someone sells his plot in a family burial site,[46] the seller's family members can come and bury him there against the will of the buyer. To silence both these claims, Yaakov says that

---

45. *Kesubos* 84a.

46. Malbim understands that this cave was already designated as Ephron's familial burial plot, perhaps even that Ephron's family members were buried in adjacent caves.

*"the acquisition of the field and the cave within it was from the Hittites,"* the sale was done in a public forum, and all the Hittites were in agreement with the sale.

# Yaakov's Final Journey

לג וַיְכַל יַעֲקֹב לְצַוֹּת אֶת־בָּנָיו וַיֶּאֱסֹף רַגְלָיו אֶל־הַמִּטָּה וַיִּגְוַע וַיֵּאָסֶף אֶל־עַמָּיו

*And when Yaakov finished commanding his sons, he gathered his feet into the bed, and he expired and was gathered unto his people.*
*(Bereishis 49:33)*

When a person moves to a different country, with the intention of permanently remaining at his new destination, he packs everything he needs and makes all the arrangements for his journey; then he gives instructions to his family regarding how to conduct their affairs in his absence. After having done so, the traveler gathers his legs up into the ship or the carriage that will take him on his way, never again to set foot in the old country.

So it was with Yaakov Avinu. *"When Yaakov finished commanding his sons, he gathered his feet into the bed,"* his feet ceased to roam this materialistic world. Then, *"he expired,"* referring to the separation of the spirit from its bodily garment, *"and he was gathered unto his people."*

> *After having made all his arrangements, the traveler gathers his legs up into the ship or the carriage that will take him on his way, never again setting foot in the old country.*

# The Mummification of Yaakov

וַיִּפֹּל יוֹסֵף עַל־פְּנֵי אָבִיו וַיֵּבְךְ עָלָיו וַיִּשַּׁק־לוֹ: וַיְצַו יוֹסֵף אֶת־
עֲבָדָיו אֶת־הָרֹפְאִים לַחֲנֹט אֶת־אָבִיו וַיַּחַנְטוּ הָרֹפְאִים אֶת־
יִשְׂרָאֵל: וַיִּמְלְאוּ־לוֹ אַרְבָּעִים יוֹם כִּי כֵּן יִמְלְאוּ יְמֵי הַחֲנֻטִים וַיִּבְכּוּ
אֹתוֹ מִצְרַיִם שִׁבְעִים יוֹם

*And Yoseph fell upon his father's face, and he wept for him and he kissed him. Then Yoseph commanded his servants, the physicians, to embalm his father, and the physicians embalmed Yisrael. His forty days was completed — for such was the full term of embalming — and Mitzrayim cried for him for seventy days.*
*(Bereishis 50:1-3)*

When *"Yoseph fell upon his father's face,"* God's promise to Yaakov was fulfilled that *"Yoseph will put his hands upon your eyes."*[47] Yoseph then kisses Yaakov, because even after his demise Yaakov's body was holy, not defiled by the impurity of death as are other corpses.

*"Yoseph commanded his servants, the physicians, to embalm his father ...."* The Torah here gives us a glimpse of Yoseph's grandeur by informing us that he had special physicians who were his servants.

The practice of embalming that was performed in ancient Egypt is well known today from the 'mummies', which are embalmed corpses that have lasted for thousands of years without any rot or decay.

*"His forty days was completed — for such was the full term of embalming ...."* According to the ancient Egyptian superstition, embalming was like a rebirth for the deceased, as though he were being conceived anew. They believed that embalming was the first stage in a process that would preserve the body until,

---

47. *Bereishis 46:4.*

after three thousand years, the soul would return to it. Therefore, they carried out the process for forty days, paralleling the forty days of the formation of the fetus in the womb. For this reason, too, they called embalming "*chanatah*," a word referring to the beginning stages of formation, as in the verse "*the fig tree has formed its unripe fruits* ...."[48]

The question, however, begs to be asked: If the idol-worshiping Egyptians of the day practiced this mummification ritual as part of their belief system, how could Yoseph allow this to be performed upon the body of his holy father?

In response, let us first understand that burial is necessary for the deceased in order to allow his body to decompose and become dust. This is important because, even though a person's Godly soul — his pure *neshamah* — separates from his body immediately upon death and returns to its Source, yet there is another level of soul, the "*hiyulian*"[49] soul, known as the "spirit" or "*ruach*," which does not disassociate itself immediately from the body upon death.

> *The question, however, begs to be asked: If the idol-worshiping Egyptians of the day practiced this mummification ritual as part of their belief system, how could Yoseph allow this to be performed upon the body of his holy father?*

This lower level of soul is what we might call the animal or animating soul, which expresses itself through a person's physical actions, thoughts, and senses. During his lifetime, a person is meant to "alchemize" and refine this soul, bringing out its true abstract spiritual essence through Torah study, contemplation of the Divine, and good deeds. Through these, the physical aspects of this soul melt away — like the dross that is smelted away from the pure gold — leaving the spiritual part pure and refined.

---

48. *Shir HaShirim* 2:13.

49. See, for example, *Ramban, Bereishis* 1:1 for his reference to this concept of "*hiyuli*."

Thereby, the spiritual part, too, acquires eternality along with the *neshamah.*

However, not everyone successfully achieves this purification in its entirety. For this *"ruach"* is born into physicality and is engaged with it constantly during the person's lifetime; and, therefore, it doesn't readily disassociate itself from physicality. Even a person's Torah study, meditation, and good deeds have physicality mingled with them; the study and meditation come through the channels of the imagination and the senses, and the good deeds are intertwined with many materialistic motives. These materialistic aspects ruin the soul's "alchemization," and the refinement process does not succeed as it should.

Because of this, even after death, some of the soul's spiritual portions do not separate from the flesh until the body returns to its original state, the dust of the earth. Then, the *ruach*, too, can return to its pure state of spirituality and to its spiritual source.[50]

This concept helps us understand why it is that a corpse imparts *tumah*, impurity: *Tumah* arises from these unfulfilled, unrefined "pieces" of spirituality that linger in the flesh of the corpse before it has decomposed totally.

The perfect ones, however, the holy ones like Yaakov Avinu, those who successfully performed this task of refinement in their lifetimes, when they die their spirit separates completely and immediately from the flesh, and there is no further impurity of the body. This is why *"tzaddikim do not impart impurity,"*[51] and their bodies do not need to decompose in the ground to refine stray portions of soul that are intertwined therein, for these have all been separated already.[52]

Based on the above, the practice of embalming was quite

---

50. For further understanding of this idea, Malbim refers us to his commentary on the verse "*Achos lanu ketanah*" (*Shir HaShirim* 8:8).

51. Cited in *Tosefos Bava Metziah* 114a.

52. Malbim does *not* say that the righteous do *not* decompose, but rather that they do not *need* to decompose *in order to separate the unfulfilled aspects of the soul.*

appropriate for the Egyptians,[53] whose souls had become totally physical through their depraved philosophy and lifestyle. Therefore, the purpose of burial, which is to separate the spirit from the body, did not apply to them, because even their spirit had become flesh.[54]

For Yaakov, however, the reason for embalming was the exact opposite, as explained above: Because in his lifetime he had already succeeded in refining every aspect of his spirituality, therefore, his body remained pure, *tahor*. Therefore, Yoseph embalmed him so that his body remain preserved,[55] like a pure garment that was once worn by this giant soul called Yisrael, called so because he "*struggled with God and with man*," and created this separation during his lifetime.

This explains why the verse here says, "*and the physicians embalmed Yisrael*," specifically using Yaakov's more exalted title, because the justification for this embalming was Yaakov's having achieved that holy sublimation that earned him the title "Yisrael."

---

53. In an ironic sense; that is, this was not the Egyptians' reason for embalming their corpses, as Malbim stated above (Editor).

54. Malbim adds that a deceased Egyptian would not even cause *tumas meis* — the defilement due to human death — similar to an animal carcass (which imparts a lesser degree of impurity).

55. Malbim implies that without embalming, Yaakov would have decomposed. As noted in the footnote above, such decomposition would not have served the same purpose it serves for people who are less than totally righteous.

# Yaakov's Self-Dug Grave

אָבִי הִשְׁבִּיעַנִי לֵאמֹר הִנֵּה אָנֹכִי מֵת בְּקִבְרִי אֲשֶׁר כָּרִיתִי לִי בְּאֶרֶץ
כְּנַעַן שָׁמָּה תִּקְבְּרֵנִי וְעַתָּה אֶעֱלֶה־נָּא וְאֶקְבְּרָה אֶת־אָבִי וְאָשׁוּבָה

*"My father made me swear, saying, 'Behold I am dying; in my grave that I dug for myself in the Land of Canaan, there shall you bury me.' And now, may I ascend, please, and bury my father, and return."*

*(Bereishis 50:5)*

Yoseph gave four reasons to justify his request to leave Mitzrayim to bury Yaakov in the Land of Canaan:

- *"My father…,"* whom I am bound to honor;
- *"Made me swear…,"* and I am bound to fulfill the oath;
- *"Saying, 'Behold I am dying…,'"* and it is a mitzvah to fulfill a dying man's last wish;
- *"In my grave that I dug for myself … there shall you bury me."* Yaakov dug his own grave during his lifetime so that it should serve as a constant reminder for him of the day of death, helping him to avoid sin and inspiring him to maximize every minute of life. That being the case, Yaakov truly desired to be buried there, so that the very grave in which he lay would testify to his righteousness.

> **Yaakov dug his own grave during his lifetime so that it should serve as a constant reminder for him of the day of death, helping him to avoid sin and inspiring him to maximize every minute of life.**

# The Beginnings of Oppression

אָבִי הִשְׁבִּיעַנִי לֵאמֹר הִנֵּה אָנֹכִי מֵת בְּקִבְרִי אֲשֶׁר כָּרִיתִי
לִי בְּאֶרֶץ וְעַתָּה אֶעֱלֶה־נָּא וְאֶקְבְּרָה אֶת־אָבִי וְאָשׁוּבָה
... וַיַּעַל יוֹסֵף לִקְבֹּר אֶת־אָבִיו וַיַּעֲלוּ אִתּוֹ ...
וְכֹל בֵּית יוֹסֵף וְאֶחָיו וּבֵית אָבִיו רַק טַפָּם
וְצֹאנָם וּבְקָרָם עָזְבוּ בְּאֶרֶץ גֹּשֶׁן

*"And now, may I ascend, please,*
*and bury my father, and return."*
*... And Yoseph ascended to bury his father,*
*and there ascended with him ...*
*all the household of Yoseph, his brothers,*
*and his father's household; only their*
*small children and their flocks and herds*
*did they leave behind in the land of Goshen.*
*(Bereishis 50:5,7-8)*

Pharaoh was concerned that Yoseph or his brothers might try to leave the land of Mitzrayim permanently. To allay these concerns, Yoseph told Pharaoh, "*And now, may I ascend,*" emphasizing that it was only *now* for the first time that he had ever requested such permission to leave Mitzrayim; and even now, he assured Pharaoh that it was only in order that he "*bury his father and return.*"

Attending Yaakov's funeral were "*all the household of Yoseph ... and his father's household,*" referring to the women and children; even they traveled to the Land of Canaan to attend. "*Only their small children*" remained behind as hostages, collateral ensuring that the rest of the Jewish people would return.

From this, say the commentaries, we see an indication that the fledgling Jewish nation desired to leave Mitzrayim permanently and return to their homeland, but that the Egyptians would not allow this.

*Thus, it was at this point that the oppression began in potential, except that it did not come out into the open until the death of Yoseph and of his entire generation.*

Thus, it was at this point that the oppression began in potential, except that it did not come out into the open until the death of Yoseph and of his entire generation.

This explains Yoseph's promise to his brothers that *"God will surely redeem you [pakod yifkod],"*[56] even though no form of oppression seems to have been initiated as yet, and it was not obvious from what they needed to be redeemed.

From the above verses, however, we see clearly that although they were prosperous upon the land, at the same time, they were prisoners within it.

# Yaakov's Funeral

וַיַּעַל יוֹסֵף לִקְבֹּר אֶת־אָבִיו וַיַּעֲלוּ אִתּוֹ כָּל־עַבְדֵי פַרְעֹה
זִקְנֵי בֵיתוֹ וְכֹל זִקְנֵי אֶרֶץ־מִצְרָיִם ... וַיַּעַל עִמּוֹ
גַּם־רֶכֶב גַּם־פָּרָשִׁים וַיְהִי הַמַּחֲנֶה כָּבֵד מְאֹד:
וַיָּבֹאוּ עַד־גֹּרֶן הָאָטָד אֲשֶׁר בְּעֵבֶר הַיַּרְדֵּן וַיִּסְפְּדוּ־שָׁם
מִסְפֵּד גָּדוֹל וְכָבֵד מְאֹד וַיַּעַשׂ לְאָבִיו אֵבֶל שִׁבְעַת יָמִים:
וַיַּרְא יוֹשֵׁב הָאָרֶץ הַכְּנַעֲנִי אֶת־הָאֵבֶל בְּגֹרֶן הָאָטָד
וַיֹּאמְרוּ אֵבֶל־כָּבֵד זֶה לְמִצְרָיִם עַל־כֵּן קָרָא שְׁמָהּ
אָבֵל מִצְרַיִם אֲשֶׁר בְּעֵבֶר הַיַּרְדֵּן

*And Yoseph ascended to bury his father, and there ascended with him all the servants of Pharaoh, the elders of his house, and all the elders of the land of Mitzrayim. ... And he brought up with him both chariots and armed horsemen, and the camp was very great.*

---

56. *Bereishis* 50:25.

*And they arrived at Goran Ha'atad, which is
across the Jordan, and they eulogized there,
a very great and heavy eulogy, and [Yoseph] made
a seven-day period of mourning for his father.
When the inhabitants of the Land of Canaan
saw the mourning in Goren Ha'atad,
they said, "This is a massive mourning for
Mitzrayim." Therefore, they called its name
"Mitzrayim's Mourning [Avel Mitzrayim]"
which is across the Jordan.
(Bereishis 50:9-11)*

When Pharaoh originally elevated Yoseph to power, he did so in three consecutive stages:[57] First, he put him in charge of all the internal affairs of the royal household; next, he made him one of the ministers of Mitzrayim, and finally, he made him the viceroy. With each elevation to a new position, Yoseph retained all the powers of his original position as well.

Commensurate with these three positions of power were the three groups who went with Yoseph to attend Yaakov's funeral: First there were *"the servants of Pharaoh, the elders of his house,"* i.e., the members of Pharaoh's household over which Yoseph was in charge. Next, in keeping with Yoseph's position as a minister, came the *"elders of the land of Mitzrayim,"* i.e., the other ministers of the land. Finally, Yoseph being Mitzrayim's second in command, came the military escort of *"chariots and armed horsemen"* prepared for battle.

As our tradition tells us,[58] Esav and his children did indeed engage this camp in battle, contesting Yaakov's right to be buried in the *Me'aras HaMachpelah*. In foresight of such an occurrence, *"the camp was very great."*

Even though they had already cried over Yaakov in Mitzrayim,

---

57. As explained in the original Hebrew Malbim to *Bereishis* 41:40-43.
58. *Sotah* 13a; *Pirkei d'Rabbi Eliezer* 38.

now their grief was renewed. For the entire time that Yaakov's body was with them, it had seemed almost as though Yaakov were still alive among them. But now that they were about to cross the Jordan River, they suddenly realized what a huge loss his death was to Mitzrayim, and they lamented now the fact that Yaakov's holy body would not be with them, buried in their land. Even in death, Yaakov's merit would shield them from harm and bring blessings to the land, just as Yaakov's blessing to Pharaoh had resulted in the famine ending early.

> *For the entire time that Yaakov's body was with them, it had seemed almost as though Yaakov were still alive among them. But now that they were about to cross the Jordan River, they suddenly realized what a huge loss his death was to Mitzrayim, and they lamented now the fact that Yaakov's holy body would not be with them, buried in their land.*

"When the inhabitants of the Land of Canaan saw the mourning," that is, when they saw them mourning now for a second time, they realized that their grief was not for the sake of the deceased but for themselves, for the people of Mitzrayim, and therefore they said, "*This is a massive mourning for Mitzrayim*"; that is, they are sad for their own sake, not for Yaakov's.

For this reason, too, the Canaanites called the place "*Mitzrayim's Mourning*," as opposed to "Canaan's mourning." The Canaanites did not join the grieving Egyptians because they did not share the reason for their grief. On the contrary, Mitzrayim's loss was Canaan's gain, for now the holy *tzaddik* would be buried among them and his merit would come to their aid.

# Yoseph's Revenge

וַיָּשָׁב יוֹסֵף מִצְרַיְמָה הוּא וְאֶחָיו ... אַחֲרֵי קָבְרוֹ אֶת־אָבִיו:
וַיִּרְאוּ אֲחֵי־יוֹסֵף כִּי־מֵת אֲבִיהֶם וַיֹּאמְרוּ לוּ יִשְׂטְמֵנוּ
יוֹסֵף וְהָשֵׁב יָשִׁיב לָנוּ אֵת כָּל־הָרָעָה אֲשֶׁר גָּמַלְנוּ אֹתוֹ

*Yoseph returned to Mitzrayim, he and his brothers*
*... after he buried his father. And Yoseph's brothers*
*saw that their father had died, and they said,*
*"If only Yoseph would hate us and surely return*
*to us all the evil that we bestowed upon him."*
*(Bereishis 50:14-15)*

As long as their father was alive, his persona joined all the sons together in a state of brotherhood. Even after his passing, the brothers were brought together by the common goal of burying their father and properly eulogizing him.

Now, however, that all this was completed, the brothers were hit with the realization that nothing external remained to bind their brotherhood together, and that the brotherhood itself would arouse Yoseph's hatred when he remembered what they had done to him.

The wise Shlomo HaMelech said in *Mishlei*, "*If your enemy is hungry, feed him bread ....*"[59] The greatest revenge a person can take against his enemies is when, in return for their hatred and the evil they perpetrated, he makes them guests at his table, treating them with pure goodness and kindness; because then his enemies will constantly remember

> **The greatest revenge a person can take against his enemies is when, in return for their hatred and the evil they perpetrated, he makes them guests at his table, treating them with pure goodness and kindness; because then his enemies will constantly remember and feel regret for the evil that they committed.**

---

59. *Mishlei* 25:21-22.

and feel regret for the evil that they committed. This is the explanation of the verse's continuation, "*... for hot coals you are pouring on his head.*"

This is how Yoseph's brothers felt: All Yoseph's kindness to them felt like hot coals poured upon their heads. Therefore, they said, "*If only Yoseph would hate us*" openly, and give us back the actual evil that we did to him, instead of his goodness which pierces our consciences like swords.

# The Brothers' Plea for Mercy

... אָנָּא שָׂא נָא פֶּשַׁע אַחֶיךָ וְחַטָּאתָם כִּי־רָעָה גְמָלוּךָ וְעַתָּה שָׂא
נָא לְפֶשַׁע עַבְדֵי אֱלֹקֵי אָבִיךָ וַיֵּבְךְּ יוֹסֵף בְּדַבְּרָם אֵלָיו ...
וַיֹּאמֶר אֲלֵהֶם יוֹסֵף אַל־תִּירָאוּ כִּי הֲתַחַת אֱלֹקִים אָנִי: וְאַתֶּם
חֲשַׁבְתֶּם עָלַי רָעָה אֱלֹקִים חֲשָׁבָהּ לְטֹבָה לְמַעַן עֲשֹׂה כַּיּוֹם הַזֶּה
לְהַחֲיֹת עַם־רָב

"*... Please, bear now the pesha [intentional iniquity] of your brothers and their chata'ah [unintentional sin], for they bestowed evil upon you; but now, please bear the iniquity of the servants of your father's God; and Yoseph wept when they spoke to him .... And Yoseph said to them, "Fear not, for am I in place of God? You planned evil against me; God planned it for the good, to do for your sake as He has done this day; to give life to a large nation."*
**(Bereishis 50:19-20)**

**B**y selling Yoseph, the brothers committed a *pesha*, intentional transgression. Yet, at the same time, their act could also be considered a *cheit*, an unintentional sin, as follows:

No matter what justifications the brothers may have thought they had, their sale of Yoseph was a *pesha*, an unjustified crime, in light of Yoseph's being their *brother* upon whom they should have shown mercy. Thus, the brothers referred to "*pesha achecha,*" the intentional iniquity of your *brothers*.

As for their intentions, however, selling Yoseph was *chata'ah*, an inadvertent sin, because they considered Yoseph the aggressor. According to their reasoning, Yoseph's reports to Yaakov were verbal attacks against them aimed at usurping their filial claims to Jewish peoplehood. They thought Yoseph was trying to manipulate Yaakov into disenfranchising them and sending them away, just as Avraham had done to Yishmael.

True, they were mistaken; yet they thought this nonetheless. In this respect, therefore, their sin was considered unintentional. Thus, in describing their *chata'ah* they do not say that they "*did*" evil to Yoseph, but rather that "they *bestowed* evil" upon him, the Hebrew word "*gomeil,*" "bestow," denoting reciprocity, a paying back of evil for Yoseph's original evil perpetrated against them.

"*But now, please bear the iniquity of the servants of your father's God.*" All the above was relevant only at the time of the sale. "*But now,*" now that the sale of Yoseph was retroactively revealed as part of God's plan for catapulting Yoseph to power, it was clearly not an act of pure free will by the brothers. Rather, they were compelled to do it through Divine Providence, and it should therefore be considered "*the iniquity of the servants of your father's God*" who acted not out of free will but rather as mere pawns, God's servants and agents. Because He is "*the God of your father,*" therefore God chose to aggrandize you and put you in position to sustain your father in his old age.

Yoseph responds to his brothers rhetorically, saying, "*Am I in place of God?*"

Yoseph agreed with his brothers' assessment that Divine Providence was behind it all, but not only for their father's sake. Such miraculous Providence, Yoseph reasoned, could not be for the sake of one lone individual, but rather "*to do for your sake as He has done this day; to give life to a large nation.*" To harm the brothers would therefore require that Yoseph be *"in place of God,"* to overturn God's obvious plan and purpose.

Furthermore, Yoseph told the brothers, he could not possibly take retribution against them, because they *"planned evil, but God planned it for the good."* To pay them back measure for measure would therefore require that Yoseph do something bad to them that would ultimately turn around for the good, and this is something that only God could know or do.

> **To pay them back measure for measure would therefore require that Yoseph do something bad to them that would ultimately turn around for the good, something that only God could know or do.**

# A Happy Ending

וַיֵּשֶׁב יוֹסֵף בְּמִצְרַיִם הוּא וּבֵית אָבִיו וַיְחִי יוֹסֵף
מֵאָה וָעֶשֶׂר שָׁנִים: וַיַּרְא יוֹסֵף לְאֶפְרַיִם בְּנֵי שִׁלֵּשִׁים
גַּם בְּנֵי מָכִיר בֶּן־מְנַשֶּׁה יֻלְּדוּ עַל־בִּרְכֵּי יוֹסֵף

*Yoseph dwelt in Mitzrayim, he and his father's household, and Yoseph lived one hundred and ten years. And Yoseph saw three generations of Ephraim; and also the children of Machir, the son of Menashe, grew up in Yoseph's lap.*

*(Bereishis 50:22-23)*

In the concluding verses of the Book of *Bereishis*, the Torah relates that Yoseph's success and happiness in regard to his extended family, in regard to matters of state, and in regard to his own children, continued all the days of his long life.

For Yoseph lived in Mitzrayim, *"He and his father's household,"* implying peace and brotherhood among all his family members. He lived *"one hundred and ten years,"* achieving the rare feat among world leaders of remaining in power for eighty

**Yoseph lived "one hundred and ten years," achieving the rare feat among world leaders of remaining in power for eighty years.**

years.[60] Regarding his own children, Yoseph merited to watch his son Menasheh's grandchildren grow up. From his son Ephraim, Yoseph saw three generations of children, four generations in all including Ephraim, which our Sages tell us is the ultimate extent of fatherly love.[61]

As an aside, the Torah informs us that Ephraim, although he was younger, had three generations of offspring while Menashe the older son had only two, in accordance with Yaakov's blessing that *"his younger brother will grow greater than him."*[62]

*Tam V'nishlam Todos l'Keil Borei Olam!*

---

60. Yoseph was 30 when he assumed power (*Bereishis* 41:46).

61. *Bereishis Rabbah* 54:2.

62. Here Malbim's interpretation of this verse seems to differ from that which he wrote earlier (*Bereishis* 48:19).